DO THEY TAKE
CREDIT CARDS IN HEAVEN?

Economics in the Afterlife

Milica Z. Bookman

Cover design by Elisa Rodriguez Vila
Cover photograph by Aleksandra S. Bookman

Cartoons from cartoonbank.com. All rights reserved. Used with permission.
Cartoon 1.1 © The New Yorker Collection 135324 Sam Gross
Cartoon 3.1 © The New Yorker Collection 133864 Emily Flake
Cartoon 6.1 © The New Yorker Collection 134001 Alex Gregory
Cartoon 7.1 © The New Yorker Collection 68259 Alex Gregory
Cartoon 13.1 © The New Yorker Collection 133978 Frank Cotham
Cartoon 15.1 © The New Yorker Collection 32250 Charles Barsotti

ISBN: 1475155700
ISBN-13: 9781475155709
Library of Congress Control Number: 2012906383
CreateSpace, North Charleston, South Carolina

Advance Praise

A unique overview of how everyone from religious leaders to cartoonists has viewed the afterlife, and why it's all about economics at the core. This book is informative, fun to read, and absolutely like no other.

-Steven E. Landsburg, Ph.D., author of *The Armchair Economist* and *More Sex is Safer Sex: The Unconventional Wisdom of Economics*

Bookman takes two seemingly dissonant topics — economic studies and afterlife theory — and seamlessly blends them into a fascinating work that is clever and compelling. *Do They Take Credit Cards in Heaven* offers the reader a wealth of interesting facts, thought-provoking sidebars and witty anecdotes about financial entanglements of the hereafter. With a range that covers everything from the role of animals in the great beyond to outsourcing the tortures of the damned, Bookman's work is a must for anyone interested in economics, life after death or who simply craves a good read.

-Miriam Van Scott, author of *Encyclopedia of Heaven* and *Encyclopedia of Hell*

There probably aren't any *economists* in heaven, but Milica Bookman shows that there's plenty of *economics*. This wide-ranging romp puts the dismal science to the ultimate test.

-Yoram Bauman, Ph.D., co-author of *The Cartoon Introduction to Economics*

Contents

CONTENTS

List of Cartoons and Sidebars

1

Introduction: Economics is Everywhere

Given the choice, most people would prefer not to die. But they don't have a choice. Everyone dies. And everyone knows there are no exceptions. What people don't know is what will happen to them after they exhale their last breath. They wonder whether there is an afterlife or whether their bodies will simply rot underground. They wonder about heaven, hell, eternity, souls, resurrection, and reincarnation.

The fact is that at some point and to some degree, everyone thinks about what will happen after they die. Concern about the afterlife is one of the most universal concerns of mankind, shared by humans across the globe and throughout history. There is evidence that Paleolithic peoples living some 50,000 years ago prepared for the afterlife, as did the ancient Egyptians and Persians some 5000 years ago. In the last millennium, religions such as Christianity, Hinduism, and Islam all had prescriptions for their followers about life after death. Myths from Alaska to South Africa, and from Finland to Japan all deal with events that take place in the netherworld. The arts have piqued imaginations with their colorful and intricate portrayals of heaven and hell. Indeed, Hieronymus Bosch inspires dread with his vivid depictions of unimaginable tortures, whereas Michelangelo inspires internal peace with his bucolic landscapes of heaven.

Literature always mirrors social concerns and so it has, throughout the ages, addressed the afterlife. The first full-length book ever written, *The Epic of Gilgamesh*, deals with the afterlife, while *Beowulf*, an epic poem of pre-Christian Scandinavia, is about four funerals and the riches buried with the characters for their use in the afterlife. Thousands of years later, the *New York Times* bestseller list includes multiple books about the afterlife, and the *Twilight Saga*, which focuses on vampires, has broken commercial publishing records.1

From rural African drummers to Mozart and the Rolling Stones, musicians have described varied versions of heaven and hell, both literally, through lyrics, and abstractly, through the notes and arrangements themselves. Movies, from the black-and-white classic *It's a Wonderful Life* to the 1970s blockbuster *Star Wars*, and then to the futuristic *Avatar*, have dealt with angels, ghosts, communicating with the dead, and life after death. Many a contemporary joke begins with, "When such-and-such died and stood before Saint Peter...", and afterlife cartoons are a staple of the *New Yorker*. Google, with its fingers on the pulse of information, in 2012 offered over eighteen million hits for the word afterlife.

This book broadens the discussion about the afterlife by introducing a new perspective: economics. It uses economic concepts, principles, and models to assess how people across the world think about the postmortem.

Far-fetched? Not really. Economists typically assert that economics is everywhere, that it is an integral part of human decision-making, and that it permeates interpersonal relationships. They claim that economic concepts and principles show up in work, business, and politics; in films, literature, and music; in marriage, sports, and leisure; in sex, crime, and war. If economics really is everywhere, it follows that it also shows up in people's visions of the afterlife. After all, views of life after death are the product of our social and individual beliefs and feelings, all of which are rooted in our daily realities and experiences. To the extent that those are permeated with economic concepts, as economists believe, then those same concepts will show up in visions of the afterlife. That, then, would support the economists' position that economics is everywhere. It would also underscore the broad reach of economics and the universality of economic principles.

By identifying economics in visions of the afterlife, this book serves to merge the universal concern with life after death with the universal relevance of economic principles. By identifying economic concepts and principles in mythology, art, literature, religion, and popular culture, it explores questions such as: do the dead compete for scarce resources, does labor productivity matter in the underworld, and is the torture equipment in hell efficient. This study of how people across time and space envision the afterlife shows that, indeed, economic concepts and principles are an integral part of many visions of the afterlife.

But this book is more than a validation of the universality of economic principles. It also underscores how views of the afterlife are influenced by prevailing economic conditions. As those conditions change, views of the afterlife also change.

Finally, the book explores the implications for 21st century United States, where over 80% of the population believes in some form of afterlife.2 It suggests that under conditions of unprecedented affluence, coupled with consumer sovereignty, believers extend their quest for happiness and fulfillment into the afterlife and make economic choices about their belief systems.

This tour of afterlife visions as seen through an economics lens begins with the answers to two questions: first, on what grounds do economists claim that their discipline is universally relevant and second, how do we know that people are universally concerned with the afterlife.

The Universal Relevance of Economics

Economists tend to be immodest when it comes to the applicability of their discipline's concepts and way of thinking. They tout it in their classrooms as well as their publications.

Economics textbooks typically begin with a discussion of how broad the subject matter is and how it reaches into all aspects of human life. The current Chairman of the U.S. Federal Reserve, Ben Bernanke, begins *Principles of Economics* by saying that the economic way of thinking permeates simple decisions individuals make every day as well as complex international markets.3 Paul Krugman, Nobel laureate and *New York Times* columnist, claims in his introductory textbook that making choices—as everyone does all the time—is at the very core of economics.4

The relevance of the discipline is also highlighted outside the textbook market, in books such as *Economics Is Everywhere, The Economics of Life*, and *Economics For Life*.5 Economists writing academic books and journal articles have identified economic principles in movies, in literature, in bureaucracies, in politics, and in crime. Economic concepts are used to explain domestic phenomena like divorce, childbearing, and infidelity, as well as "life path" decisions like going to graduate school, raising children, serving on a committee, and joining the marines. Sex and economics are also paired, most recently in *More Sex is Safer Sex: The Unconventional Wisdom of Economics*. The hugely popular *Freakonomics* brings economic principles into mainstream America, tying together the behavior of drug dealers, teachers, parents, and sumo wrestlers in a web of easily understood economic linkages. Even Dr. Seuss's books for children contain principles of economics, further underscoring how ubiquitous economics is.

The assertion that economics is universally applicable and relevant has roots in the way the discipline is defined. Economics has to do with the decision-making behavior of individuals and other units, such as households, firms, and governments. At its core, economics is about how people make choices. Choices have to be made because peoples' wants typically exceed their capacity to realize those wants. In other words, people want more than they can have. They do not have enough resources—money, time, and/or energy—to buy and do everything they want. They must choose among competing ends. Economics, then, is the study of how people choose among several alternatives, given their scarce resources. From the moment they get up in the morning to when they fall asleep at night, people make choices: what to eat for breakfast, how to get to work. There are also the broader questions: marry John or Jim, major in history or pre-med, take a job in Seattle or Miami, spend Thanksgiving with one's parents or with the in-laws.

Some of these choices may seem to have nothing to do with economics. But that is only because most people think economics is limited to topics like inflation and investing. In reality, choices like whom to marry and where to spend a holiday are choices that are made under conditions of resource scarcity and which therefore entail an economic way of thinking and are, at their core, pure economics. All human activity entails decisions, thus allowing economists to claim that economics is everywhere.

With economics defined in relation to decision-making in general, mainstream neo-classical economists have identified common behavior that has come to constitute the fundamental principles of the discipline. They have found that individuals make choices by pursuing their self-interest, responding to economic incentives, and comparing potential benefits and costs. Although this description of human activity has recently been challenged by behavioral economists (who claim people are largely irrational), it remains the staple of mainstream economic theory.

The aggregation of many decision-making individuals gives rise to another set of principles that define interactions among people. Given that no one is self-sufficient, people interact with each other in order to survive. They engage in trade by offering what they have (their supply) in exchange for what someone else has (their demand). This interaction makes everyone better off and takes place within the context of markets. Prices at which an exchange takes place are determined in the market (except for cases in which prices are set by governments). Markets represent the most efficient way of arriving at prices for all goods and services.

These economic principles apply to individuals as well as to aggregated groupings such as households, firms, and countries. All are actors on the economic stage, and all engage in economic activities. And all are linked by a complex circular flow of economic activity. Households consume in the product market, save in the financial market, and supply their labor to the labor market. Firms invest, produce, and supply goods and services to the product market. They also incur costs, innovate, and compete. Governments participate in markets for products, labor, and financial capital. Everybody participates in the money markets by saving and borrowing. When the functioning of markets fails to provide adequately for the well-being of the population, governments get involved to redistribute and rebalance. Financial and legal institutions lubricate the relationships between economic actors as they make their choices subject to their constraints.

In this way, by building on the core economic concept of choice under conditions of scarce resources, and then linking and aggregating over the economy, a way of thinking and behaving emerges that links individuals and businesses and countries.

One may question the applicability of the term *choice* to individuals across the globe. Surely not all people have equal choices. Typically, office workers do not choose their work hours and prisoners do not choose their lunchmeat. While some people have less choice than others, even they have the ultimate choice—that is, whether to participate in the transaction at all. They can choose not to work, or not to eat. Not accepting the confines of some choices is often too unpleasant to consider, but economists still count it as an alternative.

The Universal Concern With the Afterlife

The economists' claim that economic principles and ways of thinking are universally relevant is only part of the introduction to this book. The other part entails an examination of the assertion that concern with what comes after death is universal across cultures and throughout history.

Such an examination is inherently problematic. The afterlife is replete with innumerable contentious concepts, making coherent discourse about it difficult. Even the starting point of the afterlife—namely, death—is defined in a variety of ways, making it impossible to agree on when the afterlife actually begins. It is not simply a question of one being either alive or dead. Are we dead when the heart stops beating or when brain activity stops? Given modern resuscitation practices, dead hearts and dead brains no longer equal death, and people who have had near-death experiences feel they have died once and have at least one more death to go.6 There is not even agreement about terminology, as the English language has some sixty-five euphemisms for dying (including *kicking the bucket*, *pushing up daisies*, and *sleeping with the fishes*), all of which add to the confusion as to what death entails.7 In addition, some believe we can be not only alive or dead but also undead—no longer earthly but not completely dead (such as ghosts).8

After death comes the disposal of the body according to culturally determined mourning practices. Body disposal customs are hugely diverse across cultures and further blur the boundary between life and death.

And then, at some disputed point, the afterlife begins. That is, if one believes that an afterlife exists.

Belief in the afterlife is typically binary: either one believes there is no afterlife or one believes there is. People who adhere to the former view believe nothing happens after death. The buried body rots and maggots eat the decomposing flesh. Alternatively, the cremated remains are blown around in the wind, resting temporarily on random surfaces. There is no soul and there is no divine being. There is only nothingness and emptiness. Some one billion atheists across the world support this view. Their thinking is influenced by scientific evidence which (allegedly) negates the existence of the afterlife. Francis Crick, one of the discoverers of the structure of DNA, spoke from a human biochemistry standpoint when he stated that there is no afterlife (and no soul)9, while Duke University's professor of medicine, Gerry Nahum, invoked the law of thermodynamics to deny the existence of the soul after death.10 Biologist Richard Dawkins, physicist Victor Stegner, and neuroscientist Sam Harris have also denied the existence of an afterlife, and God, from the perspectives of their respective disciplines.11

In addition to atheists and scientists, some religious believers also think there is no afterlife. Those practicing Christians who adhere to the annihilationist view claim that, while a tiny number of people go to heaven and have immortality, the majority simply ceases to exist after death. They disappear. Similarly, some twenty million adherents to the Taoist religion in Asia believe that, after death, people revert to non-being, which is the other side of being according to a simple ying/yang formula. The dead are in a non-state.

Then there are those who believe in some kind of life after death. Myriad variations on such a life exist, and the discussion in this book is by no means exhaustive. For the purposes of organization, these variations can be classified into two rough categories regarding what, exactly, is said to survive death.

Some people believe that a part of the dead persona continues on after death. This part is usually thought of as the soul—yet another contentious concept. Such a soul goes on to a new existence, perhaps in a non-earthly location, or in another body as a result of reincarnation. Irrespective of where the soul ends up, the old physical body is irrelevant and does not appear in the afterlife.

By contrast, others think the afterlife entails full use of our dead bodies as they become resurrected. In this case, the dead go on to live a new life (somewhere other than earth) with their earthly characteristics. In other words, intellect, physical features, and personality cross over with the body. The dead continue life in a similar but different way. Like life, but not like life.

Among those who believe our souls or bodies are destined for a future after death, the afterlife is imagined in many different ways.

Organized religions offer reassuring frameworks of belief that answer questions such as: will I end up in heaven, and how will I get there? Inquiring minds ask even more detailed questions: in the afterlife will I have to work, or is it all fun and games all the time? Will I be reunited with my wife of forty years, or do I finally get to date Molly? If streets are paved with gold, can I take some home with me? If I have cancer on earth, will I still have it in heaven?

Such detailed questions are location specific. An Angolan herder might wonder if he will have enough cassava to fill his belly for eternity, a young Bangladeshi bride might wonder if her stillborn baby will be reincarnated in a nearby village, and a Colombian petty thief might be concerned with the fate of his soul on Judgment Day. In the North American twenty-first-century context, people might ask themselves: is there gay marriage in the afterlife? How will I access my email when I cross over? Will they have Armani jeans in my size? Will my 401k roll over when I roll over? Baby-boomers might wonder what they will do if there is a shortage of Zoloft or Viagra in the afterlife, whereas for Americans of all ages, accustomed to easy consumption and immediate gratification, a crucial question might be: do they take credit cards in heaven?

How Do We Know? The Evidence of Human Concern with the Afterlife

It is only in contemporary societies that we can learn about people's beliefs simply by asking. Segments of the population are randomly chosen to answer pollsters' questions. Their answers are then collected and aggregated over society. The final results are presented in percentages.

But Gallup did not poll the ancient Greeks, or the medieval Chinese peasants, or even the Tuareg in contemporary Mali. For some societies, such as the ancient Etruscans and Egyptians, one can only infer their afterlife views by studying their burial practices and their sacred books. For others, one can analyze the afterlife component of belief systems such as religions, mythologies, and various forms of secular communications with the dead. Additional evidence of people's belief in the afterlife is gained by observing how culture, including art, literature, and film, reflects the views of the societies within which they exist.

It has been said that Carl Gustav Jung, the Swiss psychologist, claimed it doesn't matter if the afterlife exists or not, what matters is that the human psyche behaves as though it exists. Below, a brief overview of burial practices, belief systems, culture, and polling shows that people, over time and across cultures, have behaved as though they believed in the afterlife.

Burial Practices. The earliest evidence of belief in life after death is found in burial sites that contain more than human remains. During the Stone Age (in the Middle Paleolithic era), Neanderthal peoples in France buried their dead with tools and grain, probably because they thought those items might be useful in some afterlife.12 Burial sites of homo sapiens from around 30,000 BCE point to a similar conclusion. According to Kenneth Kramer's study of death across cultures, these people had three concerns—birth, food, and death.13 He describes archeological excavations that unearthed corpses covered with red pigment, thought to signify blood that might be restored in the afterlife. These bodies were buried with tools, weapons, and food, probably to be used in a future life. Also, bodies were found in a fetal position, as though in preparation for rebirth.

Stonehenge, the prehistoric site in southern England, is known for its complex engineering based on astronomical observations. It consists of a ring of stones, built in the late Bronze or early Iron Age, that was used mostly for burials. There is very little information about the people who inhabited the area of Stonehenge, but a recent finding adds a new dimension to our sparse knowledge. The people who lived there some 3000 years ago believed in the afterlife. Unearthed bones reveal a child lying on its side, next to a toy. The toy is no plush teddy bear but rather a hedgehog made of cold stone. While there might be numerous reasons why a child would be buried curled up around a hedgehog, researchers favor the emotional one—namely, a grieving father buries the toy to provide comfort to his child in the afterlife.14

"We forgot his Teddy bear."

Cartoon 1.1: Take It With You, Just In Case

Fast forward to the couple thousand years before Christ's era and to the information provided by now-extinct societies and religions. From about 2300 BCE, Egyptians buried their dead with belongings that might be useful in the future (such as weapons, pots, and jewelry) and painted the insides of pyramids and tombs with scenes of life after death. The Etruscans of central Italy left similar hints about their beliefs, albeit less abundant and detailed. Their tomb drawings, dating from the ninth to the third century BCE, portrayed a complex vision of the afterlife that at times was optimistic, showing abundant food and merriment, and sometimes pessimistic, with scenes of war and pain. Evidence of afterlife beliefs also shows up among the ancient Greeks, the Chinese emperors of numerous dynasties, Mongolians in the era of Genghis Khan, and many others.

Even contemporary burial customs, while less elaborate than those of older societies, point to similar beliefs about the postmortem. Some Koreans bury money with their dead to use for future consumption, and some Americans bury their relatives with their reading glasses (just in case Grandpa wants to read the *Daily Eternity News*, one supposes). Lauren Bacall is said to have placed a whistle in husband Humphrey

11

Bogart's urn, inscribed with the words, "If you need anything, just whistle." Others were more dramatic: a woman was buried in her Ferrari and a Hell's Angel biker with his bike. More commonly, photos of family members are placed in coffins to provide memories and comfort for the deceased. Funeral homes report that wristwatches and cell phones are common last-minute additions just moments before a casket gets sealed.15 One man whose burial plot was near the road asked to be buried with a big nail, so if people parked on top of his grave, they would get a flat tire.16

In the past, as in the present, it is believed that the deceased will cherish, use, appreciate, and need the material goods buried alongside them. When it comes to burying their dead, implicitly and explicitly people act as though they expect a life after death.

Belief Systems. A 2008 book entitled *The Savvy Convert's Guide to Choosing a Religion* compares and contrasts ninety-nine religions by, among others, the quality of the afterlife they offer to their adherents.17 Only a handful of those religions do not place importance on the period after death. Indeed, whether eastern or western, ongoing or extinct, monotheistic or polytheistic, religions tend to embody strong opinions about the afterlife as conveyed in their religious texts and through the words of their holy messengers.

It is a fundamental tenet of Christianity that the soul survives death, that at some future time it will be re-embodied, that it will undergo the last judgment, and then, that it will either enjoy physical bliss in heaven or physical pain in hell.18 While the Bible does not explicitly describe the details of the afterlife, the Revelation contains many images of heaven, and in the Gospel of Matthew, Jesus explicitly refers to the Kingdom of Heaven.

The interpretation of this basic information by religious authorities has not been static over time. Christianity of the Middle Ages became very graphic in its portrayals of heaven and hell, and concerns about the afterlife profoundly influenced human behavior on earth at the time. In the 1400s, the *Ars Morendi*, a Christian compilation of information about the art of dying, prescribed clearly what needed to be done in order to have a good death and afterlife. Illustrations showed vivid scenes of a man on his deathbed, surrounded by a devil and an angel, both trying to appropriate his soul.19 Later, during the Renaissance, the proliferation of scientific research and overall enlightenment overtaking Europe began to challenge the belief that heaven and hell were actual locations. The Christian afterlife became a state of union, either with God or with the devil. Pope John Paul II ultimately formalized this view in 1999 when he underscored that heaven, purgatory, and hell were not places but rather states of mind and conditions of existence.20 Still, some Christian churches, such as the Eternal Perspective Ministries, continue to envision heaven as a physical location.21

A few Christian religions have developed separate views of what happens after death. Protestants, for example, do not believe there is a purgatory. Baptists do not have a single view of the afterlife but instead embrace several possibilities. Mormons believe that the spirit will reunite with its physical body and as such will go to heaven or hell. Unitarians and Quakers are scientific in orientation. The former have unspecified views of the afterlife, some believing there is none, and others believing everyone will be saved. Similarly, Quakers individually determine their own afterlife views while collectively sharing the view that there is no eternal anything.

In Islam, two possible fates await the dead: a peaceful Garden and a ferocious Fire, representing a good place and a bad place. The Muslim holy book, the Qur'an, offers graphic descriptions of this heaven and hell.22 There is no doubt that the Islamic soul survives death, that there is judgment, and that there is eternal life.

By contrast, major eastern religions envision an afterlife in the form of reincarnation. Hindus believe that after people die they will be reborn as other individuals. Buddhists have their own version of reincarnation, differing from the Hindus on the existence of the soul. In China, some 400 million believers adhere to a series of pagan indigenous folk beliefs simply called "Chinese religion."23 Broadly, it teaches that death is followed by judgment, reincarnation, or temporary hell, followed by a paradise. Variations of the reincarnation concept are also a part of the Sikh and Jain traditions. Although rare, there are non-eastern religions that also include the belief in rebirth: the Roma of Eastern Europe (previously known as Gypsies) expect to be reincarnated (as either humans or as animals), and the Wiccans (modern followers of witchcraft) believe souls get reincarnated after a brief period of recuperation in Summerland.

There are exceptions to the dominant role of the afterlife in religious thought. Confucianism and Judaism are typically less concerned about what happens after death. Their teachings focus on the present and how to lead a good life while on earth.24 Still, there are variations in individual and group views. For traditional Jews, after death the body and soul resurrect; for some reform Jews, only the soul survives. The Torah, comprising the first five books of the Old Testament, makes no mention of afterlife, whereas the Talmud explains that after death the soul is judged (but only after spending approximately one year contemplating the good and the bad deeds it performed on earth). It is the Kabala, the mystical branch of Judaism, that has filled the gap in afterlife information, with its own esoteric visions that include transmigration of the soul. Still, some Jews (American Jews in particular) pride themselves on having a religion of reason, so they tend to dismiss an afterlife existence.25

In addition to religions, secular myths and legends provide information about how people perceived what happens after death. These do not prescribe human behavior and so are not in contradiction with religions. To the contrary, in many societies myths and religions complement each other, providing parallel or reinforcing views of the afterlife. In India, mythology and Hinduism coexist, as do traditional myths and the Catholic religion in South America.

In myths and legends, several features repeatedly arise with respect to the afterlife. First, it tends to be location-specific. When people die, they go on to a place that is clearly described, with a name and a function. The ancient Greeks, for example, focused on Hades, a dark and damp underground space in which love, jealousy, and revenge played out no differently than they did on sunny and verdant Mount Olympus, where the gods resided. In Indian myths, souls go to one of the many hells (there are between 21 and 8,400,000 of them, depending on the myth). The Japanese Izanagi myth clearly describes the world of the dead and why its ties to the living are severed, whereas the Finns have vivid legends about underground spirits who live out eternity in Tuonela.

Second, myths and legends often have afterlives that describe an improved version of life on earth. Most often such improvement refers to food supply. The Maasai of Kenya believe that in the postmortem they will continue their pastoral lives, albeit in a land rich with cattle. Similarly, many North American native populations believed they will continue to hunt after they die, and the buffalo will be more abundant than they were on earth.

But improvements over earthly life extend beyond food supply. They also include the increased options the dead have. Some myths teach that ghosts of the dead will return to reside among the living (such as those prevalent among African ancestral worshippers), come back occasionally to mingle (as among the *vodun* of West Africa), or even come back in reincarnated form to get revenge on someone who previously harmed them (as believed by the East European Roma). The Inca myths topped others with respect to options, claiming the dead have not one but two souls; one can remain with the body while the other can go elsewhere.26 Since both ghosts and souls have more options than the living, these myths depict an afterlife that represents an improvement over earthly existence.

Numerous other secular sources of information describe life after death in ways that appeal to contemporary populations more than myths. Spiritualism, for example, offers its believers not only the assurance that there is no hell, but also the view that the spirits of the dead simply reside on a different plane from the living. Given their view that all living people have vibrations that continue after death, communication across planes is possible. Since the nineteenth century, when the Fox sisters in the United States first claimed to have conversed with the dead by way of rappings, mediums have been interpreting vibrations from other planes and so facilitating information about the afterlife to earthly believers.

The New Age movement, with its roots in European Christian mysticism of the 1700s, has also come to be associated with spirituality of a non-religious nature. It does not share the Spiritualist focus on communication with the dead. With respect to the afterlife, New Age adherents believe that the spirit lives on after death, and that reincarnation can occur.

While mediums or psychics offer a glimpse into the Other World by interacting with spirits, others offer a glimpse of it as a result of a temporary visit. These are individuals who by some clinical measure died, only to reawaken shortly after. While their experiences (that have come to be called Near-Death Experiences) differ in many ways, they tend to share a common denominator: the vision of a light at the end of a tunnel.27

Parapsychology has emerged as a field of study that includes near-death experiences, ghost apparitions, reincarnation memories, and psychic abilities pertaining to the dead. It deals with believers who, in the aggregate, all embrace the afterlife.

Contrast those with the believers in science, who fail to be persuaded by spirits, mediums, and stories of near-death experiences. They were driven to conduct scientific experiments to prove or disprove the existence of the afterlife. In her book *Spook, Science Tackles the Afterlife*, Mary Roach examines such experiments, including the weighing of a body before and after death to assess if a soul has slipped out.28 Other experiments entailed attempts to x-ray ghosts and listen to their inter-ghostly communications. One experiment involved installing computers above an operating table to record departing souls in case the patient dies.

The above religious and secular beliefs pertaining to the afterlife are reinforced among populations by the numerous cultural expressions of the postmortem that have emerged over time. These are described below.

Culture. The Oxford Dictionary defines culture as the customs, arts, social institutions, and achievements of a particular nation, people, or other social group.29 Literature, art, music, film, and television are all components of a society's cultural stock, and have repeatedly reflected human concerns with the afterlife.

With respect to literature, the earliest western texts dealt explicitly with life after death. Homer's *Odyssey* and Virgil's *Aeneid*, written in the eighth and the first centuries BCE, clearly defined the locations where dead people went and the lives they led there. Socrates and Plato also pondered the afterlife and immortality of souls, often reaching different conclusions (the latter believed souls are ultimately reincarnated, the former did not). The first millennium produced largely religious texts that raised questions about life after death, such as those by Augustine of Hippo. In the same vein, hundreds of years later Thomas Aquinas wrote about saved souls in heaven.

However, it was not until Dante Alighieri's epic poem, *The Divine Comedy*, that the afterlife was placed on the front burner of social discourse. It was the fourteenth century, and Dante imbued the afterlife with a new complexity, filled with imaginative subdivisions of heaven, purgatory, and hell that prescribed and described in uncomfortable detail what awaits us in the next world.

Following that, concerns and issues pertaining to the afterlife frequently dotted the classics of English-language literature. Geoffrey Chaucer's *Canterbury Tales* showed late-fourteenth-century interest in the devil, William Shakespeare's *Hamlet* in the next century left little doubt about the existence of ghosts, and, also in the sixteenth century, Christopher Marlow wrote about dealings with the devil in his *The Tragical History of Doctor Faustus*. John Milton's *Paradise Lost* described Christian afterlife in poetic verse in the seventeenth century, and William Blake introduced a new creative afterlife vision in *The Marriage of Heaven and Hell* (eighteenth century). Johann Goethe presented the world with a German version of selling the soul to the devil (*Faust*), and, across the Atlantic, the same theme was taken up by Washington Irving and later Stephen Vincent Benet (*The Devil and Tom Walker* and *The Devil and Daniel Webster*, respectively). In the *Brothers Karamazov*, Dostoyevsky describes infernal death as it appears in the dreams of a protagonist. Hans Christian Anderson wrote children's stories that directly or allegorically referred to hell, and satirical prose by Mark Twain made fun of Christian afterlife views (in *The Bible According to Mark Twain*). Baudelaire believed in the devil, Lord Byron's poetry sympathized with Lucifer, Robert Browning wrote about hell, as did William Butler Yeats. Charles Dickens gave ghosts prominence in *The Christmas Carol*, and James Joyce offered what is perhaps the most horrific literary vision of Christian hell in *The Portrait of the Artist as a Young Man*. Jean Paul Sartre's vision of hell is personal: in *No Exit*, the existentialist French playwright describes it simply as having to spend eternity with other people. David Mamet and Salman Rushdie both write about hell as envisioned worlds apart, one in the United States and the other in India (*Bobby Gould in Hell* and *The Satanic Verses*, respectively). For John Updike, *The Afterlife* is a personal struggle with approaching death and dying. Finally, in the United States, bestsellers of the late twentieth and early twenty-first century repeatedly deal with afterlife themes: Mitch Albom's *Five People You Meet in Heaven*, Ann Rice's series on vampires, Stephanie Meyer's *Twilight* series, and Alice Sebold's *The Lovely Bones*.

Visual art has been no less vivid than literature in portraying people's interest in the afterlife. Remains from ancient cultures, including the Akkadian, Assyrian, Babylonian, Sumerian, Egyptian, Greek, Roman, and Etruscan, all depict scenes of life after death as imagined by artists. In Asia, many centuries later, the Japanese drew images of the afterlife on paper scrolls, the *Tibetan Book of the Dead* illustrated what awaits humans after they die, and Chinese tomb art, from the ritual bronzes of the Shang and Zhou periods to the buried goods of the Han and Tang dynasties, gave a glimpse into their postmortem visions. In Africa, masks and figures have continued to indicate the presence of dead ancestors on earth. Among some tribes, funerary customs entail the use of decorated helmets and drums that symbolize the spirits of the dead. From the Middle East, the Islamic religion spread across Africa and competed with local tribal beliefs. Wherever Islam spread, including Europe, the Indus Valley, and East Asia, miniature drawings of heavenly gardens that promised believers an idyllic afterlife followed.

In the Western world, it is Christian art of the Renaissance that most vividly captured the afterlife. With roots in early medieval catacomb paintings and Byzantine mosaics and frescoes, West European art became focused on death, judgment, heaven, and hell.30 The afterlife was in cathedrals, it illustrated books, and it hung on walls. The great painters of the time, including Giotto, Leonardo da Vinci, Hieronymus Bosch, Jan van Eyck, El Greco, Sandro Botticelli, Michelangelo, Peter Paul Rubens, and John Martin, interpreted the Christian vision of judgment, heaven, hell, and purgatory in vibrant colors. Pieter Brueghel and sons Jan and Pieter were especially prolific in their artistic descriptions, so much so that the latter was nicknamed "Hell Brueghel." More recently, Auguste Rodin's spectacular doors of the Museum of Decorative Arts in Paris show in intricate relief what awaits us in hell.

Later, with rising atheism, Western artists focused less on the afterlife and more on death. Surrealists and pop artists produced imaginative depictions of the dying process. One of Britain's foremost contemporary artists, Damien Hirst, has made death the focus of his art, and Marina Abramovic, performance artist extraordinaire, has often used the human skeleton as a representation of death.

Like writers and artists, musicians across the centuries have also reflected people's interest in the afterlife. Early bards sang epic poems and wove legends into stories to spread local mythology about life before and after death to illiterate populations. Choruses sang about religious themes in the Middle Ages and continued doing so through to the present. Early Jews sang on earth because angels sang in heaven, and singing was believed to make people more like angels.31 The custom has retained its popularity among Jews, and is also evident among Christians. Through the ages, Jewish Kaddish and Christian hymns became part of religious rituals, and vocalizing them helped send people into the next world. *Dies Irae* (Day of Wrath), a medieval hymn written in Latin that describes the Day of Judgment, continues to be used in Catholic requiem masses that celebrate the souls of the dead. In the *Messiah*, Handel intended for the Hallelujah chorus to sound like angels singing in eternity. Slaves in the antebellum United States sang gospel music about life after death, and modern African Americans continue the practice. Peoples across Africa believe that singing invites their ancestral spirits to visit.

Classical musicians such as Chopin, Handel, and Beethoven have used instrumental funerary marches in low keys to indicate the beginning of the afterlife. Bach and Brahms set music to the death experience and the dying process, and Mozart and Verdi both wrote requiems. Franz Liszt was obsessed with death and it showed in his music, while Hector Berlioz was not far behind with his fantastical symphony of dancing souls and witches. Richard Strauss, known for his beloved waltzes, also wrote music about death and transfiguration. The notes composed by Bela Bartok and Claude Debussy seemed of another world as they instilled listeners with vivid images of hell.

Operas also tackle the afterlife theme. Radames and Aida, unhappy lovers in Verdi's opera *Aida*, prefer to go into the afterlife together than live apart on earth. In Mozart's *Don Giovanni*, the protagonist is seized by demons and taken into hell, and his *Magic Flute* allegorically deals with the passage from hell to heaven.32 In Richard Wagner's *Isolde and Tristan*, Isolde's final song describes her vision of the dead Tristan rising.

Contemporary western music has also not ignored the afterlife. Heaven is the theme of Eric Clapton's *Tears in Heaven*, Bruce Springsteen's *The Rising*, and Madonna's *Sky Fits Heaven*, and Talking Heads and Simply Red each have a song called *Heaven*. Blood, Sweat and Tears sang that there is no heaven and John Lennon agreed, adding there is no hell either. Rap music uses images and symbols of paradise. Tenacious D sings about meeting the devil in *The Pick of Destiny*, and the Rolling Stones recorded *Sympathy for the Devil*, which elicits just what the title says. Heavy Metal music is loud, seemingly meant to resemble hell, and its cover art makes heavy use of demons. One of Led Zeppelin's most famous songs is called *Stairway to Heaven*, and a contemporary hard rock band is called, quite simply, *Afterlife*.

Country music of the twentieth century also illustrates the afterlife in songs that have remained a staple of the genre, including *Ghost Riders in the Sky*, *The Devil Went Down to Georgia*, and the more recent *Hillbilly Heaven*. Stage musicals have plenty of examples, too. In 1953, *The Band Wagon* included a scene of hell with flames and moaning. A few years later, *Guys and Dolls* included a song describing what awaits a gambler after death. And later still, *Jesus Christ Superstar*, *Godspell*, and *Phantom of the Opera* continued the afterlife theme, some winning numerous awards in the process.

Starting in the early twentieth century, movies and television became mainstream forms of entertainment as well as methods for dispensing information. As the supply and demand for film and television spread across the globe, so did portrayals of the afterlife— in films like *The Green Pastures*, *Flatliners*, *Here Comes Mr. Jordan*, and *Pushing Daisies*. Ghosts are particularly popular characters (*Poltergeist*, *Ghost Town*, *Sixth Sense*, *Meet Joe Black*, *Topper*, *The Ghost and Mrs. Muir*, *Ghost*, *Field of Dreams*), as are the devil (*Constantine*, *The Passion of the Christ*) and angels (*It's a Wonderful Life*, *City of Angels*). Contemporary children are introduced to the afterlife with motion pictures featuring gregarious ghosts (such as *Casper The Friendly Ghost*), whereas teenagers can find more angst-riddled counterparts in *Buffy the Vampire Slayer*. *Star Wars* gave us a parting phrase for our dead loved ones: "May the force be with you!" *Saturday Night Live* presents innumerable skits about the afterlife, whereas *Stay Tuned* defines hell as an endless array of bad television programs. Comedians such as David Letterman and Jay Leno routinely joke about the afterlife.

Though this overview is by no means exhaustive, it shows that the afterlife theme shows up across a broad spectrum of cultural expressions. The human concern with what happens after people die continues to translate into a sustained demand for entertainment, information, and exploration of the postmortem across a variety of mediums.

Polls and Surveys. Christian religions may profess the existence of hell, John Milton may offer a vivid description of heaven, and Patrick Swayze may play a very convincing ghost, but that doesn't prove that people actually believe any of it. Afterlife words and images and songs surround us, but the mere availability of such information does not mean that it is internalized, processed, and accepted as real. Information does not necessarily translate into personal belief.

So how do we know how many people believe in an afterlife?

One way to estimate the number of believers is to count the number of people who belong to religions that proclaim the existence of the afterlife. (This assumes that all adherents to those religions believe in that particular aspect of it.) Summing the adherents of the major religions yields almost five billion people worldwide that believe in the afterlife: approximately 2 billion Christians, 1.3 billion Muslims, plus 900 million Hindus, 360 million Buddhists, and 400 million adherents to Chinese indigenous folk religion.33

But alas, this simple conclusion is invalid because the assumption on which it rests is invalid. Adherents to a religion do not necessarily believe every aspect of its teachings. Indeed, it is incorrect to assume that all Catholics oppose abortion or that all Mormons believe in eternal marriages. A survey of Italian Catholics shows that only some 68% of the respondents believed in the afterlife, despite it being a part of doctrine. (The survey also shows 19% believe in reincarnation, which is not part of doctrine).34 Similarly, 20% of Americans in 2009 claimed to believe in reincarnation, even if most of them belong to a worldview that negates the existence of rebirth.35 In other words, just because some five billion people belong to the five major world religions that tout an afterlife does not mean that those five billion people actually believe in it.

Self-reporting is our best measure of how many people think a hereafter exists. In the United States, self-reporting indicates that many do. In 2003, the Barna Research Group surveyed Americans and found that 81% believed in some kind of afterlife and another 9% were open to the possibility but were not certain.36 These numbers were roughly the same at the end of 2009, as described by a Harris interactive poll.37 Moreover, a Gallup poll in 2004 reported that 81% of Americans believe in heaven and 77% believe in hell (although only a tiny fraction of the respondents thought they were headed there).38 An Associated Press/Ipsos poll in 2007 indicated that one out of three respondents claimed to believe in ghosts.39 The following year a Harris interactive poll pegged American belief in the devil at 59% of the total population.40

It is on the basis of polls such as these that scholar Alan Segal, in his comprehensive tome *Life After Death: A History of the Afterlife in Western Religion*, concludes that in the 1990s many more Americans believe in the afterlife than they did in the 1970s.41

In conclusion, by observing burial customs, religious and secular belief systems, a range of cultural expressions, and self-reporting by polled individuals, a picture emerges of widespread beliefs in some form of afterlife. This belief, coupled with the universal relevance of economic concepts and principles, sets the framework for this book.

About This Book

When religious figures write about the afterlife, their goal is to spread the sacred message and to embrace new believers. Religious authors rarely publicly question their faith. Even more rare is an effort to prove what they write about. By contrast, academic and non-fiction writers must critically analyze their words. Their writing must reflect questioning, reasoning, proving, and testing for internal logic and consistency. Even when dealing with the afterlife, academic disciplines challenge and question to the extent allowed by the subject matter. Eschatology (that is, those aspects of religions that deal with souls, death, heaven and hell) and thanatology (the study of death) are explored within the fields of history, art, philosophy, archeology, anthropology, literature, religious studies, psychology, and medicine. All these disciplines, to varying degrees, lend themselves to a study of the afterlife.

Economic research focuses on death-related issues rather than the afterlife. The "death care industry" is an umbrella that encompasses a multitude of smaller death-related industries, including funeral homes and morphine IVs. Given that everyone dies and that social customs prescribe methods of body disposal, the death care industry tends to be huge in most countries. Economists study it from a variety of perspectives. Those interested in industrial organization focus on competition, pricing, and productivity.42 Those interested in human behavior study it with respect to intergenerational transfer of assets and estate planning. The micro and macro level implications of estate and gift taxes are addressed in the economics literature, as well as those of life insurance and the income realities of the surviving spouse and children. Some economists focus on longevity and its demographic and economic ramifications. Others focus on the economics of religion, which includes the study of religious charitable giving (that, not coincidentally, has been found to correlate positively with age and approaching death43). Comparative economists study religions (including Buddhism, Catholicism, and Islam) in the same way as economic systems, analyzing institutions and control mechanisms usually used in the study of capitalism and socialism.44 Some microeconomists study human behavior in the face of death (even identifying the best time to die on the basis of maximizing utility45), and others apply micro-economic decision-making processes to the household level and view religious activity as one of many activities competing for one's time and money. (In fact, Corry Azzi and Ronald Ehrenberg have even coined the term "afterlife consumption" as the primary motivation behind religion.46) Studies that deal with decision-making assume rational behavior, although some economists question if human behavior is in fact rational, especially when it comes to one's death.

All the above research entails economic analysis of life on earth. Only one short academic article by Scott Gordon has addressed the afterlife and the scarcity considerations therein.47

This book seeks to extend the boundary of the economic discipline. It represents an unconventional application of conventional economic theories, concepts, and ways of thinking.48 It looks at topics usually studied by the humanities and other social sciences, and applies to those topics an economic lens. This lens defines both the content of inquiry as well as its underlying assumptions.49 In terms of content, the economics lens implies that the topics under study fall within the discipline of economics. Such topics include income, consumption, recession, money, and productivity. And yes, this book deals with these issues in the context of the afterlife, and so satisfies the content requirement.

In terms of underlying assumptions, this study of the afterlife uses the economic way of thinking insofar as it seeks out evidence of rational behavior among humans who respond to economic incentives when functioning in society. An economic way of thinking is identified across cultures and over time in reference to ideas such as heaven, hell, and reincarnation. That does not mean that all the contents of the economics discipline are in all visions of the afterlife. True enough, some visions are devoid of economics. But many visions have legitimate economic content. Many more than can be presented in this text, in fact.

One way in which this book diverges from the economic discipline has to do with its method of research. Economists typically base their studies on empirical evidence. They reach their conclusions from quantitative analysis of hard data. Yet, in dealing with the afterlife, there is a complete absence of data. Instead, the researcher must deal with faith, which usually includes irrational and contradictory beliefs that do not fit into economists' efforts at modeling. Given that the examples in this book come from religions and mythology and folk tales, as well as artists' expressions, writers' narratives, and musicians' conceptualizations, the final product does not reflect fact-based positive economics. This book, therefore, explores the afterlife with respect to economic principles but does not (and cannot) adhere to strict economic methods of research and study. Nonetheless, it is those economic principles that provide a common thread that binds hugely diverse views, despite their lack of agreement on all aspects of death, burial, mourning, and the afterlife.

To the author's knowledge, there is no published book that deals with the afterlife from an economics perspective, and there is also no economics book that has an afterlife focus.

After this introduction, subsequent chapters loosely follow mainstream economics textbooks by dealing first with general principles, then moving on to microeconomics, and then macroeconomics. They are focused on topics that are typically associated with the economics discipline, including scarcity, productivity, markets, employment, recession, and money. Each chapter contains several vignettes that illustrate different aspects of the topic as it refers to the afterlife. Each group of vignettes is preceded by a one-page roadmap that ties them together. The final chapter puts afterlife visions in the context of their respective earthly economies, with a focus on contem porary American society.

This readable collection of vignettes is innovative in concept and broad in content. No prior knowledge of economics is required to enjoy it, as all concepts, principles, and definitions are explained in simple terms. The book is not meant to challenge economic theory or religious dogma. Rather, it is meant to be informative and fun. At times the reader might wonder, "Is Bookman pulling my leg?" The answer is no, Bookman is merely trying to take readers on a playful journey that is simultaneously familiar and new.

The examples from literature, art, and music, as well as from film, religion, and mythology offered to illustrate economic concepts are not necessarily more deserving than others, they are simply the ones that were selected. By no means do they represent an exhaustive list of economic concepts in visions of the afterlife.

Finally, this is not a self-help book. It offers no lessons or guidelines on how best to get into heaven. It does not make fun of afterlife beliefs, nor does it attempt to prove or disprove the existence of life beyond death. This book is written for those who believe in the afterlife as much as for those who disbelieve. To the extent that jokes and humorous satirical anecdotes are conveyed, no disrespect is intended. Rather, they are included because they are among the many expressions of what happens to us after we die.

2

Scarcity, Choice, and Opportunity Cost

Scarcity is a basic feature of all societies. There are simply not enough resources for all of us to have everything we want. Human wants are unlimited, but the resources to achieve those wants are limited. As consumers, we are constrained by insufficient money, time, and energy; as producers, we are restrained by insufficient capital, land, and labor. These resource limitations define our lives and our economic activities. In the section below, *Take it With You, Just in Case*, the burial traditions of the ancient Egyptians illustrate how their perceptions of earthly scarcity extended into the afterlife.

Limited resources imply that people have to make choices. They have to choose one outcome over another, one good over another, one path over another. The vignette *Choosing Between a Dead Shakespeare and a Dead George Bernard Shaw* describes Dionysus's journey to the afterworld in order to bring a deceased writer back to earth. Only one. He had to make a choice.

Some economists believe that when people make choices, they act rationally. This means that when they chose one good or one activity over another, they respond to incentives and pursue their self-interest. *Rational Behavior in Afterlife Choices* tackles human decision-making in matters of the afterlife.

In choosing one outcome over another, people give something up and thus incur an opportunity cost. *The Opportunity Cost of Dancing the Night Away* applies this concept to choosing among social activities in the afterlife, as imagined in mythology, literature, and religion.

Take It With You, Just in Case

Archeologist Howard Carter was just about to give up his long quest for the tomb of a little known Egyptian king when, in November 1922, he decided to dig in just one more place—directly below some ancient workmen's huts in the Valley of the Kings. It was there that he discovered a step cut into the rock, and then another, and then a blocked entrance, and then one room, and then another, until the entire tomb of King Tutankhamen was unearthed in all it's splendor. The process of excavation and exploration inside the tomb's many chambers took months, during which all things Egyptian became fashionable around the world. Tourists flocked to watch the artifacts emerge from the entry of the tomb. Progress in excavations became front page news across the globe. The excitement was palpable. Everyone was waiting to see what had been buried since 1330 BCE.

It wasn't just the precious stones and metals that evoked awe. The volume and variety of everyday things boggled the mind. The tomb of King Tutankhamen represented the most well-preserved and least plundered tomb to date, and its contents, together with those of tombs excavated before, raised questions about Egyptian beliefs. What did the burial of so many earthly goods say about Egyptian views of life after death?

In the hundreds of books and reports written about the ancient Egyptians and their afterlife views, one theme persists: they believed earthly goods would be useful to them after death. An application of the economic lens to this theme yields the following possibility: ancient Egyptians expected to need their earthly belongings because they understood the economic concept of scarcity. To explain that possibility, some background is warranted.

Ancient Egyptians lived in North Africa for some three millennia, starting in approximately 3000 BCE, in roughly what is modern Egypt today. Their economy and society and institutions developed remarkably during that time. Although agriculture was the principal industry, Egyptians also engaged in construction, international trade, shipping, and banking. They produced an intricate system of writing (hieroglyphics). Their systems of irrigation, law, and administration were more sophisticated than those of their neighbors. But it was their complex view of the afterlife that truly set them apart from others. In fact, no other society before or after has paid so much attention to preparations for life after death. To the Egyptians of that time, death was just a temporary adjustment between two different kinds of living. They believed their souls (the Ba) were immortal and would be reborn after death. During daylight, the Ba left their mummified bodies to partake in normal earthly activities, and then returned to their mummified bodies at night (by contrast, the Ka, or spirit/life force, stayed in the tomb at all times50). The Egyptians believed their lives would then continue as extensions of life on earth, but in another place (that looked and felt very much like earth).

Art in tomb wall paintings along the Nile, as well as written texts, all showed scenes of the afterlife mimicking earthly life in terms of work, leisure, family, and social life. It was believed that whatever scenes of employment and domesticity were painted on tomb walls would become an afterlife reality. It is logical then that those scenes would depict abundance and serenity. Historians have identified a consistently plentiful afterlife in hieroglyphics and drawn images. Indeed, fields tended to be portrayed as fertile, boat builders busily employed, farmers tending numerous cattle and rich harvests, and families enjoying ample food.51 The lack of hunger and drought and murder—in other words, human, social or economic ills—showed wishful thinking about the afterlife.

But what if all this optimism was not justified? Egyptians needed to rectify their hope for future abundance with the reality of scarcity on earth. Everyone faced resource limitations (for the pharaohs, the main resource was time). Given their view that the afterlife mirrors earthly life, it seems logical that Egyptians would have believed resources would be no less scarce after death. It is likely that the ancient Egyptians transferred the familiar concept of scarcity onto their view of their hereafter by thinking: if there is not enough land to grow crops, not enough cows to produce milk, and not enough slaves, gold, tools, or honey on earth, then surely it follows that there will not be enough of all these desirable things in the afterlife.

To counter possible scarcity beyond the grave, Egyptians developed ways to give themselves an afterlife advantage. They tried to get one up on the future by taking along that which would be most scarce in the afterlife and/or that which they would want and need the most. It is not clear whether they thought these items would be unavailable, rare, or expensive in the next world. But the fact is that their burial customs were in line with behavior based on conditions of scarcity, whatever its source and nature.

So what did the ancient Egyptians take along?

First and foremost, they buried a person with a copy of the *Egyptian Book of the Dead*, containing clear instructions on how to navigate the multiple afterlife hurdles before reaching a final steady state.

Food, which sustained life on earth, was assumed to retain its importance in the afterlife. In order not to risk hunger and thirst after death, the deceased traveled to the afterlife with food and drink in tow. Egyptians planned carefully with respect to provisions, packing encasements filled with honey and grains and lining buried cabinets with flasks of wine and milk. There was no reason to assume that one's appetite would be lower or one's thirst less pressing after death. Nor was there reason to assume that one's personal tastes with respect to food and drink would change.

Pots, dishes, and utensils were also packed.

Given all the stored food at the disposal of the dead, the forward-thinking Egyptians included bathrooms in their burial sites.52

Clearly the buried food and drink would not suffice for eternity. It might satisfy hunger and thirst en route to their final resting place and perhaps shortly afterwards, but then what? How would the dead souls procure food throughout eternity? For the long haul, Egyptians believed they had to bring along the means for producing food. Expectations of afterlife food scarcity led this agricultural society to focus on inputs used in crop production. Land was the principal input, so to make sure they hit the ground running in their postmortem farming endeavors, ancient Egyptians often buried a patch of grass with the deceased.53 While the patch of grass was symbolic of soil and its resources, there was nothing symbolic about the full-sized agricultural tools and implements that were included in tombs (such as scoops, hoes, rakes, and sickles).

In addition to food-related objects, Egyptians packed clothing, jewelry, and accessories for their dead to wear. They filled their tombs with furniture to ensure comfort, as well as weapons to fight enemies.

King Tutankhamen's tomb, for example, included beds, perfume bottles, shoes, razors, royal regalia, and much more.54

If a man enters the afterlife with his tools, his clothing, his jewelry and his weapons, then why not also take his servant along? After all, servants are an integral component of one's well-being and a crucial input in the maintenance of their masters' comfort. Egyptians of means who enjoyed the services of servants and slaves on earth wanted to also enjoy them after death. To ensure that they would have exactly the number of household helpers that they wanted, and who were trustworthy and trained to their liking, dying Egyptians are said to have given instructions for the burial of their staff. There is evidence that during the early part of the third millennium BCE, slaves were buried with their masters. (They were, it should be noted, dead upon burial.) In later years, wood, stone, or faience models of slaves and servants were placed on top of the corpse. These amulets, called ushabti (or shabti), were figures of men or women shaped like mummies, with hieroglyphics on their front. Each ushabti represented the person who would do manual labor for the deceased, and the writing attested that, if called upon, this person would sow and irrigate the fields, move sand from east to west, and do anything else the deceased wanted done.55 The Tomb of Seti I contained 700 such ushabti, while another nearby tomb contained of them, each inscribed to indicate the exact person who was expected to work on every day of the year in the afterlife.56

An important concern shared by individuals who could afford to take all these items to the afterlife centered on transportation. How would they and their belongings get to their eternal resting place? Simple. They buried their proposed mode of transport. In King Tutankhamen's tomb, for example, there were chariots, as well as oars and a miniature boat. Before him, King Aha of the first dynasty of Egypt (c. 2920-2770 BCE) buried the earliest known wooden boats in southern Egypt (now called the Abydos ships). These fourteen vessels were up to eighty feet long and were probably intended to carry King Aha and his entourage into the afterlife. Similarly, another Egyptian leader, Pharaoh Djoser, probably expected to walk into the afterlife and tried to reduce the distance to his heavenly abode by building a staircase towards the heavens in his pyramid at Saqqara.

It has been said that you can't take it with you, but the ancient Egyptians proved that actually yes, you could take it along when you die. They took their cherished earthly belongings because these would be useful in an afterlife that mirrored earthly life. Given scarcity in life, ancient Egyptians planned ahead by amassing the resources they expected would be in short supply in the postmortem. By taking worldly goods along, the dead were confident that they would counter scarcity and ensure the abundance they so hopefully portrayed on their tomb walls. While the quantity and quality of buried items was not equal across the population (the rich and powerful took more with them than the common folk), the belief that earthly items ensured their Ba would enjoy creature comforts persisted among the population over ancient Egypt's 3000-year history.

Sidebar 2.1: Michel Van Der Aa's Opera *After Life* – Take One Memory Only

There is something King Tutankhamen did not explicitly take into his afterlife: memories. Yet, according to a Dutch opera entitled *After Life*, a single memory is the only item that the dead can take along. Using multimedia live performances and movie sequences, composer Michel van der Aa shows the recently deceased going to an office building where resident counselors advise them and help them choose the one memory they wish to take into the next life. The afterlife then consists of the deceased spending eternity with that single memory.

Choosing Between a Dead Shakespeare and a Dead George Bernard Shaw

Fast-forward several millennia, from the Egyptian tombs along the Nile to a theatre stage in New Haven in the 1970s. Although the setting is different, the economic principles are not. Just like the Egyptians knew about scarce resources, so, too, did actresses Meryl Streep and Sigourney Weaver, when they acted in a play about scarcity. The plot that enraptured a full house at the Yale Repertory Theatre on the inaugural performance in 1974 was one that economists easily recognize: when faced with scarce resources, people must make choices.

The play under discussion is called *Frogs*. Its original version, *The Frogs*, was written by the ancient Greek playwright Aristophanes and performed for the first time in 405 BCE. In it, the main character Dionysus, the Greek god of wine, complains about how dismal drama on earth has become. Since there are no decent contemporary playwrights, Dionysus decides to go to Hades, the Greek underworld, in order to bring one of his favorites, Euripides, back from the dead. However, once he gets there, Dionysus realizes that he has a choice. There are several playwrights who are worthy of his attention. He wavers as he narrows his choice to Aeschylus and Euripides. He cannot bring back both.

In 1974, Stephen Sondheim and Burt Shevelove adapted this comedy to modern times, wrote an accompanying musical score, and dropped the article from the title. In this modern version, Dionysus again laments the state of drama in the world, although now he is referring to the 1970s. He travels to Hades, this time with the intention of bringing back the British playwright George Bernard Shaw. However, during his visit to the underworld, the modern Dionysus also realizes he has a choice. After attending a banquet where many dead playwrights discuss philosophy, he begins to waver—perhaps he should bring back Shakespeare rather than Shaw. He cannot bring back both.

In both versions of the play, Dionysus is limited by scarce resources, and so he must make a choice. As noted in Chapter 1, the necessity of choosing among competing ends is a fundamental concept in

DO THEY TAKE CREDIT CARDS IN HEAVEN?

economics. People cannot do everything and be everywhere at once. Consumers choose what goods to buy, firms choose what products to produce, and governments choose which programs to fund. In choosing one outcome over another, they face multiple constraints.

So does Dionysus. He might like to bring back to earth all the dead playwrights who so enticingly debate philosophical issues at the Hades banquet. But he is limited by prior agreement: when he went to the afterlife he was given permission to take only one soul away from Hades. Dionysus is also constrained by space limitations on the boat that Charon, the ferryman, uses for transporting souls across the River Styx, which separates the world of the dead from the world of the living.

And so, Dionysus makes his choice. In the modern musical version, he chooses Shakespeare. As the curtain goes down, the two men board the boat back to earth, Charon the ferryman sings the reprise of "All Aboard," and the audience digests a fundamental principle of economics.

Rational Behavior in Afterlife Choices

Aristophanes, Steven Sondheim, and Meryl Streep did not tell their audiences how Dionysus made his choice once he reached the underworld. They did not dwell on his thought process. They did not explain the mechanism by which a person chooses one good over another, one path over another, one dead playwright over another. Economic theory fills this void by providing a framework with which to explain what seems like an intuitive, from-the-gut process of choosing one option over another.

One of the fundamental principles of neoclassical economics has to do with rational behavior among people who consider all their options and make the best possible decision based on those options. Rational individuals respond to incentives (such as when a higher wage induces a worker to change jobs or a sale induces a consumer to buy a coat). In responding to incentives, people pursue their self-interest. They avoid activities that will hurt them (unless they somehow benefit from the hurting process, like when they smoke).

When behaving rationally, individuals (and firms and governments) make choices by weighing the benefits of each action against the costs of that action. People pursue an action if its costs are lower than its benefits; if the costs are higher, they don't. Since most choices are not all-or-nothing but rather entail decisions about incremental activity (such as the consumption of one more drink or the production of one more automobile), economists say decisions are made at the margin—that is, people weigh the marginal (or additional) costs against marginal benefits. The rule of rational choice says that individuals pursue an activity if the expected marginal benefits are greater than the expected marginal costs.

Do people really behave rationally when it comes to issues of life after death?

In answer to that question, this vignette first offers an overview of the most common afterlife possibilities (namely, spending eternity in heaven or hell), then explores the relationship between earthly behavior and the quality of one's afterlife, and lastly describes the cost/

benefit analysis believers are likely to perform when considering where to spend eternity.

The Good Place, The Bad Place

According to some beliefs, the afterlife is predetermined for everyone equally, irrespective of one's earthly behavior. The same place is inhabited both by good people as well as bad; murderers and nuns coexist side by side. Mythology of the Lapps of northern Scandinavia suggests that after death, everyone goes to the land of the dead, which is simply the reverse of the land of the living.57 There life goes on as on earth, except upside down, so trees and animals and people are all upended. Shared after-death experience is also present in Babylonian and Finnish myths, as well as among the Bagobo of the Philippines and the Ibo of Nigeria.58 Similarly, early Judaism mentions Sheol, a place where the dead go that has nothing to do with punishment for earthly behavior.

But the notion of a single afterlife for all believers is not common. Most cultures envision multiple places where the dead can spend eternity. Some of these are good and some are bad. Believers prefer to spend eternity in the good place.

In Christianity, the good place is called heaven and the bad place is hell. In the former, souls bask in the love of God; they are illuminated by it and they cannot imagine a feeling greater or a state more complete than being in the family of God. There are many offshoots of this, but they all share the idea of joy and delight. Islam is more descriptive and colorful with respect to its heaven, the garden paradise of Djanna. There, the faithful have an eternity filled with all the pleasures they did not enjoy on earth, including abundance of food and water and beautiful clothes and gold jewelry. Rivers of milk, wine, and honey flow freely. Trees are full of ripe fruits, gardens are lusciously verdant, and flowers give off a sweet aroma. Most importantly, all believers enjoy the splendor of Allah's face.

Quasi-religious views of a positive afterlife location are also common, each with its own particular features. Elysium is the paradise of ancient Greeks, the place where saved souls enjoy dancing, feasting, and festivals.

Avalon is the Celtic paradise, where good things happen to good people. Good Eskimo spirits go to the Land of the Moon, whereas the Sioux Indians believe heaven is in a tropical location (indicating that life is easier than where they reside).

Similarly, good afterlife locations appear also in secular visions depicted by popular culture. Typically these locations share little more than the name heaven. In WALL-E, the Academy Award-winner for best animated film in 2009, passengers on a space ship believe they are in heaven. Why? Because there is no hunger or illness or war, and everything is wonderful. Meanwhile, in the film *Heartburn*, Jack Nicholson is told that in heaven men get a basket filled with their socks that went missing in the dryer in the course of their lives. Eternity then consists of sorting socks.

Hell is the bad place that believers seek to avoid. According to scholar Alice Turner, hell is the largest shared construction project in imaginative history.59 Most great religions have a hell that is, to varying degrees, dark, cold, and loud. In it people feel pain, agony, and fear. There is fire and burning oil and freezing water and multiple tools with which people are tortured. Buddhists call it Avici, Muslims call it Jahannam, Greeks call it Hades, Jews call it Gehenna.

The hells of religions tend to be barren, but literature offers more opulent alternatives. Pandemonium, as described by John Milton in his poem *Paradise Lost*, is the most grand and majestic of hells.60 Dante's Dis and Hesiod's House of Styx also contain impressive complex structures.

Eskimo mythology states that Adlivun (hell) is at the bottom of the ocean and that is where unworthy spirits go, whereas, according to the Sioux mythology, hell is a freezing cold place. In the South African Zulu vision, hell's punishment is that people must walk and talk backwards. On a lighter note, Mark Twain says hell is a place that lacks oxygen so a man cannot light matches to smoke his pipe,61 and California Milk Producers floated an advertisement for their product that takes place in the afterlife and depicts hell as offering dry cookies with no milk.62

Given the prevalent view that at least two very different afterlife locations exist, how does an individual ensure entry into the preferable one?

The idea that there is something people can do to influence where they spend eternity is at the root of most religions. It is a basic premise of those religions that there is a good afterlife and a bad one, and if one leads a "good" life, then one goes to a good place after death; if one leads a "bad" life, one goes to a bad place. Most belief systems offer guidelines for proper behavior, including steps one must take and rules one must follow in order to gain access to the good afterlife. If earthly behavior follows those particular prescriptions, the reward is eternity in a good place rather than a bad place. (Limbo, purgatory, and other in-between places are omitted from this discussion).

Heaven or Hell: Rational Choice?

Those who believe in a binary afterlife consisting of heaven and hell (as physical locations or as states of mind) know they cannot go to both simultaneously, since the two options are mutually exclusive. Rational individuals must make a choice. And that choice, as the eighteenth century philosopher Emanuel Swedenborg noted, is the biggest decision people make in life, because it is the one they will live with forever.63

People make that choice long before they reach the Land of the Dead. They make it during their lifetimes, while alive and on earth. It is the choice of whether to lead the kind of life that is rewarded by heaven or the kind that is punished by hell. Their decision is the result of a rational cost/benefit analysis: they think on the margin and weigh the costs and benefits of the multitude of incremental choices that populate their lives and on which their belief system has some moral position. Do they tell an additional lie, do they steal another pack of cigarettes? Do they lead promiscuous lives and cheat their neighbors? Or do they live according to the rules set by their religions, rules that will reward their good behavior? These decisions entail weighing marginal costs against marginal benefits.

This particular cost/benefit analysis is complicated by the fact that costs and benefits are not experienced in the same time period. Costs entailing behavioral adjustments are incurred in the present, in the course of one's lifetime, whereas the benefits from those adjustments are reaped in the future, after death. Thus, rational individuals make choices not only depending on how much they value and benefit from earthly sins, but also on how they calculate their inter-temporal benefits. They consider that time on earth is shorter than time in the afterlife, so they calculate whether short-term sacrifices on earth are worth long-term benefits in heaven. Economists call this decision making process a *time preference*, or *discounting*. Those with a high time preference prefer to reap benefits in the present, while those with a low time preference are more focused on benefits in the future. In terms of the afterlife, one can say that those Christians and Muslims who choose to live virtuous lives on earth with expectations of huge benefits in eternal heaven have a low time preference.

Is it preposterous to think that we mortals have any decision-making power when it comes to our afterlife? Don't most belief systems teach that there is a superior being that ultimately determines if we go to heaven or hell?

Writers and philosophers have pondered the extent of individual choice throughout history, and many have concluded that yes, individuals do have some ability to chose. In *The Republic*, Greek philosopher Plato conveys his view that people have a choice in how they live their lives and that each individual is responsible for that choice.64 They then must face the consequences of their actions. They cannot avoid paying the price. If not in this life, they will pay the price for their sins in the afterlife. In *The Inferno*, Dante also underscores the importance of free will. He believes that every person makes a choice whether to follow the path towards heaven or hell (and those who refuse to make a choice go to hell, since, by definition, no choice is a choice).65 Lastly, English poet John Milton also extols free choice in *Paradise Lost*, claiming that nothing is predestined and everyone has the freedom of will.66

In addition to philosophy and literature, religion also weighs in on the idea of human choice with respect to the postmortem. Zoroastrians believe that all people have free will when they choose whether to align themselves with Ahura Mazda, the highest deity, or his opposite, Ahriman. Whatever choice they make will determine their future experience. Christianity is no different with respect to rational choices in this life, the tradeoffs, and the consequences to be paid in the afterlife. Good behavior on earth leads to eternity in heaven; bad behavior on earth leads to eternity in hell. Similarly, in Islam, people make choices freely, and, when their souls stand before Allah to account for their lives, they have to take responsibility for those choices. Surely in performing their cost/benefit analysis, Muslims consider that Allah rewards good deeds tenfold, whereas when they sin, they only get punished for the sins that they do.67 Clearly, the expected returns on doing good are much greater than the expected costs of doing bad.

In conclusion, choosing to go to heaven or to hell and modifying one's behavior accordingly requires what economists call *rational behavior*. But do human beings really think rationally when it comes to religion, death, and the afterlife? While neoclassical economists believe they do, Sidebar 2.2 introduces others who don't.

Sidebar 2.2: Is Human Behavior Rational?

Some economists challenge the notion of rational behavior under any circumstances, claiming instead that all human behavior is irrational. In what has come to be called "behavioral economics," researchers conduct experiments to show that in fact people do not always pursue their self-interest, respond to economic incentives, or make rational cost/benefit analyses. To the contrary, people participate in the economy as consumers, investors, producers, and traders with behavior that is emotional, passionate, and spontaneous, and not in their best interest. They change their minds, and they choose small immediate benefits over big future ones. Introducing emotions into economics represents cross-fertilization between psychology and economics, and has been the preferred framework of analysis in the research of two Nobel laureates: Gary Becker, who introduced elements of psychology into his study of crime and criminal behavior, and Herbert Simon, who claimed that people sought out satisfaction in irrational ways, coining the phrase "bounded rationality."68

Sidebar 2.3: A Rational Attempt to Trick Death: An Arabic Tale

Threatened animals attempt to trick death by mimicking the dead of their species in a process called thanatomimesis. These possum, for example, curls up in a ball and lies still until the threat of death passes. Threatened humans do the same. In the battlefield, a soldier behaves rationally by pretending to be dead so the enemy won't waste a bullet.

An Arabic tale about a (rational) attempt to trick death was brought to western audiences by Somerset Maugham in his play *Sheppey* (1933) and by John O'Hara in his novel *Appointment in Samara* (1934). The tale describes how a merchant in Baghdad sent his servant to run some errands at the local market. When the servant returned, he was visibly upset. He told his master how someone pushed up against him in the crowded marketplace. When he looked up, he saw it was Death, and, terrified, the servant ran home. He begged his master to lend him a horse so that he could gallop out of town, to Samara, where surely Death wouldn't find him. After he rode away, his master went to the marketplace. He also ran into Death and asked, "Why did you frighten my servant?" To that, Death responded that he didn't mean to frighten anyone. He was merely surprised because he had an appointment with the servant later that day in Samara so he was wondering what the servant was doing in Baghdad.

The Opportunity Cost of Dancing the Night Away

You choose, you lose. By this economists mean that when people behave rationally and select one outcome over another, they are by definition giving something up. By choosing one path, people lose the possibility of the other. There is a tradeoff. The loss that is incurred has a value, namely the *opportunity cost.*

The concept of opportunity cost is typically used in conjunction with the time resource, such as the value of income lost when one takes an unpaid vacation or works for free. It is also used to measure the loss incurred when investing money in one way rather than another (such as buying IBM stock rather than a government bond).

The concept of opportunity cost appears in afterlife visions with respect to the activities that fill the days of the deceased.

If there is nothing to do, if the deceased spend all their time literally doing nothing, then the value of their time is zero, because there is no alternative way they could be spending it. (The musical group Talking Heads sings about this option in their song *Heaven.* See lyrics in Sidebar 2.4). However, if the dead have something to do, some activities that fill their days, then the opportunity cost of their time is not zero.

How Do the Dead Spend Their Time?

Many visions of the afterlife portray an active eternity. According to David Letterman, for example, in winter there are sign-up sheets posted all over hell for hayrides (with Hitler).69 What is remarkable about this view is not only that there are activities in the afterlife but also that the dead have a choice. They can sign up for the rides. Or not. They can do something else instead. The idea that multiple leisure activities exist simultaneously in the afterlife has been a recurring theme from antiquity to the present. From ancient Greek and Etruscan art and mythology to twenty-first century films and novels, the afterlife is shown as filled with physically and intellectually active shades, ghosts, and souls.

Socializing with family and friends is often associated with heaven. The late senator Edward Kennedy, in his eulogy for his nephew John Kennedy, Jr., said, "He and his bride have gone to be with his mother and father."70 Kennedy, like many others, believed that the dead get reunited with their friends and families. Winston Churchill also looked forward to meeting up with his family and friends, and said, "Only faith in a life after death is a brighter world where dear ones will meet again…".71 According to Socrates, the afterlife is filled with conversations with old friends as well as the new people one meets after death. Perhaps it is this human desire to have meaningful interpersonal relationships in the afterlife that led to the huge success of Mitch Albom's bestseller, *Five People You Meet in Heaven*, which promotes that very idea.

Dancing is another activity often associated with heaven. The Greeks, Romans, and the Celts all imagined their ancestors dancing. There is hardly an ancient society that did not portray its dead in various dancing poses. Such dancing was an integral part of a celebratory postmortem atmosphere including feasting (Greeks and Romans), listening to music (Celts), and engaging in contests while at banquets (Egypt). So too today, the Ashanti of Africa believe that the dead go to Asamando where, among other activities, they dance and sing for eternity.72

Then there is the option of participating in sports. According to drawings on vases and reliefs on walls, the ancient Greeks expected to compete in horseback riding and gymnastics in the Elysian Fields.73 Similarly, the elaborate wall drawings in Etruscan memorials for the dead indicate an athletic afterlife filled with competitions and games. Sports show up in ancient visions of the afterlife because ancient societies believed it mirrors earthly life. For that same reason, sports also show up in the New Earth, the contemporary heaven described by Randy Alcorn, an American pastor of the Eternal Perspective Ministries. Alcorn reinterprets the Scriptures to argue that life in heaven includes the best of life on earth, and since there is nothing sinful about physical competition, sports, too, will exist in the afterlife.74

Using the same reasoning, Alcorn suggests that there will be leisure travel in the afterlife, that people will move around and visit places outside their residences.75 While Alcorn bases his view on reinterpretations of the Bible, contemporary secular afterlife visions share the possibility of afterlife travel. In his book *The Travel Guide to Heaven*, Anthony DeStefano describes heaven as Disneyworld, Hawaii, Paris, Rome, and New York all rolled into one, since the afterlife is an all-inclusive vacation that never ends.76 And, like other afterlife activities, leisure travel also appears in visions of ancient societies. Indeed, the Egyptians believed that if they had elaborate funerals, their afterlife would be filled with travel in boats on the Nile, enjoying the view of nearby deserts and lush greenery around the river banks.77

Finally, a variety of cultural and educational activities are also available to the dead. While the ancient Greeks believed people played the lyre in the afterlife, some Americans of the 1800s outdid them. They believed souls played in orchestras. Such an afterlife was proposed by Elizabeth Stuart Phelps in her widely read book *The Gates Ajar*, first published in 1868. It offered a comforting view of heaven to the families who lost their loved ones in the American Civil War. With a secular and materialistic perspective, Phelps described the afterlife as similar to a small New England town, full of shops and libraries, schools, museums, and, yes, concert halls in which the dead played as well as sat in the audience.78 Afterlife cultural and educational activities also show up in the twenty-first century vision offered by Sylvia Browne in her latest book *Afterlives of the Rich and Famous*.79 In it, the prolific psychic reveals that the soul of Michael Jackson gave sixteen concerts once he got to the afterlife and that of John Lennon still continues to write music and perform.

Opportunity Cost of Time is Positive

If leisure activities such as sports, travel, socializing, and cultural enrichment are all available, then do the dead incur an opportunity cost when they chose one over the other?

The answer is provided by economist Scott Gordon in a short academic paper about scarcity in heaven.80 Gordon argues that time is a scarce resource in heaven because one is faced with a multitude of activities that could be pursued at any given time. Even though people have an infinite amount of time to pursue those activities, still, each individual must decide which of the many activities to pursue at any given time.

Gordon's argument rests on the fact that we cannot do all things at once but must prioritize them; therefore, there is a sequence to our activities. Even though the deceased have forever to do things, they cannot do things simultaneously so one activity must be given up in order to pursue another. In other words, the opportunity cost of time is positive.

Specifically, by choosing to socialize with neighbors, a dead person gives up the possibility of attending a concert or playing a game of soccer. The opportunity cost of socializing then is the value, to the dead person, of the activity given up.

Sidebar 2.4: Lyrics of *Heaven*

If there is nothing for the dead to do, then they have no choices to make, and so they do not incur opportunity costs. A vision of such a heaven is offered by David Byrne, the singer of Talking Heads, and Jerry Harrison in their song entitled Heaven (see lyrics below81).

Everyone is trying to get to the bar
The name of the bar, the bar is called heaven
The band in heaven, they play my favorite song
Play it one more time, play it all night long
Heaven, heaven is a place, a place where nothing, nothing ever happens
Heaven, heaven is a place, a place where nothing, nothing ever happens
There is a party, everyone Is there
Everyone will leave at exactly the same time
When this party's over, it will start again
It will not be any different, it will be exactly the same
Heaven, heaven is a place, a place where nothing, nothing ever happens
When this kiss is over it will start again
It will not be any different, it will be exactly the same
It's hard to imagine that nothing at all could be so exciting, could be this much fun
Heaven, heaven is a place, a place where nothing, nothing ever happens
Heaven, heaven is a place, a place where nothing, nothing ever happens

3

Supply, Demand, and Markets

In the 1970s, *Saturday Night Live* featured a humorous character by the name of Father Guido Sarducci. He introduced the concept of the Five-Minute University, claiming that people can learn, in only five minutes, as much as the average person remembers five years after graduating from college. Sarducci then proceeded to teach several subjects. When it came to economics, he suggested that all one needs to know is supply and demand. Just two words: supply, demand. Many contemporary economics professors would probably agree, believing that if a student remembers those two concepts five years after college, their teaching efforts have not been wasted.

Indeed, supply and demand are at the core of economics. They are also at the core of the vignette *Don't Know Much About the Afterlife,* which deals with the information about the afterlife provided by priests, mediums, and book authors, as well as the demand for such information by Odysseus, Dr. Faustus, and millions of religious believers.

Supply and demand come together to form a market. In addition to the market for information, there is also the market for products that ensure a high quality afterlife. *The Market For Indulgences* describes how the fourteenth-century Catholic Church offered believers such a product.

Same Wife in the Afterlife explores the marriage market in the netherworld by putting an economic spin on the Mormon view of eternal coupling.

When markets are in equilibrium, the quantity demanded of a good is equal to the quantity supplied. That is a rare occurrence. More often than not, there is market disequilibrium, resulting in a shortage or a surplus. In *Queuing For a Cauldron in Hell and a Halo in Heaven,* Michelangelo and Mark Twain illustrate the shortages that occur in the afterlife.

Don't Know Much About the Afterlife

Hamlet, the Prince of Denmark, and Joseph Heller, the author of *Catch-22*, both exhibited a lack of information about the afterlife. In his famous existential soliloquy, Shakespeare's Hamlet wondered about more than whether to be or not to be. He wondered about death and its aftermath, noting that no dead man has ever returned to share his experience with the living. In Shakespearian English, Hamlet says, "...the dread of something after death, the undiscover'd country, from whose bourn no traveler returns, puzzles the will..."82 Hamlet was confused and somberly admitted he had no clear idea about the postmortem.

Joseph Heller used contemporary American English to say, quite simply, "Dying is like having children—you never know what will come out."83 With humor, Heller also revealed his confusion about the postmortem.

Although Hamlet and Heller missed the tsunami of afterlife information offered by the Internet, they could have turned to literature, religion, and mythology of their time for answers to their questions. There is no evidence that they did, so, despite all their ponderings, Hamlet and Heller did not have what economists refer to as "demand" for knowledge about life after death. In order for such a demand to exist, people must be willing and able to pay to obtain it. They must be willing to exchange money (or a substitute thereof) for the product they want. Throughout history, people have willingly paid for afterlife information, going to great lengths to glimpse the other side, to obtain hints as to what it is like, despite the lack of any proof about the quality or veracity of what they were getting.

And who are the suppliers of these glimpses and hints? They are mediums, writers, priests, artists, researchers, and ordinary folk who provide what information they have through verbal communications, books, and religious teachings. They do not offer their product for free, but rather they exchange it for money or its equivalent.

Demand and supply of afterlife information have both existed throughout history. They took repeatedly reinvented forms and they repeatedly reinforced each other. Perhaps demand for information came first, and entrepreneurial individuals responded by offering supply. Or perhaps supply came first, creating a demand where none existed before. Irrespective of the sequence, supply and demand together make up the market for afterlife information in several ways.

Single Demander, Single Supplier

In 1604, British author Christopher Marlowe published a play by the name *The Tragical History of Doctor Faustus*. In it, he described the main character's insatiable curiosity and quest for information on a wide variety of subjects. Faustus was bound by the times in which he lived, times in which knowledge and information were hard to come by. One day he befriended Lucifer, the devil, who was presumed to possess extraordinary breadth and depth of knowledge. They made a pact: over the course of the next twenty-four years, Faustus will get all the information he desires, including forbidden knowledge about what happens after death. Mephistopheles, a minor devil, will live by his side during this time and answer his questions as they arise. In exchange, at the end of twenty-four years, Faustus will turn his soul over to Lucifer.

Marlowe's drama of Doctor Faustus illustrates a situation in which there is a single demander for afterlife information, Faustus, and a single supplier, Lucifer. The price is agreed upon (Faustus's soul) and the transaction goes forward.

A modern spin on this exchange uses the Internet to identify the sale price for a soul, thus avoiding the *sotto voce* negotiations in a darkened room that were part of Dr. Faustus's experience. In 2001 Alan Burtle tried to sell his soul on e-bay.[84] He was a sole supplier of souls—one soul in particular—looking for a single buyer. E-Bay headquarters closed the bidding because it deemed the sale raised too many complicated issues, but not before the bidding reached $400. By contrast, in 2008 Wally Scott put his soul up for sale on the New Zealand version of e-bay, TradeMe. Bidding reached $189 and the sale was permitted to proceed. For the exchange to take place, all it took was a single supplier and a single demander.

Multiple Demanders, Multiple (Direct) Suppliers

Florentine poet Dante Alighieri visited the afterlife. Or so he told his readers in his immensely popular book *The Divine Comedy*, published in the early 1300s. With its colorful prose and descriptive drawings, Dante's book provided the most detailed vision of the afterlife to date. It described his journey through hell and purgatory, guided by the long-deceased Roman poet Virgil, as well as through heaven where his guide was Beatrice, the love of his youth. In the course of his travels, Dante interviewed the dead and observed their surroundings. Then, upon his return, he wrote about his underworld experience. He became a supplier of afterlife information.

Hundreds of years later, Don Piper, a Baptist minister from the United States, also claimed to have visited heaven. It happened after he was hurt in an automobile accident. Paramedics arrived to his rescue and pronounced him dead. At first it seemed an accident no different from numerous others, but then, just before Piper's body was removed, another Baptist minister happened upon the scene and knelt by Piper's body to pray. When he began singing a hymn, Piper joined him. Everyone present at the scene was astonished, the sense of magic increasing when Piper opened his eyes and claimed to have visited heaven while lying on the highway. Soon thereafter, he published a book about his experience called *90 Minutes in Heaven*.85 Since Piper had less time in the afterlife than Dante, his descriptions are incomplete by comparison. But still, he, too, became a supplier of afterlife information.

Since both men claimed to have personally crossed over, witnessed the lives of the dead, and returned safely, armed with the mission to spread information about their respective experiences, they are direct suppliers. Since there is no go-between in the supply of their message, each author is both the producer of information as well as supplier of the final product to the consumer.

Both Dante and Piper faced huge demand from readers during their lifetimes. We know that because the popularity of Dante's book is said to have put food on his family's dining table.86 Similarly, the fact that Piper's book spent years on bestseller lists, first as a hardcover and then as a paperback, points to the magnitude of demand for afterlife information among contemporary readers.

Multiple Demanders, Multiple (Indirect) Suppliers

While Dante and Piper supplied afterlife information that they personally collected, others have supplied indirectly obtained information, making no claim of personal experience. They served as intermediaries in the information market insofar as they collected, compiled, and then published the impressions of heaven and hell obtained by others. Homer, for example, never claimed to have visited Hades, the world of the dead, but instead described Odysseus's journey there in *The Odyssey*. Similarly, Virgil's *Aeneid* traces Aeneas's visit with his dead father, never claiming personal experience.

Such indirect supply of afterlife information is not limited to fiction writers. There is no small number of non-fiction authors who write books and articles about real people who claim to have crossed over. Crossing over, as Don Piper did, has come to be called a near-death experience (NDE). Such short and unanticipated visits to the afterlife are a relatively common phenomenon in the early twenty-first century. Fifteen percent of Americans reported having what could be interpreted as near-death experiences.[87] According to the medical journal *Lancet*, some nine to eighteen percent of people near death in 2000 claimed to have had an NDE.[88] Some said they passed through a long dark tunnel, encountering light at the other end. Others reported being greeted on the other side (by people they knew or by strangers), finding themselves outside of their bodies, and finally returning to their bodies. While most describe feelings of peace and love, and so assume they went to heaven, some had painful experiences, concluding that they had visited hell. Even though scientists are largely skeptical about such claims, attributing the described sensations to biochemical changes possibly due to life-sustaining drugs, most dying patients are happy to share their experiences. And many want to listen and learn. Raymond Moody's pioneering 1975 book *Life After Death* described the experiences of some one hundred fifty people who had NDEs. His book was followed and confirmed by research conducted by Karlis Osis, Elizabeth Kubler-Ross, Kenneth Ring, Melvin Morse, and, most recently, Jeffrey Long, all of whom compiled information provided by others who had NDEs, organized the information, and analyzed it before supplying it on the market to satisfy readers' demand. It is unlikely that Raymond Moody ever thought of himself as Homer, but, in effect, both are suppliers of information about how others have experienced the afterlife.

Another kind of afterlife information is supplied by mediums. By claiming to communicate with the dead, mediums offer the living a channel through which to ask their loved ones not only how they are doing but also about life on the other side. Attempts at two-way conversations between the living and the dead have been common throughout history. (Witness the time and effort Thomas Edison invested in developing electrical equipment for that very purpose.89) Where those efforts failed, mediums claim to have succeeded and to provide answers for the 21% of Americans who believe people can talk to the dead.90 Mediums rely on tools such as Ouija boards and crystal balls to elicit responses from the other side. Sometimes they fall into a trance and use pencil and paper to write out what a spirit tells them. Alternatively, they tap on a table. Whatever aides and mechanisms they use, mediums serve as intermediaries between the living and the dead insofar as they facilitate cross-communication. They are empowered to perform that function because they are believed to possess special capacities. In medieval Japan, blind people were typically mediums since it was believed their blindness gave them the ability to see into the afterlife.91 In contemporary Western societies, believers think mediums are born with special powers that can then be honed and supplemented through appropriate schooling. Whether in historical Japan or in contemporary United States, mediums supply a product to the afterlife information market. Like book authors, they, too, are indirect suppliers, with no claims to personal experience in the afterlife.

In that way, mediums are similar to religious emissaries, such as priests and monks, who serve as intermediaries in the supply of afterlife information by providing their religion's vision of eternity. Serving this function is fundamental to their mission as God's representatives. The demanders for their services—namely, their congregation—turn to organized religion for many reasons, not the least of which is an interest in their own postmortem. Believers have a demand for information that will help them navigate through life in order to maximize their chances of securing a good afterlife.

If mediums use Ouija boards to supply their product, religious emissaries rely on sacred texts. Priests in ancient Egypt read relevant passages from the *Book of the Dead* to the dying, the first how-to book for navigating eternity. People demanded this information since they believed that if the soul did not know the right hymns and incantations, it would not be able to pass through the seven gates blocking the path to the afterlife. In the absence of that knowledge, their souls were destined to be swallowed by Ammut, the eater of the dead. In the contemporary world, Muslims seek out information about the afterlife and holy men teach, interpret, and explain the holy book in order to provide it. The Qur'an, whose content was dictated to the prophet Mohamed by the angel Gabriel (Jibril), is meant to comfort people about the postmortem. It describes the paradise Djanna, the final judgment and the eternal life that lies ahead for believers. Buddhists also rely on their monks and their holy books to spread information. The *Tripitaka* is the most important of these as it contains the earliest scriptures that were then altered over time to adjust to the national realities of the countries where the religion spread. But it is the Tibetan Buddhists, in their *Tibetan Book of the Dead* (also known as the *Bardo Thodol*), that offer one of the most detailed descriptions of what follows death. Its contents are recited by priests at the time of death, and the information is expected to guide the soul through the good and bad that awaits it. In this way, the *Tibetan Book of the Dead* is a guide for the living, the dying, and those who tend to the dying, as it describes the forty-nine day journey of the soul while it is in limbo (or bardo), before rebirth.

By contrast, in Christianity it is the religious emissaries rather than the holy books that offer most afterlife information. The Bible does not provide much of a road map; the Old Testament offers no practical information and what the New Testament contains is sparse. It is the philosophers and theologians that followed the compilation of the Bible, including Augustine of Hippo and Thomas Aquinas, who amplified the descriptions of heaven and hell with their own visions. Moreover, priests personalized their sermons and described punishment in hell and the rewards of heaven in ways that changed over the course of the centuries. By the 1400s, the *Ars Morendi* (The Art of Dying) compiled information about death and judgment and heaven and hell into one coherent whole. This illustrated book was used to guide the dying out of earthly life and contained practical prescriptions to ensure a positive afterlife experience. It served to remind believers that both the devil and an angel will vie for their soul at the time of death. With all this information, it is understandable that demand for the *Ars Morendi* was virtually universal among believers.

Whether afterlife information comes from religious figures, mediums, or book authors, it is not given freely. Suppliers offer it to consumers who are able and willing to pay the price. While it is obvious that a visit to a medium or the purchase of a book requires a payment, the financial exchange with religious representatives is less obvious. Yet it exists, as collection boxes and membership dues in churches, temples, and synagogues attest.

No Demanders and No Suppliers

Skeptics, non-believers, and those who have no curiosity about life after death obviously have no demand for afterlife information. Then again, there are curious, non-skeptical believers who also have no such demand. The reason is that they can get afterlife information for free, without having to pay for it. Two examples from across the world show conditions under which this occurs.

According to Chinese indigenous beliefs, everyone visits the world of the dead while they sleep. This happens because people have two souls, the *p'o* and the *hun*. The former represents the physical world and the latter represents the spiritual world. It is the hun that can separate from a sleeping body and visit the land of the dead. Upon waking, the individual remembers what the soul witnessed. It knows everything there is to know about the afterlife.

Similarly, the Wagawaga people of Papua New Guinea believe that living people can visit the dead any time they want.92 The onus to visit relatives is on them, since the dead cannot come back to visit the living. The living travel to an underworld place called Hiyoya that is located below the ocean There are specific flowers that are believed to come from the underworld, so whenever they sprout from the ground or show up in a vase, it is believed that someone has visited and brought them back.

Given the possibility of regular visits to the afterlife, the Chinese and the Wagawaga easily obtain information about conditions in on the other side, as well as news of their ancestors. As a result, there is no demand for afterlife information, and no one will supply it since cannot be exchanged for money. It is simply not a tradable good.

"It's like texting, but for dead people."

Cartoon 3.1: Ouija- Texting for the Dead

Sidebar 3.1: An Eskimo Learns About Hell

Writer Paul Arden describes a fictional exchange between a Christian missionary and an Eskimo about afterlife information.93 After a missionary described the numerous tortures of hell, an Eskimo asked if it was possible for him to go to hell if he didn't know about it. The missionary, somewhat perplexed, said no. To that the Eskimo, also perplexed, responded, "Then why did you have to tell me about it?"

The Market for Indulgences

The Pardoner in Geoffrey Chaucer's *Canterbury Tales* regales his fellow pilgrims with stories about demand and supply.94 While those exact words are never uttered, their meaning is implicit. The Pardoner boasts that when he preaches, he induces believers to buy his relics. He tells them the relics will absolve them from their sins so they can enjoy a good afterlife. In the course of his narrative, the Pardoner describes the demand by his parishioners, his supply of relics, and the price at which the exchange takes place. With no knowledge of economics beyond the intuitive, Chaucer is in effect describing the functioning of a market.

A market represents the interaction between buyers and sellers of a particular product. It is where consumers express their demand for something, producers offer their supply of it, and they interact through exchange. Markets offer the potential for efficient trade, a process that makes everyone better off. The sellers are better off because they get compensated for their product; the buyers are better off because they get a product that they cannot or wish not to produce for themselves.

Such mutually beneficial trade occurs in numerous markets having to do with the afterlife. One of these is described by the Pardoner in the *Canterbury Tales*: the market for indulgences.

Indulgences are a product of the medieval Catholic Church. According to Catholic doctrine, believers can plead with religious authorities for something and the authorities can hear their pleas and decide to grant it. When believers plead for the pardon of some of their sins and the remission of some portion of their afterlife punishment, they are asking for an indulgence. Such an indulgence is granted when the believer prays, does good deeds, and does penance.

Over time, a full-fledged market for indulgences developed across Europe, culminating in the 1500s. It consisted of popular demand for a product that was believed to improve the quality of the afterlife, and the supply of it by the medieval church representatives. The resulting transaction pleased demanders and suppliers alike.

That there would be a demand for indulgences is obvious. By the early 1000s, Christians across Europe were terrified of the final judgment that awaited them, as well as the torture they expected to experience in hell and purgatory. People believed that if they committed venal sins during their lifetimes, upon death their souls would go to purgatory for a period of cleansing. It was possible for venal sins to be cleansed and therefore forgiven because they were considered minor (as opposed to mortal sins, which were so grave they were unforgivable; a mortal sinner went directly to hell). The period of cleansing in purgatory was unpleasant, and by purchasing an indulgence for oneself or a deceased loved one, an individual got a promise from the Church that the cleansing period would be shortened. It makes sense that believers coveted a product that promised to decrease or bypass the anticipated agonies, and anyone who could afford such a promise had a demand for it. Over time, as word spread and people learned about such easy salvation, the demand for indulgences grew. This growth was also aided by the realization among the population that there were no substitutes for indulgences. Nothing but an indulgence could, with absolute certainty, shorten a soul's time in purgatory. Relying only on good earthly behavior did not provide a guarantee.

That the supply of indulgences existed is also easy to understand. For centuries the Church had given out indulgences when people said specific prayers and engaged in specific good deeds. Increasingly, these came to be accompanied by monetary donations. Such donations represented an inflow of cash into the Church coffers. This revenue enabled purchases, construction, and the expansion of activities and programs. The fact that the Catholic Church was the most important and powerful institution of the time lent credence to the products it offered. When a religious emissary proclaimed that punishment in the afterlife was shortened, his words were not challenged. And so, over time, offering indulgences became a painless way of increasing Church revenue.

Demand and supply together defined the market for indulgences. It was a clear and dynamic market in which trade between buyers and sellers made everyone better off. Christians got what they wanted—a good afterlife. The Church got what it wanted—a seemingly endless source of revenue. Both sides had incentives to trade, and the market thrived.

Until it no longer thrived. A major bottleneck was reached, and activity came to a standstill. Supply could not keep up with demand, since the preparation of each physical indulgence was a labor-intensive, time-consuming project.

The market for indulgences was saved by a revolutionary technological advancement that enabled mass production of supply. In the fifteenth century, Printer Johannes Gutenberg invented the printing press in Germany, and within a short time the world changed. Not only did the press enable the Renaissance and the wide dissemination of knowledge, it also enabled the mass printing of indulgences. Although Gutenberg also printed bibles, given the prevailing illiteracy among medieval populations it was not the sale of bibles that made it a lucrative business. It was the printing and sale of indulgences (that did not require reading).

The subsequent manifold increase in supply of indulgences enabled the market to expand and the industry to spread into previously unreachable territories. But once again, supply could not keep up with demand. This time, it was the bishops and priests who were stretched beyond their limits. Ever resourceful, the Church eliminated this bottleneck by increasing the number of suppliers of indulgences. It granted authority to so-called "pardoners" and sent them out across Europe to meet with believers and facilitate the market transaction.

Soon it became clear that this new system of product delivery was susceptible to abuse. Pardoners became greedy and began to act on their own accord, supplying more indulgences than permitted and charging higher prices so as to pocket the difference. Given that they were out on their own, there was no opportunity for supervision but ample opportunity for illegal and immoral behavior. The Church leadership in Rome had lost control and had no effective way of reimposing it and reigning in the pardoners.

Still, despite the corruption and greed, the indulgence market continued to function, with highly responsive supply and demand that adjusted to social, demographic, and technological changes of the times. Until it no longer did. As with any market, an external disruption can cause havoc. In the case of indulgences, that external disruption came in the form of Martin Luther, a German priest and professor of theology, and the havoc was a social movement that forever changed the indulgence market.

Luther did not support promising a decreased time in purgatory for a price, nor did he support Pope Leo X's granting of indulgences to those who contributed to rebuilding St. Peter's Basilica in Rome.95 The lack of effective and sincere restraint on the ballooning abuse of trust and power led Luther to write the Ninety-Five Theses that called for a theological debate on indulgences. A movement against the Catholic Church came together that later led to the Protestant Reformation. It wasn't until 1564 that the sale of indulgences was terminated by the Council of Trent, which thus brought an end to a thriving market by choking off supply.

Sidebar 3.2: Buddhist Ritual of Releasing Ghosts With Burning Mouths

The medieval Catholic Church is not the only religious institution to have supplied a product that is claimed to improve the quality of the afterlife. In Asia, it is believed that some people become ghosts with small mouths after they die.96 As a result of their mouth size, such ghosts are unable to eat or drink, making them perpetually hungry. Having the bad luck of becoming a ghost with a small mouth is a fate feared by all. Families of the deceased do not know if this fate has befallen their relatives. They turn to Buddhist priests or Taoist monks for help. They have a demand for a service that could correct this problem.

The priests and monks supply such a service. They perform a ritual called "Releasing [Ghosts] with Burning Mouths." With the aid of magic instruments and incantations, these religious emissaries make their way into hell, where they open the mouths of those with the condition, enabling them to eat and to be reborn as normal people in the future.

Upon their return from the hereafter, the priests and monks accept monetary donations from the grateful families. The exchange is mutually beneficial.

Same Wife in the Afterlife?

The market for indulgences was an earthly market, one in which an exchange took place on earth for a payoff in the afterlife. The marriage market, as discussed in this vignette, is made up of two markets: one that is entirely earthly, and another in which both trade and payoff take place in the hereafter.

Viewing marriage as a market, where supply and demand come together as they do for medical services or tractors, may seem preposterous to non-economists. On top of that, extending the concept of a marriage market into visions of the afterlife may border on the fantastical. Unconventional as they seem, both ideas are explored in this vignette by focusing on afterlife marital relations as viewed through an economics lens.

Marriage as a Market

Nobel laureate Gary Becker was the first economist to apply economics principles to the marriage institution. In his pioneering 1973 study, he set the groundwork for subsequent research on marriage under conditions of scarce resources, the costs and benefit analysis of marriage, and the terms of the marriage contract.97 From this research, a view of marriage emerges that closely resembles the functioning of a firm, insofar as people come together, typically to produce a household experience and offspring. Such coupling may or may not entail romantic love, exclusivity, and permanence. It might be legally binding or not. Irrespective of its nature, the formation of the couple results from the interaction of supply and demand. Men and women have a demand for coupling; men and women supply themselves for that coupling. They demand (and simultaneously supply) affection, companionship, economic security, social status, and much more. Each person supplies a particular set of physical, economic, and intellectual characteristics; each person demands some particular set of physical, economic, and intellectual characteristics. People pay a price for their marriage partner. Payment is valued in terms of the loss of independence, the necessity for compromise, supporting another individual, and housekeeping for another individual, as well as giving up the possibility of marrying someone else (the opportunity cost). People consider all this when they perform a cost/benefit analysis to determine whether to marry or remain single, and, also, how long to search for a mate.98 Among the benefits, they consider that marriage allows them to produce goods and services they cannot produce alone, and to do so more efficiently, because each partner can specialize and then exchange.

People marry if the outcome of their cost/benefit analysis points to an improvement over their current single state. When a person with the right set of characteristics comes along, one for which another person is willing to pay the price of marriage, then an exchange occurs in the marriage market (and a contract is signed at the wedding ceremony). Just like businesses and countries that trade, people marry because they expect to be better off than they were before marriage. If they didn't, there would be no incentive to marry. While it is intuitively easier to apply the fundamentals of supply and demand to non-Western arranged marriages or Western matchmaking services, characteristics of a marriage market show up even in love marriages.99

Marriage in the Afterlife

According to the Vikings, if the warrior's wife wants to be reunited with her husband in Valhalla, the heaven for soldiers, she has only one chance to achieve her goal. She must kill herself at the time of his death. Failing that, she is destined to spend eternity in a different location and will never see her husband again.

That is a high price to pay for reuniting with one's spouse. Several contemporary religions posit husband and wife afterlife reunions without extracting such a price. In Islam, it is believed that a man will meet up with his wife after death, and since he is allowed up to four simultaneous wives on earth, he can meet up with all of them in heaven (his wives, however, can only have one husband, on earth and beyond). By contrast, Christianity has no single position on afterlife marriages.

Most Christian churches adhere to the view espoused by the Bible: in Mark 12:25, Jesus states there is no marriage in the afterlife, that marriage is part of the old order, the one on earth.100 Catholics and Orthodox Christians believe everyone will be together in the family of God, that there are no private groupings such as husband and wife.

In the intellectually turbulent eighteenth century, a Christian philosopher and scientist named Emanuel Swedenborg offered what continues to be the most comprehensive and elaborate view of afterlife marriage. On the basis of revelations from the Lord that were transmitted to him by spirits from the hereafter,101 Swedenborg authored twenty-five books over twenty-seven years. He distanced himself from mainstream Christianity by claiming that the boundary between earthly life and the life of spirits is very thin. The world of spirits, where afterlife marriage occurs, is the halfway point between heaven and hell, and it is where the dead reside. There, people live like they did on earth.102 Swedenborg claimed to have been told by spirits that some people don't even realize they are dead.103

Elements of Swedenborg's philosophy show up in the teachings of the Mormon Church, whose contemporary customs pertaining to afterlife coupling most clearly mirror the earthly marriage market.

The Mormon Church, formally known as the Church of Jesus Christ of Latter Day Saints, is based on the teaching of the prophet Joseph Smith, who wrote the religion's spiritual text, the *Book of Mormons*, around 1830. It differs from mainstream Christianity in several ways, including the view that, after death, body and soul reunite for eternity. Mormons also believe that the souls of people on earth have preexisted, since human life is longer than the time spent on earth. There is a forever backward and a forever forward, as people come from eternity and return to eternity.104 Before coming to life on earth and after leaving life on earth, every Mormon lives with the Heavenly Father. Mormon heaven consists of three parts, one of which is the Celestial.105 It is there that families from earth come together after death and live as spirits.

To ensure that husbands and wives actually meet up in this heaven, they participate in a special ceremony called the Celestial Marriage. The couple kneels in the Mormon Temple, facing each other, each in front of a mirror that reflects their image into eternity.106 At the conclusion of the ceremony, husband and wife are said to be Forever Sealed, as this binding marriage contract carries over into the afterlife.107 A couple that fails to have a Celestial Marriage on earth can still expect to meet up in heaven, where their souls can remarry if they want. George Smith, in his extensively researched book on Mormon polygamy, *Nauvoo Polygamy*, explained that celestial marriage was first used to describe plural marriage on earth, but, under pressure from authorities and internal dissenters, by the 1880s came to refer to marriage in the postmortem.108 It was then specified that if a man or woman dies, the surviving spouse can remarry, but that marriage is only good until death, since the person will spend eternity with their sealed spouse.109

The Afterlife Marriage Market

Applying the economics lens to Mormon teachings entails identifying the demand and supply for afterlife spouses.

Eternal marriage can be achieved *ex ante* or *ex post*. In the former, a couple performs the celestial wedding on earth, so each spouse is sealed when he or she reaches heaven. In the latter, a man and woman have the option of voluntarily participating in the postmortem marriage market, as spirits.110

While both Mormon men (MM) and Mormon women (MW) are simultaneously demanders and suppliers, for the sake of simplicity, let us assume that MM are the demanders of afterlife marriage and MW are the suppliers.

Let us also assume that the determinants of men's demand for afterlife spouses are the same as men's earthly demand for spouses, which is similar to that for any good or service. According to economic theory, individual demand is determined by taste, availability and price of substitute goods, expectations about the future, and income.

Taste. Taste is simply a question of likes and dislikes. If MM and MW like their earthly spouses sufficiently to want to spend eternity with them, then they will want to be sealed. If an MM doesn't like or want his spouse, he will have no demand for her in the afterlife. He will view death as a *de facto* divorce, a liberation of sorts. He may then decide to stay single in the afterlife or to enter the marriage market and seek a new partner to marry, depending on his taste. As a single soul not bound by marriage vows, the

MM has the possibility for variety in new romantic encounters. It is likely, however, that the taste of the MM is inclined towards a new marriage, since Mormons believe only married people can become "godlike" in the hereafter, and for eternity.111 No single person can aspire to that state, making Celestial Marriage a very desirable institution.

Availability and Price of Substitutes. In the marriage market, the term "substitute goods" refers to spousal candidates other than the earthly wife. If MM reach the afterlife unsealed and choose not to re-wed their earthly spouses, they will consider other options. In their search for substitute soul mates, MM will consider both the availability of alternatives as well as the price of pursuing them. The availability of alternate spouses depends on female souls' taste for sealing: if many MW souls are interested and in the market, there will be more choices for MM souls. The price of a substitute soul mate is more difficult to estimate, because it is not known if MM souls incur explicit costs of finding and getting acquainted with a potential spouse (analogous to the earthly costs of dating or matchmaking services). However, they do incur an opportunity cost, since the time spent in the search and in courtship can instead be used for other heavenly activities (a Celestial Marriage ceremony on earth eliminates that opportunity cost).

Expectations About the Future. The way in which an MM envisions the future determines his demand for sealing. If he is concerned about locating his earthly spouse in the afterlife, he will demand a celestial ceremony on earth. Also, if he is concerned with encountering a shortage of other possible spousal candidates in the hereafter, he will demand a celestial ceremony on earth. If he fears having a bad marriage with another spouse, for eternity, then he will have a demand for an eternal marriage with his earthly spouse, since she is, in essence, a pre-tested product that comes with no surprises.

Income. The available information on Mormon eternity does not lend itself to economic interpretation when it comes to income. Economic theory states that income and demand are positively related.112 Applied to the Mormon afterlife, that would mean that the more income a MM has, the greater his financial capacity to expand his household and to pay for associated costs of the marriage, and so the greater his demand for it. But alas, income does not feature in Mormon afterlife teachings.

Let us now focus on MW who, for the purposes of this vignette, are suppliers to the afterlife wedding market. The product they supply is themselves as potential spirit wives. According to economic theory, the determinants of supply for any good or service include the cost of inputs used in production, the profitability of alternative pursuits, expectations about the future, and technology. These are also relevant when MW supply themselves to the eternal marriage market.

Cost of Inputs. The costs incurred by MW in order to make themselves desirable as eternal spouses include the study of the Mormon holy book and adjusting one's lifestyle so as to live according to Mormon princi-ples. These self-improvement activities take place both before and after death. In both cases, they entail an opportunity cost of time and energy, since MW could be spending their time in other ways.

Profitability of Alternative Pursuits. Given the costs entailed in becoming a desirable potential spouse, an MW might consider pursuing the alterna-tive, namely the single state. By remaining single, she can avoid incurring those costs. Since profits are defined as the residual left over after subtract-ing costs from revenue, pursuing the single state might be more profitable than pursuing the married state.

Expectations About the Future. MW are likely to consider the fact that there are afterlife activities not open to them if they remain single. Like MM, they will miss out on the possibility of a "godlike" existence if they fail to become sealed. This expectation about the future is likely to increase their demand for afterlife marriage.

Technology. Technology refers to how things are made. The more effi-cient the technology used to make herself desirable as an afterlife spouse, the more likely an MW is to supply herself to the marriage mar-ket. Specifically, the faster she can learn the relevant Mormon teach-ings, the less time she has to spend on study, so the lower her opportunity cost and the more likely she is to offer her product—namely, herself—to the market.

Finally, the demand by MM and the supply of MW come together in the market for eternal marriage. Each seeks to become better off than each was before, and the exchange is expected to be mutually beneficial (or it would not occur voluntarily). The transaction is finalized at the wedding ceremony.

Does Afterlife Marriage Entail Afterlife Sex?

Do visions of afterlife marriage include afterlife sex? And if so, is it a tradable commodity, with clear supply, demand, and rules of exchange?

Given the multifaceted and enduring importance societies place on sexual activities, extrapolation to the afterlife is logical for those who believe that life after death mirrors life on earth. The Austrian psychoanalyst Sigmund Freud has said that the drive to reproduce (and thus engage in sexual activity) is one of the most basic drives of human beings. If life after death is viewed as life on earth, there is no reason to believe that this fundamental drive is lost when crossing over. And indeed, some visions of the afterlife assume that drive is not lost and that sexual activities do take place.

There are myths with explicit reference to sex, leaving little to the imagination. According to the Kalapalo Indians of central Brazil, the afterlife begins with sex. When people die, their shadow goes to the village of the dead, where it must first recuperate from its journey. That period of rest is filled with sexual activities: men have sex with Sakufenu (the woman from whom all people came), whereas women have sex with the dead shadows of the village.113

Other belief systems encourage the dead to go forth into the afterlife and copulate. While they are explicit in their recommendation, they do not prescribe with whom sexual relations should take place. The ancient Egyptian beliefs illustrate such recommendations. A copy of the *Book of the Dead*, prepared for an individual named Horemakhbit, provides instruction on spells that must be said in order to engage in intercourse. These spells have the purpose of "gaining control there, becoming a blessed one there, ploughing there, reaping there, eating there, drinking there, *copulating there*, doing everything that is done upon the earth…[italics mine]."114

Alternatively, for some cultures it is not written text but burial customs that point to sexual activity in the afterlife. An ancient Greek grave relief from the island of Kos, dated approximately 530 BCE, shows the dead engaging in a variety of sexual activities with each other,115 possibly as an indication of what lies in store for the dead. On the other side of the globe, Chinese gravesites from some 4000 years ago contain coffins with life-size wooden phalluses laid next to or on top of women's bodies,116 probably indicating the expectation of future sexual pleasures. In the same country, but millennia later, men have similar expectations and are often buried with bottles of Viagra within reach, as well as paper models of prostitutes that mimic reality.117

Organized religions have tackled afterlife sex either by categorically denying it or condoning it with varying degrees of muteness. Early Christianity denied the existence of any physical affection or sexual sensation after death. According to the Bible, sexual relations occur in the context of marriage, and since there is no marriage in heaven, it follows that there is no sex. Augustine of Hippo, who lived at the turn of the fifth century in the Roman province of Africa, claimed people appreciate each other's bodies in heaven, albeit for aesthetic pleasure only not in sexual ways.118 This view remained almost unchallenged into the present.

A dissenting view was offered, in the fifteenth century, by a Dominican friar called Girolamo Savonarola. He described paradise as containing the best earth has to offer, including sensual pleasures.119 The other challenge to Christian views came from philosopher Emanuel Swedenborg who claimed that the hereafter offered opportunities for sexual relations more exquisite than anything possible on earth.120 And, he claimed, the dead experience no decrease in potency after the act or over time. Indeed, one spirit who appeared before Swedenborg told him he had lived with his wife for a thousand years and was as sexually potent as when they first met.

As the twentieth century progressed and sex became a topic of open discussion on television and in print, some churches chimed in on the existence of afterlife sex. James Garlow, pastor of the Skyline Church, in California, softened the harshness of the Christian categorical denial of sex by claiming instead that it was merely obsolete. Sex is about intimacy, and in heaven there will be emotional intimacy for everyone.121 He also explains that sex will be unnecessary for procreation, which is absent in heaven, and for ecstasy, which will already be constant and abundant. Christian Pastor Randy Alcorn believes God does not discard aspects of earthly life without replacing them with something better. This leads him to postulate that while there is a replacement for sex, it will be so much better and greater that we cannot even imagine it.122 Jennifer Wright Knust, professor at Boston University, wrote a book entitled *Unprotected Texts: the Bible's Surprising Contradictions About Sex and Desire*, in which she offers a more sexually liberal interpretation of the sacred book.

However, it is the Mormon Church, the only among contemporary Christians, that professes the belief that when souls get to heaven, they can marry, procreate, and make spirit children.123 Since family on earth is the key to happiness, it follows that to be happy in heaven one must also be surrounded by family—the more the better. Some of these offspring will inhabit other realms, while others will be reincarnated as earthly babies.124 While spirit children play a large role in the Mormon vision of eternity, the way in which they are made is not explicitly stated.

Perhaps Islam is the best-known example of a belief system that has a sexual afterlife component. It has become a topic of speculation among believers and non-believers alike, because it, too, is implicit rather than explicit, allowing interpretations to suit an individual's personal inclinations. At its core is the belief that, in addition to their earthly wives, seventy beautiful maidens await the men who have faithfully observed their religion during their lifetimes. These maidens represent the men's award, to be enjoyed for eternity in the Islamic paradise. They are called *houri* (also known as *hur* and *jouri*) and are mentioned in the Qur'an several times, albeit without much detail. According to scholars Smith and Haddad, it is the subsequent religious writings that have expanded on the concept of houris, differing somewhat in their descriptions.125 Houri complexions have been described as translucent, white, or creamy, and their eyes have been described as ebony, pearl, or almond-shaped. But those are small differences. The broad agreement is that the houri are beautiful, that they are virgins, and that their raison d'etre is to provide pleasure to men. Miriam Van Scott, in her *Encyclopedia of Heaven*, notes that the pleasure provided by the houris is carnal, the kind forbidden during earthly existence.126 (Incidentally, one characteristic of the houris that is often overlooked has to do with age. According to Smith and Haddad, the houris are of the same age as the male for whom they are intended.127 This little caveat favors early death among Muslim men.)

The preceding illustrations indicate the existence of afterlife visions that are peppered with references to sexual activities. For the purposes of this chapter, the relevant question is whether those visions can be explained in terms of demand, supply, and a market that offers the possibility for mutually beneficial trade.

It turns out that the evidence of afterlife sex is so sparse that applying an economic lens to it is a stretch. While it might be argued that the Chinese woman buried with a phallus and the man buried with Viagra provide evidence of expected sexual pleasure, there is no evidence of demand in the economic sense—namely, a willingness to pay for a desired good or service. There is also no evidence of a corresponding supply which, together with demand, would define a market. While Islamic houris might be said to be suppliers of pleasure and deceased men are demanders, there is insufficient evidence of a functioning market mechanism.

Mormonism offers the closest approximation of a market for afterlife sex. Mormon teachings stipulate that the purpose of celestial marriage is procreation and the production of spirit children. Even though Mormons have accepted some of Emanuel Swedenborg's ideas, they did not embrace his view that souls engage in sexual relations.128 Yet, spirit babies are somehow created within the context of celestial marriage. The creation process need not be sexual, but it does entail some activity that is not open to those outside the marriage. Mormon men and Mormon women are simultaneously demanders and suppliers of that non-sexual activity. The activity is then traded among spouses under conditions of monopoly and monopsony (which mean the market has only one seller and one buyer, respectively). Participation in the market is limited to the two people or the two spirits who underwent the sealing ceremony.

Sidebar 3.3: Ernst Hemmingway, William Blake, and the Etruscans on Afterlife Love and Marriage

Nobel laureate Ernst Hemmingway told his friend F. Scott Fitzgerald that he expects his afterlife to be full of sex.[129] He described it as a place where he will have two houses, one in which he will keep his wife and children and have a great loving relationship with them, and another where he would keep nine mistresses, one on each of nine different floors.

As far as we know, British poet William Blake did not hope for such a sexually active afterlife. What we do know is that he illustrated the cover of his book on the afterlife with a couple kissing in the underworld. Such an amorous pose of a man and a woman surely indicates Blake's belief in afterlife love and physical relations. (Or not? Perhaps Blake was merely carrying over the irreverent wit reflected in his poetry onto his cover illustration.)

What about the Etruscans, those enigmatic peoples who left evidence of their afterlife vision before being swallowed up by history? Did they believe in afterlife marriage? On the walls of their tombs there are remnants of detailed activities that awaited the dead. But between all the feasting and the sports, there are no couples in amorous embraces. Instead, the Etruscans left behind sarcophagi with two figures—a man and a woman—sculpted on the top cover.[130] On the basis of the inscriptions, we know that the figures represent a married couple. Typically, their names and the man's profession are listed. We can infer that the corpses of both husband and wife were placed inside a matrimonial sarcophagus, but we don't know for sure. We can also infer that by being buried together, husband and wife believed they would share the postmortem, but that, too, is not known with certainty.

Disequilibrium: Queuing For a Cauldron in Hell and a Halo in Heaven

Medieval European artists depicted the endless torture and excruciating pain that Christianity had in store for its sinners.

One of these artists is Giotto. In his *Last Judgment,* the pre-Renaissance Italian painted a fresco in Padova's Arena Chapel, vividly portraying the multitude of torture methods that await the damned in hell. On the chapel walls, some souls hang, others simmer in cauldrons, and others still are being eaten by the devil. Despite also showing Jesus enthroned and souls ascending to heaven, for centuries viewers have overwhelmingly responded to Giotto's fresco with terror.

Most viewers, that is. Most people look at any of the medieval depictions of hell and think of torture. However, those using an economics lens see something entirely different, something others are likely to overlook. They notice the waiting. They notice that souls queue to get into hell, and, once there, they queue to be eaten by the devil.

Giotto's *Last Judgment* is not alone in its depiction of an afterlife filled with lingering and waiting. *The Inferno,* a mosaic lining the cupola of the baptistery of San Giovanni, made by an anonymous Italian painter in approximately 1270-1300, shows a terrifying devil devouring people who have sinned. Even though the devil holds one soul in his mouth, one in each hand, and one in each foot, there are others, on the sidelines, waiting their turn. This scene is repeated in Michelangelo's fresco, *Last Judgment,* in the Sistine Chapel. On the lower right side, he depicts the damned getting off Charon's boat, having crossed the river into hell. Many others are waiting to get off and then to face judgment. Souls wait to be torn by demons on the façade of Orvieto's Cathedral in Lorenzo Maitani's *The Damned in Hell.* Souls wait to be thrown into the cauldron full of boiling liquid in Fra Angelico's 1435 triptych *Last Judgment.* They also wait for the cauldron in *Satan Enthroned in Hell*, a Book of Hours by the Brussels Initials master.

In these medieval Christian art scenes, waiting is a reflection of market disequilibrium. It indicates a shortage—namely, a situation in which there are insufficient means of torture with which to torment all the damned souls slated for punishment. If there were no mismatch between the number of sinners and the capacity of the torture equipment, there would be no waiting around before getting dropped in boiling water or devoured by a devil. Hell would be in an equilibrium state, a state that economists describe as "stable," from which there is no inherent tendency to move, and in which the quantity of sinners to be punished is exactly equal to the torture supply.

Do shortages in hell have an equivalent in heaven? Most believers think of heaven as a place of infinite bounty. Christians imagine that in heaven they will have everything they want, in whatever quantities they want. Muslims believe that they will have lots of honey to eat and beautiful clothes made of expensive brocade. The Katha Upanishad teaches Hindus that there will be no hunger or thirst when they reach one of the heavenly plains.131

Mark Twain disagrees. The American writer and social critic of the 1800s does not portray heaven as a place of infinite bounty. While he stops short of using economic terms, those versed in economic theory are likely to read a clear message between the lines of his prose: there is disequilibrium in heaven! Over his lifetime, Twain wrote a series of irreverent short stories that make fun of Christian afterlife views. These have been posthumously collected and published under the grandiose title *The Bible According to Mark Twain*. One of the stories, "Captain Stormfield's Visit to Heaven," describes the fantastical experiences of an elderly captain who manages to reach heaven after his death. Once there, he arrives at a distribution center where heavenly clerks outfit new arrivals with halos, harps, hymn books, and wings. All the dead must check in at this center, and it is there, according to Twain, that "thousands of Yanks and Mexicans and British and Arabs" wait to be fitted with halos.132 If there were sufficient halos for everyone, no one would have to queue to receive their allotment. The market would be in equilibrium and there would be no shortage.

4

Prices

When people buy information about the afterlife, whether in the form of a tangible good (such as Don Piper's book, *90 Minutes in Heaven*) or a service (a medium's communication with a deceased relative), the purchase inevitably involves an exchange. A product is exchanged for money or a substitute thereof. A crucial question economists ask is, "how much money?" Specifically, what is the price of the product and how is it determined?

In market economies, prices are largely determined in the market where supply and demand come together. When the quantity demanded is equal to the quantity supplied, the market is in equilibrium and the price per unit is determined.

Prices associated with the afterlife are not so straightforward. This chapter explores some of their complexities.

The vignette, *The Price of Entry Into the Land of the Dead*, describes how the ancient Greeks paid for entry into the afterlife, and how that price was determined.

Ancient Egyptian Priests Practice Price Discrimination illustrates the rationale behind charging different people different prices for the same afterlife good.

How is a Halo in Heaven Like a Dog in a Shelter? draws on Mark Twain's description of the free distribution of halos in heaven to explain the economic consequence of getting a good at a price of zero.

Price of Entry Into the Land of the Dead

People pay for entry into national parks, movie theatres, and college. Why don't they pay for entry into the afterlife?

Actually, they do, according to numerous belief systems.

In Christianity, the fee for admission into heaven consists of undergoing the baptismal ritual and of leading a life of goodness. Similarly, in Islam the fee for entry into Djanna is knowledge of the Qur'an and also a life of goodness. Both prices of entry are implicit and non-monetary. They are nevertheless prices, since leading a good life entails opportunity costs of time, as well as the emotional price associated with constant evaluation and modification of one's behavior.

By contrast, there are ancient societies in which the price of entry into the afterlife is both explicit and monetary. The ancient Greeks, for example, buried their loved ones with coins to be used as payment at the gates of their final resting place. Such payment was considered indispensible for getting into Hades, the Land of the Dead, where shades, as souls were called, spent eternity.

According to legend, the River Styx was one of several rivers thought to encircle Hades, forming the boundary between the living and the dead. The river was believed to have magical properties, perhaps best known for being the water into which the mother of Achilles dipped his body, holding him by the heel, in order to make him invulnerable. The only way to cross this magical river and reach the land of the dead was to take a boat steered by the ferryman Charon. Many a painting and drawing depict his arms (sometimes skeletal, sometimes muscular) working the oar, as well as his long beard and unruly hair (such as in Michelangelo's portrayal in the Sistine Chapel). In order to pay Charon, family members placed a coin in the mouth of the deceased just prior to internment.133 In the absence of such payment, the dead were condemned to roam on the outskirts of Hades for eternity, unable to get themselves across the river. Those shades would never have peace.

The price of the crossing and the subsequent entry into Hades has been described in Greek mythology as one coin per person. During the

centuries that Greece was an empire, and across all its imperial territories, this price seems to have been uniformly accepted.

While legend specifies the amount, it leaves unexplained how
the price was determined. It is unlikely that it was determined by
the market mechanism—namely, by the interaction of supply and
demand for river crossings. If it had been, there would inevitably
have been fluctuation in the price. The demand for the crossing
would not have been constant over time, as the number of dead
was rarely constant. There were periodic wars and famines, causing
an increase in deaths and the subsequent increase in demand for
Charon's services. This would have caused an upward pressure on the
price of the crossing. By contrast, during peacetime and prosperity,
there would be fewer deaths, resulting in a decreased demand for the
crossing, pressuring the price downwards. These demographically
induced shifts in demand, together with the subsequent changes in
price, would in turn affect Charon's supply of his service. According
to the Law of Supply, if the price of the crossing were to increase,
Charon would be motivated to increase the number of crossings so
as to maximize his earnings. But in reality he cannot continue to
increase his supply forever, even if the price of the crossing were to
keep going up. At some point he will tire and get old and be unable
or unwilling to row any more. Or he might worry about the depreci-
ation of his only asset, his boat. Or, given that he is the sole provider
of a service—he has a monopoly—he might adopt a take-it-or-leave
it attitude towards the dead. In any of those cases, Charon's supply
would have been set at the quantity of crossings he chooses. Then,
a change in demand would not change the number of crossings but
would only change the price at which the exchange takes place.

This discussion about prices is an exercise in the exploration of the
market mechanism. The fact is that, no matter how much demand for
entry into the afterlife might have changed over the years and over the
Greek territories, the payment remained one coin. Thus we can infer
that the price of entry into Hades was not determined by the market
mechanism. Rather, it was set by tradition and custom. Each family
conformed to social rules because it had no definitive information on
the price of the service their members were purchasing. They never
met Charon, they never saw his services advertised. Instead they faced
what economists refer to as a situation of asymmetric information—in

which people behave extra cautiously because they know someone else has more information than they do. In the context of Greek mythology, Charon knows the acceptable price of crossing the Styx, but the family members of the deceased do not. As a result, they prefer to err on the side of caution and send off their loved ones with a payment they believe will be sufficient to ensure entry into Hades. How much is sufficient? It is an amount that has evolved over time as a reflection of what Charon's service is worth to the families of the deceased. While families might ask themselves if it is too little, or too much, given asymmetric information, in the end they abide by the price set by social custom.

And social custom also serves to police the payment process. Lest they are tempted to pocket the coin instead of placing it in the mouth of their relative, families of the deceased are under social pressure to conform to burial rules. This pressure is reinforced by the belief that there might be unknown punishments on earth if a shade wanders for eternity, without reaching Hades. Fear is an important motivator for those left behind. The buried coin can be viewed as the price of fear alleviation just as much as the price for a seat on Charon's boat.

Ancient Egyptian Priests Practice Price Discrimination

It has been said that Thomas Becket, the Archbishop of Canterbury, offered to resurrect people in exchange for money. Rather than being shocked by this, economists are likely to ask, "how much money?" Given the terror of the afterlife shared by medieval Christians, it is understandable that the demand for resurrection was high. We do not know if the supply was infinite or if there was a self-imposed restriction to the number of resurrections offered by Becket. It is possible that his price was high—so high, in fact, that only the wealthiest people in society could pay it. It is also possible that his price was low—so low that ordinary folk could afford to buy it. Or perhaps there was a sliding scale, enabling high and low prices to co-exist. That would be a logical outcome, since different people are willing and able to pay different amounts for the same product. In other words, people have different price elasticities of demand.

Elasticity measures how sensitive people are to changes in price. When the price of a good goes up, we know from the Law of Demand that the quantity demanded by consumers will decrease. Economists refer to the change in quantity demanded due to the change in price as the *price elasticity* of demand.

There is insufficient information about Thomas Beckett's pricing policies for us to assess whether he faced different elasticities among his demanders and so charged them different prices. However, there is sufficient information about the ancient Egyptians to use their market for a high quality afterlife to illustrate the concept of elasticity.

Given the importance of the postmortem in their worldview, Egyptians went to great lengths and incurred great expense to maximize their chances of a good eternity. They purchased a copy of the *Book of the Dead* for eventual placement inside their coffins. (Although called a book, this was actually a papyrus containing spells compiled and written by a commissioned scribe, thus ensuring no two books were the same.) People studied the magic spells before death so as to learn how their Ba can overcome obstacles in the netherworld and arrive safely to its final resting place. They memorized the names of the guards and the gates through which it would pass; they memorized hymns and prayers so as to seek protection from the gods. Although memorizing the contents of the *Book of the Dead* was necessary, it was not sufficient to ensure a good afterlife. Egyptians also hired and paid priests to mentor them on their afterlife journey and to pray for their souls both before and after death. They built burial sites and they collected goods to bury alongside their bodies. And then they paid for special embalmment, also known as mummification.

However, not all Egyptians had the same demand for this package of afterlife commodities. Demand requires both the willingness and the ability to buy something. While Egyptians were all willing to buy afterlife commodities, they did not all have the ability to do so. Their society was highly stratified, characterized by sharp income and wealth inequalities. Under those circumstances, the rich could, and did, pay more than the poor. Also, as a result of their wealth, the rich were less sensitive to price increases than the poor. In other words, their price elasticity of demand was relatively low (or inelastic) while that of the poor Egyptians was relatively high (elastic). The poor were more sensitive to an increase in prices of mummification and priestly fees than the rich, and would have responded by decreasing their demand more sharply than their wealthy compatriots.

The fact that Egyptians had differing price elasticities enabled the priests, who were the suppliers of afterlife commodities, to charge them different prices. This was not a common practice in the years associated with the Old Kingdom period (c. 2686-2181 BCE), when a good afterlife was believed to be the prerogative only of rulers, the wealthy, and the powerful. However, by the New Kingdom period (c. 1550-1069 BCE), more commoners began demanding a better afterlife, and priests began to make it available to more people, albeit at a different, lower price. Economists refer to such a pricing policy as price discrimination.

Suppliers practice price discrimination because they can. As long as buyers have different price elasticities, suppliers will charge them different prices for the same good. By doing so, they will maximize their revenues as they sell a greater quantity, albeit at a lower price. Since revenue is equal to the number of goods sold times the price at which they are sold, then, when selling to commoners, the priests offset lower prices with a higher volume of sales.

The policy of price discrimination reflected rational behavior on the part of Egyptian priests, just like it reflects good business practices on the part of airlines in the twenty-first century, which charge passengers different prices for essentially the same good (a coach seat that transports them from point A to point B). Business travelers and leisure travelers are willing to pay different amounts for airline travel because the former typically have inelastic demand while the latter's is elastic.

Price discrimination does not work if people can buy the product at a lower price and then resell it at a higher price and pocket the difference. Just like airline tickets are not transferrable, so, too, a commoner cannot resell his afterlife package to a rich man. By personalizing each *Book of the Dead*, Egyptian priests introduced minor alterations to the chants and magic spells in a process of product differentiation. This practice prevented the resale of books, and since services of priests and mummifiers by definition could not be resold, priestly revenues were protected.

The persistence of price discrimination practices over millennia, ranging from ancient Egyptian priests to contemporary airlines, attests to its success as a business pricing policy.

How is a Halo in Heaven Like a Dog in a Shelter?

People don't voluntarily pay more for a good than the value they derive from it. If they value it five dollars, they will not pay more than five for it; if they pay five dollars for the good, it means they value it at least five dollars.

Does this link between willingness to pay and perceived value hold for goods whose price is zero? In other words, how much do people value goods that they get for free? "Not much" might have been the likely answer given by Thomas Paine, the eighteenth century British author and thinker who is known for saying, "What we obtain too cheap we esteem too little: it is dearness only that gives everything value."134

Mark Twain would probably have agreed with Paine. In his description of the afterlife, he suggests that the dead do not value what they get for free. The rationale for this view is embedded in Twain's story of Captain Stormfield's heavenly adventure.135 Specifically, when the deceased captain makes his way to the distribution center, he meets up with other dead souls. The center distributes a pair of wings, a hymnbook, a halo, and a harp to each soul. For free. Yes, all these items are courtesy of the heavenly administration. While waiting patiently in line, the perceptive captain observes an activity, repeated over and over again in his vicinity. The more experienced, longer-dead souls approach him and the others who wait in line, and thrust their wings at them with the words "Here, hold this for a moment." Hymnbooks, as well, are pushed at him, accompanied by the request "Please hold this for me." Then the souls go away, never to return. Stormfield's initial puzzlement gives way to an "a-ha!" moment. He realizes that no one wants any of the heavenly paraphernalia. Wings are heavy, halos encumber, hymnbooks shackle the arms. The dead are freer without that *stuff.*

If the souls in Mark Twain's story had to pay for wings, the scene at the distribution center would have been different. Those who didn't want to pay the going price would not wait in line. If they did pay for the wings and subsequently changed their minds, it is likely they would have valued them more because their payment, monetary or non-monetary, would have had an opportunity cost. As a result of the implicit and explicit cost incurred, it is unlikely that the dead would have given the wings away so readily. Rather, they would have sold them in the secondhand market. Entrepreneurial souls might have started a business to sell wings at a discount to newcomers who didn't want to wait in line. A lucrative market for used hymnbooks might have emerged, perhaps with those of the rich and famous fetching the highest resale prices.

Halos in heaven are like dogs in animal shelters. Shelters collect stray pets and nurture them until a potential owner comes along. Experience has shown that when the pets are turned over, for free, to eager pet lovers, they are not valued highly and are given up at the first sign of difficulty. To avoid such irresponsible adoptions and revolving-door visits by Fido, most shelters now impose a price to the adoption. It consists of the explicit cost associated with the medical check up and the fee, as well as the implicit cost of the owner's time while forms are filled, payments are made, and medical procedures are followed. Having paid explicitly and implicitly for their new dog, an owner is more likely to value and commit to ownership.

The distribution staff in Mark Twain's heaven can learn from dog shelters and impose a positive price on halos. Doing so would indicate exactly how much the dead value halos, wings, and prayer books, and at the same time it could generate some beneficial spin-off economic activity.

5

Utility Maximization

Why do people do what they do? Economists answer this question differently than do sociologists, philosophers, and psychiatrists. They use the concept of utility, which is defined as the satisfaction derived from the consumption of a good or service ("consumption" is the term used to indicate spending). People spend in order to get satisfaction. However, as they do not have unlimited resources, they must consider their constraints. Since the most pertinent constraint has to do with money, economists say that people seek to maximize their utility subject to their income constraints. Applying this utility theory to answer a simple question about human behavior, such as "why do people eat chicken?" or "why do they vacation in Cancun?", would yield the following answer: they do it because it gives them the most satisfaction, given how much money they can spend on that category of goods. By maximizing their utility subject to their income constraints, people eat chicken rather than filet mignon and vacation in Cancun rather than Paris.

Evidence from literature, mythology, and religion indicates that people strive to maximize the utility they will derive after they die. They do this both *ex ante* and *ex post*. While still living, believers adjust their behavior to ensure the best possible afterlife. These *ex ante* considerations were raised in the discussion of rational behavior in chapter 2. By contrast, this chapter explores *ex post* maximizing behavior as it takes place in the afterlife.

In *Harry Potter's Near-Death Experience and Utility Valuation*, the young man's actions following a partial death are explained using economic terms.

Pet lovers derive utility from owning pets. *Will Fido Join Me in the Afterlife?* explores ways in which they strive to continue deriving utility after death—theirs and their pets'.

In *Reincarnated Souls in Search of New Homes,* Hindu views of reincarnation are used to illustrate how a soul maximizes its utility when it seeks to be reborn into a wealthy and privileged family.

Harry Potter's Near-Death Experience and Utility Valuation

Harry Potter and the Deathly Hallows is the seventh and last book in the Harry Potter series, with which J.K. Rowling introduced an entire generation to magic and witchcraft. In anticipation of the book's publication in 2007, pundits were abuzz with calculating the odds that Harry will die together with the series.

(Spoiler alert.)

Harry does not die. During a battle towards the end of the book, the evil Voldemort tries to murder him, and thinks he has succeeded. However, the Killing Curse aimed at Harry only kills that part of him in which some of Voldemort's soul resides. As he lies face down on the ground, his magic wand tucked into his belt under his robes, Harry does not die but instead he has a near-death experience. He travels to another place, where he encounters dead people, including his former professor, the old Albus Dumbledore. After lengthy conversations, Harry realizes that he cannot stay in the netherworld. He will have no peace there because he has unfinished business on earth. He must go back and deal with Voldemort, the killer of his parents.

In deciding not to stay dead and instead to return to earth, Harry is maximizing his utility. He gets more utility out of avenging his parents' death than from remaining in the afterlife.

When his consciousness returns to earth, Harry looks through the slits in his eyes to appraise the situation. Voldemort and the Death Eaters believe him to be dead. Harry plays along, all the while concocting a plan. He allows his limp body to be carried through the thick forest and into the castle. He waits for the opportunity to do what he has lived to do.

By playing dead, Harry is again maximizing his utility. He could have jumped up immediately upon coming to, grabbed his wand, and tried to kill Voldemort on the spot. While killing his nemesis this way would have given him immediate gratification, Harry was unsure of the outcome. By collecting his wits and carefully plotting his next move, Harry was able to analyze which action was more likely to give him the greatest utility. He evaluated the constraints that bound his choices. The most important of these was that his magic wand was under his robes and the Invisible Cloak was stuffed under his stomach. This meant that he did not have easy access to either and that would constrain his actions.

Harry's decision to wait for his revenge was the one that maximized his utility subject to his (non-income) constraints. It also ended up being the one that brought the most benefit to most of the good people in Harry's life.

Will Fido Join Me In The Afterlife?

When heiress Gail Posner died in 2010, she left her pet Conchita $3 million, along with the right to live out the rest of her dog life in Posner's $8.3 million mansion on Miami Beach. That seems cheap by millionaire Leona Helmsley's standards. She had raised the bar in 2007 by leaving her dog Trouble $12 million. Such estate planning says a lot about how the dog owners maximized their utilities. Both women derived more utility from naming their pets in their wills than they would have had they left their entire estates to relatives or charities.

Pet lovers would surely derive even more utility if they had some assurance of an afterlife reunification with their beloved animals. In some cultures, such future meetings are an integral part of the mainstream worldview. The Aztecs, for example, believed that a man makes his final journey to the eternal house of the dead, Chicomemictlan, with the aid of his dog, and there they will spend eternity together.136 Ancient Egyptians also buried the dead with their dogs, sometimes mummified and at other times just lying by their feet, so they would be together forever.137 Medieval European dog owners carved out lapdogs at the foot of their tombs, probably indicating the belief that pet and master were destined for an afterlife together.

By the twenty-first century, beliefs pertaining to animals in the postmortem world have become more tenuous and more complicated. According to a poll by ABC news and beliefnet.com, 43% of Americans think they will reunite with their pets in heaven.138 There are approximately 73 million cat owners and 68 million dog owners in the United States,139 and it is likely that many of these people have wondered if their animals have souls, whether there a heaven and hell for them, and what determines where they will end up.

In an effort to maximize the utility they derive from owning animals, pet lovers seek to give their pets the best possible send-off into the hereafter. Their demand for options has stimulated creative supply responses, resulting in a lucrative market for dead pet paraphernalia. Depending on their personal inclination, pet owners choose home burial, cemetery burial, or cremation. They choose caskets, grave markers, headstones and urns. They decide about embalming, obituaries and memorial services. And then they send off their beloved pets with little trinkets they might enjoy in the afterlife. Animal cemeteries report that chocolates, collars, and teddy bears have been placed with pets in gravesites.140 Hallmark offers animal sympathy cards, mediums specialize in communicating with pet ghosts, and bereavement groups are available for psychological therapy. Books about pet heaven and reincarnation are available to comfort the grieving owners. (Author Ptolemy Tompkins writes that animals have souls and enjoy an eternal afterlife,141 while Cynthia Ryland claims that, in dog heaven, pets get dog biscuits and are petted all day and told how wonderful they are.142)

While it is unclear whether chocolate-filled caskets make the deceased animals feel good, we can infer that it makes their owners feel good. They might be tempted to spend even more on pet-related postmortem activities and services but are constrained by their income and the opportunity cost of their time.

In addition to the monetary constraint, there is yet another constraint on the behavior of pet owners. It has to do with a question that remains unanswered: do pets go to heaven (or hell) on their own merits or on those of their owners? If it is the former, then owners should make sure their dog's nightly barking doesn't infuriate neighbors and thus increase Fido's chances of going to doggie hell. If it is the latter, then owners who seek to maximize their utility by ensuring a reunion with their pets have yet one more reason to behave properly during their lifetimes. Such moral behavior might be too a high a price to pay for afterlife reunion with Fido, and thus may act as a *de facto* constraint on a pet owner's utility maximization.

Reincarnated Souls In Search of New Homes

There are some 900 million Hindus in the Indian subcontinent for whom reincarnation is fundamental to their beliefs. While Hindus reject immortality of the body, they embrace immortality of the soul, believing it will continue being reborn, transmigrating from one body to another, in a process known as Samsara. Then one day, individuals become freed from this cycle of birth and death. According to the Hindu philosophical texts, the Upanishads, a person can escape from reincarnation when he/she attains complete knowledge of themselves and understanding of life and reality. If a person dies without such awareness, his/her soul will be reborn. Whether it is reborn in a human or an animal depends on how good its behavior was during its most recent earthly life. Hindus believe that their friends, neighbors, and family members, as well as their politicians, teachers, and nurses, have all had previous lives. How many of those lives intersected in the past is a matter of much speculation.

Using an economics lens, one can also speculate about utility maximization in the course of reincarnation. A story about an Indian boy, described by the American psychiatrist Ian Stevenson in the 1970s, serves to illustrate how utility theory might apply to reincarnation.[143]

Stevenson documented numerous case studies of children that, in his view, had previous lives. He offered three types of supporting evidence.[144] First, he collected testimonies of children who remembered details of locations and people they never saw during their short lives. Second, he found some phenomena that cannot be explained in any other way, such as a child who speaks another language—to which the child had never been exposed—fluently. And third, he identified birthmarks on children that correspond to injuries that they claim to have had in previous lives.

One example of the first type of evidence entails a young Indian boy called Aishwary, who was believed to be the reincarnation of a factory worker, Veerpal, from a nearby village.[145] As most cases in which Past Personalities are reborn in others, Veerpal's death occurred just before the new birth, and it was due to an accident. When Aishwary was three years old, he began to describe events and situations that he could not have known about had he not been to Veerpal's village. Aishwary's parents collected all his ruminations and identified a family that fit his descriptions. Contact was made, and Veerpal's family happily embraced the reborn soul of their dead relative. They got the benefit of thinking that a part of their son/husband/sibling was alive while Aishwary's family got the benefit of belonging to a second family, since the two became socially and emotionally joined. It was a win-win situation.

Examining this reincarnation with an economic lens, it might be said that Verpaal's soul was rational and sought to maximize its utility. It sought to be reborn into a body that it deemed to be the best it could have, given the constraints it faced. What is considered the best? One soul might think family wealth is important, whereas another might be swayed by the location of the family residence. And what are the constraints it faces? The choice of a new body for the soul is constrained by earthly behavior. Good behavior opens up human reincarnation possibilities, bad earthly behavior limits the options to rebirth in animal form.

It is likely that Aishwary's parents also sought to maximize their utility, that they were rational and that they responded to economic incentives. To the extent that parents can chose the family into which their child's soul will be reborn, they will maximize their utility by claiming connection to a family of a higher socio-economic level than their own. This is due to a Hindu custom according to which the discovery that souls are bonded carries with it financial responsibility towards the less advantaged family. They don't want their dead relative living in conditions worse than those to which he was accustomed.146

Still, Aishwary's parents cannot pursue a connection to a wealthy family indiscriminately. Their efforts are subject to constraints. These are not the usual budget constraints, but rather they are non-monetary, logistical, and operational in nature. The family must find someone who died shortly before their baby was born—not too long before, not too recently. More importantly, they must also provide some proof, such as descriptions supplied by their child that refer to a past life. The more detailed and unknown the information, the more credibility they will have and the more likely they are to achieve success in their search for a linkage of souls.

The nineteenth century French author Voltaire said that it is no more surprising to be born twice than to be born once.147 Economists might say that it is also no more surprising that souls maximize their utility than that souls are reborn in new bodies.

6

Production, Inputs, Innovation, and Externalities

Production takes place in every economy. On earth, output is produced using inputs such as labor, capital, raw materials, and land. The afterlife is no different.

According to medieval Christianity, the most abundant output in hell is a service, not a good. It is torture by fire. This service, delivered to the soul that has sinned, uses capital inputs such as furnaces and cauldrons. The labor input consists of demons that stoke the fire and stir the pots of boiling liquids. Entrepreneurs think up innovative ways of producing the torture, energy is used to light and maintain the fire, and raw materials such as water, wood, and coal serve as supplements. All these inputs are combined in a specific way, described by a so-called "production function," in order to generate output.

Torture by fire is just one of the outputs produced in the afterlife. Others are analyzed in this chapter, together with the inputs they require, the technology they use, and the side effects they create.

The production of food is essential on earth, as it enables the sustenance of life. Numerous myths show this importance extends into the afterlife (*Food For the Dead: Produce It, Store It, Eat It*).

In *Don't Leave Earth Without Your Capital Inputs*, the role of machinery and tools in afterlife production is underscored by Native American burial customs.

Water Makes the Grass Greener on the Other Side describes the importance of water resources across numerous afterlife beliefs.

Homer Simpson, William Blake, and Assembly Line Production in Hell illustrates the use of efficient technology in afterlife production.

Innovation and technological change are not limited to industrial production. They also occur in medicine, resulting in improved treatments and new cures. *Stem Cell Research and a Sinner's Liver* refers to Greek afterlife myths about medical advancements that predate contemporary research.

Sometimes there are side effects of production that are borne by people who are not involved in the production process. *Plastics and Pollution: the Dead Know About Externalities* describes these side effects.

Conspicuously missing from this chapter is a discussion of labor, a crucial input in production. Because of its importance across afterlife visions, an entire chapter is devoted to it (Chapter 7: Human Capital).

Food For the Dead: Produce It, Store It, Eat It

The Bible refers to manna as the food provided by God to the Israelis while they were crossing the desert.

Does that mean there is food in heaven? And if so, does it mean that food is so abundant that some can be given away to those outside heaven? According to some people's beliefs, the answer to both questions is yes.

Food features prominently in numerous visions of the afterlife, both in its absence as well as its abundance. An undesirable afterlife is characterized by food scarcity. In Tibetan Buddhism, for example, hell is a place where people crave to eat and drink, but all food and drink turns to ash when they approach.148 In the Hindu hell Nakara, the dead must eat each other for lack of alternatives.149 By contrast, having access to tasty food in abundant quantities is considered a feature of a good afterlife. Those in Islamic heaven expect to eat and drink one hundred times more than they could have on earth, and they expect to enjoy it one hundred times more.150 Banquets where delicious food is laid out for all to enjoy until sated appear in Nordic and Celtic mythologies, as well as in ancient Greek and Roman beliefs.

Afterlife myths that feature food often also describe the food collection and production processes. Greek, Native American, and Maasai myths describe hunting for game, whereas Welsh myths envision a heaven, Avalon, as a place where the dead grow fruits and vegetables. But it is the ancient Egyptians that had the most elaborate beliefs about food collection and preparation. According to their beliefs, the dead gather food, catch fish, and grow grains, fruits, and vegetables.

When the soil and the rivers and the game yield enough food to satisfy the daily consumptive needs of the population and have excess left over, then there is enough to share with those outside heaven's borders (such as the manna God gave to the Israelis).

Moreover, such a surplus serves an important economic function: it frees up souls to devote their time to non-food production and/or to leisure activities. They are assured of having sufficient food even on days when hunting and fishing are unsuccessful.

But there is a condition that must be met. Souls must come up with a way of storing food so that it is preserved until it is consumed. Since food is perishable, appropriate and effective storage facilities are imperative to prevent it from rotting. This crucial detail is addressed in afterlife myths of the Kalapalo Indians.

The Kalapalo are a group of indigenous peoples who live in central Brazil. Due to the geography of their habitat, they have remained largely isolated from missionaries and settlers. Depending on the land they occupy, some tribespeople practice hunting and gathering, and others rely on agriculture or fishing. Manioc (also known as cassava) is the principal cultivated grain, responsible for most people's livelihood. And it is this crop that features prominently in their intricate view of life after death. According to Ellen Basso, an anthropologist who lived with the tribe and studied their customs, the Kalapalo believe after they die, their shadows continue living.151 The first night after burial, a shadow stays with the family, eating a last meal together. Then it travels towards the east until it reaches the Village of the Dead, in the sky. Following a short period of adjustment, during which the shadow rests to regain its strength from its long journey, it joins the village community in their continuous ceremonial singing and dancing. How is it that they can sing and dance for eternity? Don't they need to think about subsistence? The Kalapalo have made provisions for that in their afterlife mythology. They believe the dead shadows are liberated from crop cultivation because there is a preexisting storage facility where abundant manioc flour is stored, enough for all their collective consumptive needs. Specifically, a large silo sits in the middle of the village. It is never empty. As some manioc gets used up, more appears. No matter how large the Village of the Dead becomes, and no matter how many households it contains, the resident shadows are never hungry, because the storage facility ensures their food demands are met.

In the absence of adequate storage, the Kalapalo peoples would have no food security and would be unable to continuously sing and dance. Some of their time would need to be diverted to food production and procurement activities.

Don't Leave Earth Without
Your Capital Inputs

Advertisements for American Express warn people not to leave home without their credit card, foretelling calamitous events that can befall them in remote parts of the world should they become stranded without the ability to pay. While credit cards may provide security in the twenty-first century, pre-modern societies derived similar security from the tools and implements they took with them into the afterlife. For the dying Native North Americans of the eighteenth century, not having those tools was believed to negatively affect their postmortem experience.

The role of capital inputs in afterlife production was described by a colonel in the U.S. army, Richard Irving Dodge, in his book *The Plains of the Great West and Their Inhabitants.*152 As was common in the 1800s, Dodge lumped all Native peoples into a single category called "the Indians."

According to his description of the Indian worldview, the afterlife is simply a continuation of life on earth (the dead will hunt for sustenance), peppered with some wishful thinking (there will be plenty of game and birds and other animals). In the place of final repose (that has since come to be called the Happy Hunting Grounds153), activities such as hunting, cooking, and producing the necessities of daily life require inputs no less than they did on earth. Therefore, rifles, pistols, bow quivers, gunpowder, lead, caps, knives, and iron pots were all buried with the dead for their future use. By contrast, skins (with which to make clothing) and ropes (with which to make beds) did not accompany the dead into their graves. It was believed that these goods could easily be produced by the dead, in the afterlife. In other words, only tools and implements (manufactured goods that were expected to be unavailable in the Happy Hunting Grounds), were taken by the deceased.

According to Dodge, Native Americans understood that the actual productive inputs do not follow them into the afterlife. Rather, they believed that if the material articles remain with the body until it decomposes, then the spirit of the dead will have the phantoms of the articles at his/her disposal in the next world.

In the absence of capital inputs in the afterlife, the production of everyday items is hindered. The dead could not hunt or cook in the way they were accustomed. They would have to change their production methods in order to survive.

Economists use the concept of a production function to describe the maximum quantity of output that can be produced using different combinations and quantities of inputs. In the absence of their earthly capital inputs, the deceased Native populations would have to adopt a new production function in the afterlife, one that relies on substitutes for the capital inputs no longer available to them.

Water Makes the Grass Greener on the Other Side

Like capital inputs, water is a resource used in afterlife production. Unlike capital inputs, water is ubiquitous in afterlife visions, showing up in myths, religions, art, and literature.

It appears as an input into the production of afterlife food. According to ancient Egyptian tomb paintings, fishermen relied on it for their catch, farmers harnessed it to irrigate their crops, and everyone used it to prepare their meals.

In the form of rivers and seas, water is fundamental to the provision of transportation services as envisioned in Viking mythology. These seafaring peoples also relied on water to provide national security in the afterlife, which they believed entailed battling their enemies on open seas and protecting their shores and ports.

Ancient Greeks and medieval Italians are among the many populations that envisioned water-based torture in the afterlife. In the *Odyssey*, for example, Tantalus is condemned to standing in water up to his chin but when he bends down to drink and quench his thirst, the water disappears. Water is again used to produce torture in Dante's *Inferno*, where it serves as a prison for traitors who are condemned to live out eternity in the frozen lake Cocytus.

Of all the possible uses for water in the production of afterlife products, none surpasses that of the creation and maintenance of heaven's bucolic landscapes. In those visions of heaven where rural scenes predominate, water plays an implicit and explicit role. The Christian heaven, as portrayed by Renaissance painters, includes green pastures and abundant foliage. In order to achieve the verdant color and the fecund vegetation, water resources are implicit. Somewhere there, hidden from the viewer, is an underground irrigation system necessary for the maintenance of what lies above. The use of water is explicit in Renaissance paintings, where it is portrayed in fountain scenes, typically bursting in the air and/or cascading down multi-tiered constructions.

No afterlife vision places as much importance on water as that of Islam. The Muslim heaven is a multi-level lush garden called Djanna. Many rivers run through it, most of which are made of water, although some consist of milk, wine, or honey. Surrounding the rivers and throughout the garden are fruit trees with colorful ripe fruits as well as blooming flowers. It is water that gives them the color and water that nurtures the fruits. In their study of Islamic art, Sheila Blair and Jonathan Bloom point out this importance of water: the phrase "rivers of paradise" appears forty-six times in the Qur'an.154

In addition to the Muslim holy book, Islamic art also portrays heaven as a garden. The first instance was in the Great Mosque in Damascus, built in the early eighth century. The mosaic on the walls shows lush landscapes in which gardens, plants, rivers, and architectural structures underscore the water theme.

That water would be a crucial input in afterlife production is not surprising, given the arid land in the Middle East where both Christianity and Islam first developed. The region was agricultural, dependent on water resources for its very sustenance. In the absence of water, food production was impossible, as were spin-off activities such as trade. The populations appreciated how difficult and expensive construction and maintenance of gardens were, as was the plumbing that irrigation required. But the benefits in terms of productivity and fertility were great. Given that water supported life on earth, believers assumed it would do the same in the afterlife. And in the afterlife, water was the main input in the production of abundant food and beautiful landscapes. Water enabled afterlife abundance in a way unrivaled by other productive inputs.

Homer Simpson, William Blake and Assembly Line Production in Hell

There are two ways to increase output. One is to use more inputs in the production process, and the other is to adopt innovative methods. Innovation refers to the introduction of more efficient production techniques that use newer technology and/or that combine inputs in new ways.

Applying this to the production of torture in hell tells us that increases in output can be achieved by using more cauldrons, stakes, coal, and demons. It can also be achieved through the application of innovative technology.

Such innovation appears in the popular animated television series *The Simpsons*, which has captivated American audiences since the late 1980s. In an episode entitled "The Devil and Homer Simpson," the father character, Homer, personally experiences technological innovation in hell.155 It happens after he sells his soul to the devil, in exchange for one donut, and is ordered by his new master to go to hell. Given the nature of his crime, Homer is condemned to an eternity of eating donuts. But his punishment does not include a leisurely bite here and there, whenever he feels like it. To the contrary, a highly efficient machine is used to force-feed Homer. Such a machine can produce more torture in a shorter amount of time and at lower cost than could be accomplished if the devil's workers fed Homer donuts by hand. The mechanization of torture increases the efficiency of the production process in hell.

But that is not Homer's only experience with innovative technology. When he needs to be moved from one location to another, Homer is placed on a conveyor belt. He is transported up and down and left and right through hell's many rooms and passages. The conveyor belt ensures speed and efficiency in the transportation of punished souls far surpassing what could have been achieved by, for example, hiring demons to accompany Homer by foot.

Innovation can take the form of organizational changes in the production process, as well. The now ubiquitous assembly line production represents such a change. When first introduced, this method of producing a good in stages, by adding additional parts, consecutively, by different specialized workers, represented a major technological breakthrough since it enabled a drastic increase in output and a per-unit reduction in production costs.

This type of production also shows up in visions of the afterlife. One in particular comes from the late eighteenth century. It is the vision offered by William Blake, one of England's foremost Romantic poets and the author of *The Marriage of Heaven and Hell*. This poem is a satire, an assault on the Christian morality of the times. In one section, Blake writes about witnessing a production process in hell: the production of books filled with knowledge.156 In the printing house of hell, Blake writes, knowledge is transmitted and compiled in six stages. In the first five, a dragon, a viper, an eagle, some lions, and then some unnamed forms each add their particular input, consequentially, to the package of knowledge that has come to them. In other words, at each stage of production, something of value is added, and then the newly improved product passes on to the next stage, where another entity adds its mark. Finally, in the sixth chamber, Blake states that man receives the knowledge and puts it into book form. These books are then arranged in libraries.

This production process is eerily similar to assembly line methods popular in contemporary earthly manufacturing industries. Assembly line production did not exist when Blake described hell. It did not become a reality until around 1910 when entrepreneur Henry Ford applied it to his automobile factory. While it is unlikely that Blake had efficiency in mind when he described his *de facto* assembly line production, there is no doubt that his vision offered a cost-reducing method of compiling knowledge.

In conclusion, one of England's finest poems and one of America's most popular television shows share a vision of hell characterized by innovative technology. But, truly, such visions are rare. Usually, hell entails torture produced by outdated and inefficient methods. The punishment of Sisyphus, for example, consists of rolling a stone up one of hell's hills, and when he reaches the top, the stone rolls back down and he must start all over again, and then again, for eternity. Similarly, the Danaid sisters were condemned to fill a water jug in hell. The jug has a hole in the bottom, so their job is never done. The fact that Sisyphus and the Danaids continue to perform repetitive tasks for eternity, and do not introduce more efficient, perhaps mechanized ways of achieving their goals, shows that innovation is not always possible. For these mythical characters, perhaps the most torturous aspect of their torture is its eternal stagnation, with no possibility for replacement with innovative methods.

"Two bars—how about you?"

Cartoon 6.1: Mobile Phone Reception in Heaven

Stem Cell Research and a Sinner's Liver

Innovation and technological change are not limited to manufacturing. They also occur in the production of medical goods and health care services. A promising source of such advances in medicine involves stem cells. In the twenty-first century, stem cell research worldwide seeks to use these regenerative cells for innovative forms of healing. If successful, such innovative research might one day enable people to grow a new arm if one is severed, grow hair on bald heads, grow breasts after mastectomies, and so on.

Scientists enthusiastically emphasize the potential of this new and exciting stem cell research. But while it is undoubtedly exciting, it is not new. Evidence of cell regeneration first appeared in the ancient Greek vision of the afterlife over two millennia ago, and later, in the seventh century, in the Islamic vision.

According to Greek mythology, Tityus was a giant who was born underground where Zeus, his father, hid his pregnant mother so that Zeus's wife Hera would not learn of the affair. When he grew up, Tityus raped Leto, the mother of several of Zeus's children. As punishment, he was sent to Tartarus, the part of Hades where the gravest sinners go. There he was condemned to lie stretched out on the ground while two vultures peck at his liver, for eternity. No matter how much they pecked, Tityus's liver grew back to its normal size overnight.157

Mythology provides no clarification of the mechanism by which the liver continuously and cyclically re-grows and re-generates. One wonders whether the ancient Greeks knew something about organ regeneration that Western medicine did not begin to understand until the early nineteenth century. That question was posed by three scientists—Dina Tiniakos, Apostolos Kandilis, and Stephen Geller—in a study published in the prestigious *Journal of Hepatology*.158 They claim there is no evidence that ancient Greeks, despite their elaborate myths, had any knowledge about liver regeneration. Yet, with limited medical knowledge, the ancient Greeks integrated organ regeneration into their mythology, making the concept simultaneously familiar and fear-provoking.

106

Greeks are not alone in describing organ regeneration in hell. Another example is found in the Islamic religion. The Qur'an explicitly portrays hell as full of fires in which sinners wail as they burn. An interesting feature of the burning is the repetitive replacement of people's skin. As soon as the skin gets burnt, it is replaced with new skin so that it, too, can be burnt. As a result, the pain and torment is experienced over and over again, as though for the first time.159

In the twenty-first century, scientists study skin regeneration in order to achieve faster healing from burns.160 They would greatly appreciate understanding the mechanism by which sinners in Islamic hell have been growing new skin so rapidly and over extensive body parts, for centuries.

Stem cell research that leads to the regeneration of multiple human organs would, if successful, treat diseases and prolong life. It would represent technological change in medicine no less radical than assembly line production was in manufacturing over a century ago. It is noteworthy that both organ regeneration and assembly line production were featured in afterlife visions before they became earthly realities.

Plastics and Pollution: The Dead Know About Externalities

The production of goods and services sometimes affects random people who are in no way involved with the production process. They may bear indirect costs or they may reap indirect benefits. When factory emissions pollute the air, innocent bystanders that breathe it incur a cost. When a neighbor invests in luscious landscaping, nearby homeowners reap a benefit because their property values rise. Such costs or benefits, borne by individuals who have nothing to do with production, are called externalities.

In the 1978 American movie *Heaven Can Wait*, a dead man returns to earth to prevent a negative externality from taking place. Actor Warren Beatty plays a football hero called Joe Pendleton who is taken from earth by an angel, by mistake. It was not yet Pendleton's time to die. To rectify the mistake, the heavenly authorities allow Pendleton to return to earth for a while longer. He is allocated to the body of a recently deceased man. That man happens to be millionaire Leo Farnsworth, of Farnsworth Industries, whose drive for profit maximization entailed unscrupulous and unethical business behavior.

Just before his death, Farnsworth was negotiating a controversial project: the expansion of his business in England and the building of a refinery. That expansion was expected to displace several communities and permanently alter the lives of their inhabitants. In addition, the refinery was slated to produce plastic bottles using a production method that entailed the release of acrylonitril, a toxic substance.

One of the town's residents, Betty Logan (played by Julie Christie) travels to America to implore Farnsworth to reconsider his investment. She meets with him to explain the potentially devastating effects of his proposed business venture. But the man she speaks to is not the callous, unfeeling businessman she expected. It is Joe, a nice guy.

With Hollywood flair, the dead Joe Pendleton, now inhabiting Farnsworth's body, sets out to right the wrong about to be committed in England. Even though he is a football player with no background in economic theory, he intuitively understands all about externalities. He realizes that the population about to be displaced, and perhaps even poisoned, is poised to bear the costs of industrial production without participating in any of its benefits. And so, at a Farnsworth Industries board meeting, Pendleton shocks the board members when he announces his intention to pull back from the British project. He asks, almost innocently, "Why do bad things?" Why displace innocent people and produce goods of questionable toxicity when the company is doing so well and does not need to engage in risky behavior to improve its bottom line? In reality, Pendleton is asking, without using economics language, why produce negative externalities if it is not necessary? In this way, Joe Pendleton, back on earth for a temporary second chance at life, saves the English communities at risk.

(Lest it seem like Joe is altogether a selfless environmentalist, it must be mentioned that he developed a crush on Ms. Logan and went to great lengths to impress her. The Board's decision to relocate the refinery can be viewed as a positive externality of Pendleton's romantic interest in Ms. Logan.)

7

Human Capital

Like capital, land, and natural resources, labor is also an input in the production of goods and services. It is an umbrella term that includes a heterogeneous grouping of workers with differing skills acquired through different formal education, specialized training, and work experiences. Economists refer to a highly skilled labor force as "human capital." Like physical capital (machinery, tools, and implements), financial capital (resources for investment), and natural capital (natural resources), human capital is positively related to productivity, efficiency, and output.

Does the role of education in creating human capital carry over into the netherworld? In *Educated Souls Rock*, ancient mythologies and a short story by Isaac Asimov provide an affirmative answer to that question.

Learning By Doing: Souls Fly With Wings describes one way that the dead are believed to acquire skills.

The vignette, *To Maximize Productivity in the Afterlife, Die Young*, introduces Native American mythology about afterlife labor productivity.

Human capital represents a stock of wealth for societies. When people move from one place to another, they take that wealth with them. In *Immigration: Skilled Souls Cross Over*, the economic costs and benefits of migration to the netherworld are discussed.

Educated Souls Rock

Educated souls contribute to afterlife output by producing services uneducated workers cannot provide. By definition, they have mastered literacy and numeracy, and have enhanced thinking and communication skills. As such, they are well suited for afterlife tasks that require reading, writing, and basic math. Record keeping is one such task that shows up in visions of the netherworld. Scribes note afterlife events such as harvests, but most commonly they keep track of souls. Using writing materials and surfaces common in their earthly cultures, these dead scribes record the coming and going of souls, as well as the good and bad deeds that filled their lives. According to Egyptian mythology, the heart of the deceased, believed to be the home of the soul, is weighed against a feather in order to determine the nature of the afterlife it deserves. Scribes sit nearby and write the outcome of the scales in a ledger. Similarly, in Indian mythology, after a person dies, a list of their sins and good deeds must be prepared and read to the god Yama who stands in judgment. It is a task that requires literacy.[161] It is a task that must be performed by an educated dead person.

The postmortem usefulness of earthly skills carries over into Western literature. Prolific author Isaac Asimov underscored how earthly education enables the dead to have unique jobs in the hereafter.[162] In his short story "The Last Answer," the main character Murray Templeton is a physicist with numerous educational achievements and robust intellectual capacities. He is plucked out from the multitude of dead by the leader of the afterlife and put to work as his thinker. In other words, Templeton becomes the provider of intellectual services. He is among the chosen as a result of his education, not his good earthly behavior.

Reaching the netherworld with insufficient education and skills is a shortcoming that can be rectified. Religious and secular visions of the afterlife offer plenty of opportunities to explore and learn and improve oneself while dead. In Judaism, heaven is viewed as a quiet place where people study and learn so as to be able to solve life's mysteries. (In the words of a religious scholar, "Heaven is a Talmud class, without recess and without lunch."[163]) The Islamic view of the afterlife also emphasizes learning and study. Believers who are sent to hell have the opportunity to learn and improve on themselves, thereby purifying themselves from their sins. When they accumulate sufficient knowledge, Allah can rescue them and take them to heaven.164

Non-religious conceptualizations of heaven as a place that encourages self-improvement have persisted from ancient times to the present. Writing in the fourth century BCE, Socrates taught that the afterlife is filled with study. How and where does such study occur? While Socrates did not elaborate, Elizabeth Stuart Phelps provided the answer. Writing after the U.S. Civil War, she offered solace to many bereaved families by describing her temporary visit to heaven and the bucolic hereafter she witnessed. In the book *Beyond the Gates*, Phelps describes the myriad afterlife educational opportunities available to the dead. There are schools and universities, with options of lectures and classes, all of which are in high demand. Phelps reports how "the proportion of persons pursuing some form of intellectual acquisition struck me as large."165

The idea that we will continue learning in the afterlife has persisted into the present. In his comprehensive tome *Life After Death*, religious scholar Alan Segal wrote how contemporary American views of heaven include the belief that people will grow intellectually. He claims that self-improvement through education has become part of who we are and how we see ourselves, both in life and after death ("Our American notions of...continuous education *are deeply enshrined in our contemporary notions of heaven*" [italics mine]166).

"I need someone well versed in the art of torture—do you know powerpoint?"

Cartoon 7.1: Appropriate Skills For Afterlife Employment

Learning By Doing: Souls Fly With Wings

In the previous vignette, the physicist in Isaac Asimov's story was chosen for preferential afterlife treatment because of his extensive university education. But formal learning, in a classroom setting and with the goal of earning a diploma, is not the only means of accumulating human capital. Important skills are also acquired outside of formal educational institutions, through practice and experience.

An example of such postmortem skill acquisition is learning to fly with wings. Although Socrates was the first to say that souls have wings, he failed to provide directions for their use.167 He left no blueprint indicating how souls should fit, attach, and operate the appendages. Centuries later, Mark Twain added to the discussion by noting that flying with wings takes a lot of practice and does not come easily.168 Human souls are not born with the instinct to fly, like birds. It must be learned. In his story about Captain Stormfield's visit to heaven, Twain describes the experience of some one million dead people struggling with their wings. Captain Stormfield says, "Most of us tried to fly but some got crippled, and nobody made a success of it. So we concluded to walk, for the present, till we had some wing-practice."169

Wing-practice is an example of what economists call "learning-by-doing." The more practice one has performing a task, the more self-improvement there is, and with minor tweaking and learning as one goes, the task gets accomplished faster and better over time. The person becomes more productive as he/she becomes more efficient, producing more output with less inputs in a shorter time period.

When workers do not have sufficient on-the-job training and have not done sufficient learning-by-doing, then output problems arise. Some one hundred years after Mark Twain underscored the need for practice in afterlife tasks, an American movie described the unfortunate consequence of insufficient learning-by-doing. *Heaven Can Wait*, the film introduced in a previous vignette, depicts how a newly employed Escort, responsible for taking souls from their dead bodies and escorting them to their next life, made a grievous error due to his lack of experience. Observing earth from the perspective of the postmortem, the Escort saw Joe Pendleton riding his bicycle while a car headed straight towards him. The Escort wrongly swept onto the scene and took Pendleton's soul. He assumed there would be a crash, followed by a death. But he was mistaken. Had he been less eager, the Escort would have witnessed the bicycle swerving away and the head-on crash being averted. Had the Escort been more experienced, he would have known that even if there is a high probability of death, a new soul must not be seized until the outcome is unmistakable. The more souls the novice Escort rescues, the better he will become at his job.

Whether learning to use wings or learning to recognize crucial moments, inhabitants of the afterlife benefit from experience that makes them more efficient and productive in the completion of their tasks.

To Maximize Productivity in the Afterlife, Die Young

Labor productivity measures how much output a worker produces per unit of input. The healthier the person, the more output she can produce in a given time period. Also, the healthier the person, the more skills he can acquire and the more efficiently he can use supporting inputs (such as machines), both of which contribute positively to productivity. All aspects of health are important for production: physical stamina and energy levels, mental and emotional balance, access to clean water and health care, age and frailty levels, and absence of chronic disease and susceptibility to acute illnesses.

This direct relationship between health and productivity also exists in the hereafter. Myths and belief systems have focused on age as a determinant of afterlife productivity, citing the obvious fact that a healthy young man is able to carry more wood, work the fields for longer, and be more nimble with a weapon than a frail old man whose eyesight is failing, who suffers from pneumonia, and whose energy levels are low. In his book about the Native Americans of North America, *The Plains of North America and Their Inhabitants*, Colonel Richard Irving Dodge implicitly addressed the role of age and productivity, adding to his implicit discussion of capital inputs described in an earlier vignette.170

According to Dodge, "Indians" believed they will continue to hunt after they die. They also expected to wage wars against their enemies in the competition for resources such as land and animals. Hunting and warfare both rely on the labor input, so the younger and healthier the deceased man was at the time of death, the more successful he will be in those afterlife activities. (Indians believed their age at the time of death remains fixed for eternity.) It is for this reason, Dodge explained, that many Indians did not regret dying young, while they still have their strength and their vigor. Using economic terminology, they wanted to die while the marginal product of their labor was at its peak, and when the additional output they produced (the buffalo they hunt or the enemy they kill) per unit of their time was the greatest. As Indians aged, they would have to expend more time and energy to

117

achieve the same output as before. (When this happens, economists say that "diminishing marginal returns" have set in).

Dodge also suggested that Indians viewed all efforts to decrease the productivity of their postmortem competitors as important as efforts to increase their own. Indians strived to ensure not only that they were at the peak of their form when they reach the netherworld but also that their enemies were at the lowest of theirs. By cutting off the hands of dead enemy soldiers who died in battle, the Plains Indians ensured that these men would be less dangerous opponents if fighting them became necessary in the postmortem world. This belief was illustrated with an anecdote about Major Elliot, an officer of the United States cavalry. Elliot and sixteen of his men were surrounded and killed by the Plains Indians, despite their superior weapons. The sixteen men were scalped since, according to Indian beliefs, only unscalped people can get into the Indian afterlife known as the Happy Hunting Grounds. However, Major Elliot was left unscalped. This was not an oversight. In deference to his impressive fighting skills, he would be invited to enter that afterlife. But in order to ensure he would be at a disadvantage in afterlife battles with the Indians, the major's right hand and foot were cut off. Thus, Elliot's afterlife productivity was artificially decreased and his ability to compete for food and land in the Happy Hunting Grounds was lowered.171

Immigration: Skilled Souls Cross Over

Educated and skilled workers represent a society's human capital stock. The size of this capital stock fluctuates with changing conditions. When people relocate into or out of a country, the capital stock changes because they bring in or take out all their embodied skills. Economists study the ramifications of such immigration by measuring the value of the loss of human capital to the losing region (known as brain drain) as well as the benefit to the receiving destination (known as brain gain).

The concepts of brain drain and gain are illustrated in a hypothetical example of migration from the world of the living to the world of the dead.

A physician named Dr. Justin Innis-Prime is killed in an automobile accident at the peak of his career. While his corpse makes the voyage from his Park Avenue apartment to the nearby Woodlawn Cemetery, New York begins to adjust to the brain drain his death has caused. Dr. Innis-Prime's skills are lost to the world of the living. He will never again operate an appendix or teach a medical student. Given his roles as worker and producer in the earthly economy, the doctor's passing affects both the earthly labor market (in terms of the supply of his labor) as well as the product market (in terms of his supply of medical services). On a broader level, society also loses the economic benefit of Dr. Innis-Prime's taxes (that contribute to government revenue which in turn funds public sector expenditures), of his consumption activities (that contribute to the national aggregate demand), and of his fertility (that contributes to the future labor force).

At more or less the same time that Dr. Innis-Prime's corpse travels to the cemetery, his soul travels to the afterlife. It is imbued with all the skills, knowledge, and experience that the doctor had at the time of death. The nature and extent of the brain gain experienced by his new abode depends on the characteristics of that abode. If it is similar to the ancient Egyptian afterlife, then Dr. Innis-Prime is likely to continue treating patients, adding the value of his medical skills to his new residence. If instead the afterlife is similar to the one envisioned by Chinese popular religion, then the gain is primarily in the form of taxes that Dr. Innis-Prime's soul is required to pay. If instead the doctor's afterlife is in line with Mormon beliefs, then his soul's contribution is demographic, insofar as it will add to the creation of spirit babies. And if his afterlife resembles the heavenly small New England town that Elizabeth Stuart Phelps described after her return from the hereafter, then Dr. Innis-Prime's soul will continue training residents at local hospitals.

In all these permutations, the afterlife stands to gain from the human capital the doctor's soul carries over.

Sidebar 7.1: James Cameron's Avatars Cross Boundaries

The Maya of Central America believed the World Tree trunk provides the link between the underworld, the earth, and the heavens.172 In James Cameron's futuristic movie Avatar, a tree trunk plays a similar role. At the center of the Navi universe, the Tree of Souls provides a direct line to all ancestors and enables the souls of the recently deceased to join them in the afterlife. The powerful tree uses electrochemical communication and the synapses in its roots to produce a network of 10^4 connections. Surpassing the human brain in the number of connections, the Tree of Souls can "breathe in" both chief protagonists in the movie, Grace and Jake, so as to permanently transfer their souls to avatar bodies and welcome them into the Navi afterlife. In the movie, the values of the brain drain and brain gain are clear.

8

Costs

People incur all kinds of costs throughout their lifetimes. There are costs of production and costs of consumption. There are costs associated with working and costs associated with not working. Some costs are explicit, some are implicit; some are borne directly, others are borne indirectly.

Are cost considerations relevant in the afterlife?

Late Night Show host David Letterman suggests that they are. He implies that dead producers are no less rational about cost containment than the living when he offers the following joke: "One of the signs that summer is over in hell is when Satan begins his annual fretting about whether it is cheaper to switch the whole system over to natural gas."173

The vignettes in this chapter support Letterman's view and show that, yes, cost considerations show up in numerous visions of the netherworld.

Energy Consumption in Hell examines the total cost of producing fire in hell, according to a staff writer at the *New Yorker*.

Fixed costs, variable costs, and marginal costs appear in the vocabulary of economics textbooks. They also appear in the vignette, *Be Nice To Your Kids—Your Afterlife Depends On It*, in reference to the cultures that tie complex funerary rituals to the quality of the afterlife.

The average cost of production is often determined by the size of operation. In some visions, large units of concentrated souls have low average costs of operation, whereas in others, large size leads to high costs of operation (*Does Size Matter? Economies and Diseconomies of Scale*).

The difference between implicit and explicit costs is highlighted in *Death Omens: Opportunity Cost Revisited*, by drawing on Irish, French and Fijian myths.

Finally, *Don't Cut Out the Middleman* explains how priests, mediums, and angels cut costs incurred by souls.

Energy Costs in Hell

Ian Frazier published an article in the *New Yorker* in 2009 about the cost of energy in hell ("The Temperature of Hell: A Colloquium"). The article is tongue-in-cheek, poking fun at real world characters. While it is clearly not a serious depiction of how a society perceives the afterlife, still, as a clever portrayal of one man's humorous view, it contributes to popular culture and as such warrants inclusion in this book.

Frazier reports on an interdisciplinary conference on climate change in hell that was recently convened by former Vice President Gore. The impetus for the conference was the realization that hell's temperature had risen by 3.8 degrees since 1955, causing more than necessary discomfort for all its residents. The conference was attended by experts in the field of climate and environment, as well as the satanic leadership and representatives of souls in hell.

One of the speakers, Dr. Hansen, an environmental specialist, honed in on the rising cost of energy. He explained how there are many burning fires in hell that require energy for their sustenance. In the past, it was brimstone that burned (brimstone is essentially sulfur, which produces the unpleasant odor). However, brimstone is more expensive than coal, so authorities eventually switched over to the cheaper energy source. But there are several grades of coal, the cheaper ones being the most damaging environmentally (hence their name: dirty coal). Due to cost considerations, energy demands are increasingly satisfied by the lowest grade of coal available.

Dr. Hansen notes that in the future, even dirty coal will be prohibitively expensive. Why? Because the energy demands will increase as more souls go to hell and require more fire. He made careful calculations that he offered to the conference participants. There are some 6.5 billion people in the world, all of whom will die, he claims. He then estimated that only .0001 will go to heaven, and the rest will go to hell. The existing infrastructure in hell will not be able to accommodate such an influx. The increased demand for coal will push its price even higher, to unsustainable levels. Therefore, Dr. Hansen suggests, a new long-term energy policy in hell is needed. He concludes his argument by calling for immediate changes in the use of fire on its resident souls, and the need for planning for future sustainability. In his recommendation, hell must "convert as soon as possible from a coal-based soul-scourging system to one that relies on clean-burning, plentiful, and inexpensive natural gas."174

It turns out that cheaper sources of energy would also solve another problem that has arisen in hell. As a result of rising energy costs, Satan's assistant devils can no longer afford the best titanium pitchforks and instead must "poke the sinners with their pointy fingernails."175 This has led to an outcry and added pressure on the leadership to resolve the energy crisis. Cheaper energy would enable scarce funds to be diverted to other products such as state-of-the-art pitchforks.

In a single page, Ian Frazier manages to identify key economic concepts that describe the production process in hell. Without using economic language, Frazier describes the many ramifications of increases in input prices. He shows that producers alter their production function when input prices change (use coal rather than brimstone, use dirty coal rather than clean coal). He describes how those price changes have spillover effects on substitute industries (such as pitchforks) and lead to negative spillover effects on the environment (from the use of cheaper, dirty coal). In addition, those price changes are reinforced by movements in supply and demand that in turn bring about new equilibrium market prices (more dead people translates to more demand for coal, resulting in a higher equilibrium price of coal).

Be Nice to Your Kids—Your Afterlife Depends On It

The costs of burial in the United States can easily reach tens of thousands of dollars. Goods such as caskets and floral arrangements, as well as services such as body preparation and administration of religious rituals, easily add up and even surpass weddings as the most expensive ritual marking a life milestone. However, this analogy to weddings does not extend to the payment of expenses. In most cultures, wedding expenses are incurred by the parents of the bride and/or groom, whereas for burials the reverse is true: funeral expenses are typically borne by the adult children of the deceased.

Some cultures clearly specify which rituals the children are expected to perform and which arrangements they must make and pay for. Among the Burmese Buddhists, for example, it is the children who arrange the cremation, as well as the monks' ritual chanting that facilitates the soul's passage from the material world to the spiritual.176 Tibetan Buddhists specify that children must arrange for passages from the *Tibetan Book of the Dead* to be read to the corpse so the soul can be guided by the information contained therein. In addition to bearing the costs of the sendoff, a Chinese daughter is expected to wail the moment a parent expires, in order to break down obstacles the deceased will encounter on the way to the other world. An Angolan child, on the other hand, stays in the bed of the deceased, unwashed, with closed windows, and he/she can only break silence during the funeral wail, done at prescribed times of the day for several months.177 Eldest sons also have prescribed duties. Among Hindus, they must crack the skull of an almost cremated parental body with a bamboo stick in order to release the soul from its bodily entrapment. 178 And among Jews, offspring are the ones to recite the funerary prayer, the Kaddish.

The Costs Of Sending Off the Deceased

Rituals that send off the deceased into the afterlife are culturally determined and entail a package of goods and services that range from the rudimentary to the elaborate. The sendoff is not free, and the costs incurred by adult children and family members across the world differ in quantity, method of payment, and conditions of payment. Despite these differences, all these costs can be observed through an economic lens.

Economists distinguish between several measures of cost. *Total cost* refers to the market value of all the inputs used to produce a good or service. It consists of *fixed costs* (that don't change when the rate of output changes) and *variable costs* (that do change when the rate of output changes). Both fixed and variable costs are evident in the production of a sendoff.

Fixed costs refer to the expenses that do not depend on the number of people participating in the funeral or the number of funeral-related activities. In Western societies, burial plots, caskets, and body preparation are examples of fixed costs. They are constant, whether the sendoff occurs within the confines of a private family-only gravesite gathering or it entails multiple ceremonies over multiple days and is open to the public. Similarly, the Hindu corpse has to be prepared for cremation, and the funeral pyre and fire has to be paid for, no matter how many grievers attend the ceremony. So, too, the cost of mummifying ancient Egyptian corpses did not depend on the number of loved ones who congregated to say goodbye.

By contrast, the variable costs of the sendoff change when the quantity of some variable changes. This variable may refer to the mourners who must be accommodated, or the religious emissaries who perform rites, or the burial paraphernalia, such as candles and flowers, that adorn funerary environments.

Economists use the term *marginal cost* to refer to the addition to total cost incurred by producing one more unit of output. Since the output in question is the sendoff of the deceased, the marginal cost then refers to the cost of an additional sendoff for the same person. From the modern Western perspective, the idea of having multiple funerary rituals may seem odd. However, it is not an uncommon occurrence across the world. In some societies, culturally appropriate customs dictate that family and friends congregate at the gravesite of the deceased on a particular day or on the anniversary of death. The expense incurred in executing that ritual would be defined as the marginal cost.

In Mexico, on the Day of the Dead (November 2), the family of the deceased brings food, drink, flowers, and candles to the grave, where friends are invited to gather. (Incidentally, these goods are all left for the dead who, it is believed, will come to collect items unavailable in the afterlife.) Similar marginal costs are incurred in Japan during the Bon festival, when souls are believed to return to earth so their families can feed them.179 In addition to food, the marginal costs incurred by the Chinese include the paper items purchased from local temples for presentation to one's ancestors during the Festival of Ghosts. These items, such as paper mansions with paper servants, paper cars, and paper clothing, represent goods that the ancestors might have difficulty obtaining in the afterlife and are burned at the gravesite to facilitate their reaching the dead.180

Congregating once a year with some minor donations for the dead amounts to a small marginal cost compared to the multiple full funerals that some societies offer their ancestors. In these cases, the marginal cost of the additional sendoff is often no less than the total cost of the original one. The Maori of New Zealand, for example, exhume the body of a loved one a year or two after death in order to scrape the bones clean. They then paint them with red ochre, take them around the village for a second mourning, and finally rebury them. Among the Malagasy peoples in Madagascar, the Famadihana (aka "Turning of the Bones") happens about once every seven years for each family. It is a time when loved ones unearth the bodies of their ancestors and re-wrap them in new shrouds. Lastly, the Toradja of Celebes also give the bones of the dead a second funeral.181 The marginal costs of these subsequent funerals do not consist only of the paint and the exhumation, but also include the traditional celebrations, full of food and drink, to which entire villages are invited.

Failure to Incur Sendoff Costs and Follow Traditions

Religious norms and social customs dictate the arrangements and rituals that the family of the deceased should follow and pay for. If these rules are not adhered to, it is believed that there will be negative consequences. Some of these will be borne by the dead, and others will affect the living.

With respect to the former, the first and gravest consequence for the dead is that their souls have no peace and are condemned to an eternity of wandering about, never finding a home. We know from the *Iliad* that when Achilles killed Hector and desecrated his body, Hector's father, Priam (the King of Troy), pleaded for the return of his son's body in order to bury it and prevent it from roaming forever. In the *Aeneid*, Virgil wrote how souls go to the banks of the River Styx after death. Charon the boatman will only take across those who, in addition to having a coin to offer in payment, have received a proper burial. Those whose families did not give them a proper burial are stranded on the river bank for eternity.

Contemporary societies hold similar views about afterlife unrest. The Hindus believe that after cremation the soul embarks on an eleven-day journey to other worlds. To make sure it gets there, the loved ones must perform Shraddha.182 That is, they must make daily offerings of pindas (rice balls). These are symbolic of a home for the dead while they journey. On the twelfth day, the soul reaches its ancestors and the family merges a small pinda with a larger one. Without this ritual, it is believed the soul is unlikely to ever reach the afterlife. Similarly, adherents to Haiti's Voodoo tradition believe that without a burial that follows carefully prescribed sacred rites, the dead cannot reach their ancestors in the afterlife, and any subsequent gravesite rituals performed for them are useless. When Haiti suffered a devastating earthquake in January, 2010, many of the 250,000 people who perished did not receive a proper burial. Since bodies could not be found or recognized, children slated to perform rituals for their parents had died, and the poverty and devastation precluded traditional (and costly) burials, the earthquake effectively severed the links to the spiritual world in a society that pays a lot of attention to the afterlife.

The second consequence of an inadequate burial is that the soul of the deceased becomes hungry. This is believed to happen in societies where the prevailing afterlife vision includes the consumption of earthly foods. According to Finnish mythology, the dead go to a place called Manala, where they eat what is given by the living as offerings on the grave. If those offerings stop, then the souls die a second time, this time of hunger. After that death, they simply fade away.183 Similarly, the ancient Egyptians also believed regular food offerings by the living sustained the dead. If they stopped, then the souls were driven by hunger to roam around foraging for food. In the end, the souls died a second death, this one in what Egyptologist Wallis Budge referred to as "the Other World."184

A third consequence of an unsatisfactory sendoff is unhappiness of the soul. Such a sentiment arises when surviving children fail to place the coffin of their parent in the correct way. Positioning is especially important among the Chinese, where Feng Shui started as the study of how to place coffins so as to maximize the free and natural flow of life energy. If the dead are incorrectly placed, it can disrupt the yin and yang energies, which in turn will make the buried souls unhappy.185

While the dead may experience hunger and unhappiness if improperly buried, the living experience fear. They fear the consequences of an unsatisfactory sendoff, one that is not up to the traditional or social standards that are expected of them. Some survivors believe the ghosts of their ancestors will come back to earth and hurt them in retaliation. Some fear the poltergeist—that is, unexplained events that myths attribute to angry ghosts who come to earth to cause problems. Others fear they will reap what they sow, and inadequate burial of their parents will lead, by example, to their own neglect by their offspring. Many in China fear that a disrupted yin and yang energy will make a soul dangerous for those left on earth.186

If children of the dying are sufficiently bound by traditions and customs, then apprehension about these negative consequences provides incentives for giving their parents a proper sendoff. But they must also have the capacity to incur the costs that are entailed. They must have sufficient resources and they must be physically present and capable of performing the necessary rituals. In developing countries, where many of the strongest filial traditions are found, young people have emigrated, leaving their parents alone at the time of death. Their capacity to arrange and pay for their parents' sendoff, and often their incentive to do so, both tend to diminish as their distance from the ancestral home increases.

In modern Western societies, where the filial sense of obligation towards one's ancestors is typically weak, institutions have emerged that ensure a person's final wishes are respected. People leave written instructions that are legally binding, they pay in advance for their burial plot and casket, and they pre-pick their funeral home. In that way, they do not depend on their offspring's goodwill to ensure a proper sendoff.

Does Size Matter? Economies and Diseconomies of Scale

Like variable costs, average total costs are also associated with the scale of operation. While variable costs of burying the dead increase as the number of mourners increases, the average (per person) total cost of the burial decreases as more people partake in the funeral activities. This is because total cost includes fixed costs that remain constant. Economists use the term *economies of scale* to describe this inverse relationship between average total costs of production and the size of operation. Economies of scale are evident in many earthly industries, including automobiles and wheat. They are also evident in some visions of the afterlife.

As described in an earlier chapter, both Christian and Islamic heavens are often depicted as gardens. The irrigation that provides the verdant color and the lushness of these gardens can more cheaply be administered and maintained when gardens are contiguous and large in size than when they are fragmented and small. Moreover, the cost of every gallon of water, as well as the cost of its distribution, decreases as the garden acreage rises.

Also, both Christian and Islamic heavens contain a variety of constructions. A literal interpretation of both the Book of Revelation and the Qur'an points to walls, gates, and towers in heaven. There are also streets and there are buildings. Using an economic lens, it can be said that the total costs of construction and materials, per unit, decrease as more buildings, walls, and gates are constructed. The heavenly construction industry exhibits economies of scale.

Using the same logic, it can be inferred that similar economies appear in the production of torture in hell. Both Islam and Christianity envision a hell where sinners experience torture by fire. The more souls are tortured, the more the per-unit cost of producing the torture declines.

Yet increasing size of operation does not always result in decreasing total average costs. Just like in earthly production, when a productive unit becomes too large and unmanageable, then marginal product begins to fall off and average total costs begin to grow. In other words, diseconomies of scale set in.

There is a view of the afterlife in which such diseconomies are evident. Neuroscientist David Eagleman describes it in his creative book *Sum: Forty Tales From the Afterlives.*

Without using economic terms, Eagleman envisions a heaven so large and complex that God lost control. Overwhelmed by the magnitude of the workload, He soon realized that, "He had no concept of the skills required to run an organization of this magnitude. Because of the excessive procreation of His humans, the population was doubling at a blinding rate, and the managerial load for a hereafter became staggering. A file had to be kept on every individual, planet-wide, with constant updating of new sins and good deeds."187 Eagleman goes on to describe the anarchy that results, as adultery and crime flourish. By implication, the per-soul cost of maintaining peace in heaven has increased as size increased, and diseconomies of scale have set in.

The appearance of both economies and diseconomies of scale in visions of the afterlife raises the question of optimal size of the hereafter. Is there a size of hell or heaven that is just right, one that is large enough to reap the benefits of economies but small enough so diseconomies do not set in? If such a size could be identified, it would surely be the quantity associated with the lowest average cost.

Death Omens: Opportunity Cost Revisited

The energy costs incurred by hell's administration are explicit, as are the ritual send-off costs borne by children of the deceased. They both entail direct payments to somebody, in exchange for something. By contrast, implicit costs are incurred without an associated direct payment. An example of such costs was introduced in Chapter 2 in reference to rational behavior, specifically in choosing how to spend one's scarce resources in the afterlife. These opportunity costs are now revisited in another context, one that links mythical death omens to forgone wages. (Omens and wages? It is not as much of a stretch as it first appears.)

Omens portend future events. Through the ages, people have sought out signs of future events they cannot predict, such as a ground-hog's appearance portending the timing of spring. Omens have been especially important when it comes to death, a life event shared by all but whose timing and circumstances are (usually) unknown. To deal with this uncertainty, people have identified a series of omens believed to announce upcoming death. Among medieval Christians, the appearance of the Grim Reaper (the spirit of the latest person who died in a village) in one's dreams meant that death was approaching. More recently, deathbed apparitions of angels, or of deceased friends and celebrities, are seen as signs that an afterlife emissary is en route to take the dying away.

Applying an economic lens to death omens highlights the economic purpose they serve. Omens that appear in three national myths illustrate this purpose.

In the remote Pacific island of Fiji, it is believed that Rati-Mbati-Ndua is the god of the underworld. In addition to his ruling duties, he also flies across the skies with broad wings and no arms, and when he finds someone who is about to die, he sweeps down to earth to devour him or her.188 Given that he leaves a train of fire behind him when he flies, people see him arriving before he actually lands. In this way, death announces its arrival.

In the Brittany region of France, where sleepy villages and bucolic hills dot the landscape, a local myth about a male ghost was born. His name is Ankou, and he is believed to look like a skeleton, with long white hair protruding from under a big hat.189 He drives a wooden cart, and when a person is about to die, he pulls up in front of the home, thereby announcing his arrival. Although villagers close shutters and doors to avoid him, they sometimes peek and report seeing him.

The Irish, rich in colorful folklore, have their own version of the Ankou. It is the Banshee, a female ghost with long hair, often carrying a comb.190 She is the death messenger who shows up to wail when someone is about to die. For centuries people have believed that her wailing is heard by the dying. Although she is rarely seen, family members report hearing her at times.

In each of these myths, death gives fair warning to families of the dying before it comes to take away their loved ones. Such information invites action no less than the words of a twenty-first century western physician who tells a terminal patient to get his affairs in order. The recipients of such information act upon it because it is rational to do so. As a result of death omens, loved ones are able to get a head start on the laborious tasks that await them in death's aftermath. Bodies need to be prepared for disposal, be it cremation or burial. Mourning rituals need to be organized. Eulogies need to be composed, friends from afar need to be congregated, and food needs to be cooked.

By providing advance notice, omens decrease the future opportunity costs of grieving family members. Since opportunity cost is defined as the value of what one gives up when choosing one outcome over another, families of the deceased must trade off time spent on death-related activities against time spent at work. Opportunity costs are incurred by family members of the dying when they spend time on burial arrangements instead of their paid jobs. When death announces its arrival, a Fijian fisherman, a French farmer, and an Irish metalworker can all get a head start on the logistics of the burial and, therefore, decrease the time they spend on it later. They can start making funeral arrangements before death occurs; they can start gathering relatives together before the dying draw their last breath. With *a priori* information in hand, they can make cost-effective choices and execute them more efficiently than if they were operating *a posteriori*. Ultimately, they can get back to work faster and give up fewer productive hours, thus forgoing less income. The opportunity cost is the value of the fish the Fijian fisherman did not catch (and sell) while tending to funeral arrangements. It is the value of the cheese the French farmer did not produce, the cabbage he did not tend, and the wine he did not sell at the market. For the Irish metalworker, it is the value of the fence that he could have built but didn't. By announcing death's arrival, Rati-Mbati-Ndua, Ankou, and the Banshee unintentionally show consideration for the opportunity costs of grieving family and friends.

Sidebar 8.1: Death Omens of Early Buddhists

According to Jason Boyett, the author of Pocket Guide to the Afterlife, early Buddhists believed that death was approaching if an individual dreamed any of the following: wearing black clothes made of yak hair; eating feces; being trapped in a wicker basket or inside a tall, red-colored castle; having one's head cut off and carried away; being disemboweled; being dragged by dead people; jumping into a pit; and repeatedly picking red flowers.191

Don't Cut Out the Middleman

When the business press publishes stories about "angels," they are not referring to the cherubic, sexless creatures typically associated with heaven. They are referring to financial intermediaries, real world individuals who provide entrepreneurs with their first infusion of money. These angels put financial capital into the hands of those who will use it creatively. They give life to good ideas. They bring people together. They facilitate, they lubricate. Financial angels are middlemen, and, as such, they perform an important function in the economy.

Yet "real" angels are also middlemen, albeit their sphere of operation is the spiritual world. In Christianity and Islam, they serve as go-betweens, linking the world of the spirits with the world of the living. In addition, they guide and they guard. They are messengers and they are mediators. They connect, they bring together, they lubricate, they facilitate. They inform.

Angels are not alone in those roles. Religious emissaries such as pastors, priests, bishops, and imams, also serve as middlemen between believers and their God. They provide information about the afterlife and guide believers to position themselves for the best possible eternity. Psychic mediums also serve as middlemen between the world of the living and that of the dead. Although they are not believed to cross the boundary, they provide information to the living about the dead and they facilitate communication between the two.

Intermediary services are not free. Earthly middlemen take a portion of the transaction they facilitate (witness the commission paid to real estate agents, travel agents, and investor angels). So, too, middlemen services involving the afterlife are not free, although the directness of the monetary exchange varies. The cost of a medium's services are overt, direct, and immediate, but the cost of a priest's afterlife information, embedded in a Sunday sermon, takes the form of indirect donations to the church, often given with a lag. The cost of the angel's guidance and messenger service is neither direct nor explicit, taking place instead in private. Any given individual estimates the opportunity cost of the time they spend believing in angels.

When buying guidance and information, some people try to cut out the middleman. They do this in an effort to reduce their costs. Yet that is often a mistake, because middlemen, whether facilitating earthly or afterlife matters, can actually lower total costs. They can add the value of their service to the exchange. They can provide information where there was none before, information that is costly for a non-specialist to obtain. They can put economic actors together who otherwise would not find each other. They can reduce the opportunity cost of time spent in the search. For all these reasons, middlemen can serve to cut costs and increase efficiency.

9

Rule of Law

Production and consumption do not take place in a vacuum. They take place in environments that are more or less conducive to economic activity. The rule of law is among the most important features of such environments. Laws set guidelines for economic behavior and, in the process, protect the rights of producers and consumers. Typically, governments are responsible for maintaining the rule of law and ensuring that contracts are enforced and rights are protected. Widespread rule of law creates an environment in which free market economic activity can thrive. In this chapter, rule of law is observed in several visions of the afterlife.

Rights to physical and intellectual property are fundamental to the functioning of market economies. In *This Cloud is My Cloud, That Cloud is Your Cloud*, property rights of the dead are examined.

Under the Western legal system, guardians protect the interests of minors. *A Dead Legal Guardian* describes the relationship between a ghost guardian and a living child as described in an American bestseller.

Where there are laws, there are attempts to break those laws. The vignette *Death and Taxes* shows that tax evasion is illegal in the afterlife as it is on earth.

Embezzlement is another way of breaking the law. *All Embezzlers Go to Hell* describes how financial fraud is punished in Dante's vision of the afterlife.

This Cloud is My Cloud; That Cloud is Your Cloud

When the Rolling Stones sang, "Hey, hey, you, you, get offa my cloud," it is unlikely that they were referring to a squabble over property rights in heaven. Yet those listeners who interpret the lyrics literally might imagine puffy cloud homes resembling cotton balls, and a resident soul yelling to a trespasser to keep away.

Such a vision of cloud abodes raises the question economics textbooks typically ask in chapter one: who gets what, when, and how. Specifically, how are clouds allocated among demanding souls, who gets which particular cloud, and how do they ensure it stays theirs? Is there a market mechanism that distributes cloud housing, one in which suppliers and demanders come together in a market for clouds and the equilibrium price (monetary or non-monetary) determines who gets what? Or is there a command system, in which some higher authority awards clouds to souls? If the latter, is it done on the basis of first come, first served? Or do good deeds on earth translate into preferred cloud property in heaven? Whether distribution of cloud homes takes place through a market mechanism or a command system, there are additional questions to be answered: once souls get a cloud, do they keep it for eternity? Can they lease it out? Can they give it away? If they go for an afternoon stroll, how are they assured no trespassers will move in during their absence?

All these questions have to do with property rights—that is, laws about property that define the rights of owners. Typically such laws grant individuals the right to hold property and do with it what they like, including sell it, lease it, and pass it on as inheritance. While property rights are easily understood on earth, it is far less clear how they transfer to the afterlife. Although classics scholar Robert Garland claims the idea that the dead possess legal rights is enshrined in Greek legal history,192 there are no specified modifications for contemporary property disputes in which one or more of the parties reside in the hereafter. To fill this void, Hollywood's creative screenwriters and movie directors stepped in. One product of their imagination is the 1995 children's movie *The Story of Casper*, in which the struggle between the dead and the living over property rights fills the screen from beginning to end. The main character, known from earlier screen appearances as Casper the Friendly Ghost, has touched the hearts of generations of American children, and in *The Story of Casper* he teaches them about property rights. Here's how.

In the movie, flashy and obnoxious Carrigan Critterdon inherits a haunted mansion in Maine (Whipstaff Manor) from her estranged father. She has no intention of moving in or restoring it. She only wants to find a treasure she erroneously came to believe was hidden in the house. Carrigan has no idea that ghosts inhabit the property, ghosts with strong convictions about their right to use the land and the house. The moment she first approaches the property, Carrigan's nastiness and greed make themselves felt to these resident ghosts who, in turn, make their presence felt to her. In an effort to fend them off, Carrigan first hires a pseudo-religious figure that claims extensive ghostly experience. He makes a speedy exit out of the manor. Carrigan then hires an exterminator armed with poisonous gases. He, too, makes a speedy exit. In desperation, she calls in a demolition crew to raze the manor to the ground, thinking that ghosts could be turned into dust. After their first encounter with the ghosts, the crew drives their vehicles, bulldozers, and cars off the property, in panic.

The plot thickens when Carrigan learns about Dr. Harvey, a psychiatrist who specializes in the afterlife. He treats souls who have unfinished business on earth and have not yet crossed over. Simply put, he is a ghost doctor. Carrigan urgently hires him to deal with the ghostly residents of Whipstaff Manor. In order to complete his assignment, Dr. Harvey moves into the mansion, together with his young daughter Kit. Soon after their arrival, father and daughter have their first encounter with the ghosts who call the mansion their home. The young one is Casper, a lilly-white ghost with big eyes that radiate innocence and charm. To say his uncles Fatso, Stinky, and Stretch are not friendly would be an understatement. Casper's case for home ownership rests on solid ground. The mansion was his family home before his untimely death. The playroom is full of his toys, his mother's clothes are in the closets, and his father's inventions are on display. Casper and his uncles lived there for many decades, undisturbed, until Carrigan showed up and threatened their rights.

From that moment onwards, the movie becomes a standoff between two parties, both of whom claim to have property rights on the old mansion and surrounding land. Carrigan inherited the property and has a legal deed to prove her ownership rights. In modern market economies, such as the one in which Carrigan operates, property rights give holders the right to own, sell, or do what they wish with their property. A legal environment exists to protect those property rights. In it, contracts (such as deeds) are drawn up to define them and institutions (such as courts) are created to enforce them.

On the other hand, Casper has lived in Whipstaff Manor for decades. If he were alive, he would be the one holding the property rights. But even without formal proof of residency, if Casper were alive he would have squatting rights by virtue of his *de facto* possession. Since he is a ghost, his rights are not respected by the living. Carrigan has a deed and *de jure* ownership, and, therefore, her rights trump Casper's.

When Dr. Harvey explains this legal point to Casper and his uncles, the ghosts respond by trying to drive him away, as they did with previous intruders. In the end, Dr. Harvey is overwhelmed by the complexity of a legal situation that entails claimants on different sides of the life divide. He gives up and tells Casper and his uncles that as far as he is concerned, they can stay in the manor because possession is nine-tenths of the law.

This movie about ghosts ingeniously treats a legal issue made infinitely more complex by the boundaries imposed by death. And it does more than that. The movie also shows that Carrigan's failure to evict the ghosts from her property, despite her earthly legal rights, has diminished the economic value she derives from her inheritance. She will have difficulty selling Whipstaff Manor as long as its peculiar ownership question remains unresolved.

A Dead Legal Guardian

When people are deemed incapable of looking out for their best interests, or those of their property, a legal guardian is appointed. That guardian has the responsibility and the authority to make decisions on their behalf, and is legally empowered to act in their best interest in all affairs, including all economic activities. Legal guardians of minors are typically their parents, although if they are incapable of performing that duty, a substitute guardian is appointed. Every minor must have a guardian. It is the law.

According to author Neil Gaiman's vision of the afterlife, legal guardians of living minors can be dead. In his book, *The Graveyard Book*, the 2009 Newberry Award winner describes how a dead legal guardian was chosen to represent a minor in the world of the living.

The story goes as follows. A little baby boy crawls to the local graveyard after his family is murdered in their nearby home. Mr. and Mrs. Owens, two ghosts who had inhabited the Graveyard for several hundred years, find him and hide him. After the pursuing murderer walks away in frustration, unable to locate the escaped boy, an emergency meeting of ghosts is called to decide the baby's fate. The ghosts did not deliberate long before choosing Mr. and Mrs. Owens to be the boy's new parents. (By now, he'd been named Nobody Owens, nicknamed Bod.) However, since they are dead and the baby is alive, someone had to be identified to represent Bod's interests in the world of the living, where the ghostly Owens cannot function. Silas steps in for the task and proclaims himself willing to serve as Bod's legal guardian. Silas can perform such a function because he is an Inbetween Person, or one who is dead but inhabits both worlds. Not only can he easily visit the world of the living to procure food for Bod but he can also look out for Bod's interests in other ways until such a time as the baby becomes a man and can take over responsibility for himself. As Bod's guardian, it is Silas who later administers and oversees Bod's education. It is he who determines the extent of Bod's interactions with humans as well as with ghosts. When circumstances require it, Silas even decides with whom Bod should socialize.

It is not odd that guardianship matters would be of concern to the ghosts. Guardianship has to do with law, and according to Neil Gaiman's description of the Graveyard, its citizens are all law-abiding ghosts. Indeed, there are clear laws that govern inter-ghostly behavior, as well as the rights that all residents enjoy. As Bod grows up, he is taught the laws and granted the rights, little by little. First he got the right of abode, meaning that he could reside at the graveyard even if he was not buried there. Later, he was granted the Freedom of the Graveyard, namely the ability to see in the darkness and to learn skills such as "sliding" and "fading," which allow him to go places where the living cannot go. In the Graveyard, as in societies of the living, rules and rights exist in order to avoid anarchy. By the time Bod grew up, he was familiar with the Graveyard rule of law and abided by it no differently than he would have abided by earthly rules had he grown up among the living.

Death and Taxes

Most societies have laws that require their members to pay taxes. Taxation is the means by which governments collect revenue from their subjects, which is then used to fund expenditures that benefit society. Government expenditure provides individuals with goods and services they cannot otherwise obtain. Such products fall under the government domain because they cannot be provided on a small scale (such as waste disposal) or without a coordinated effort (such as military defense). Some goods are shunned by the private sector because they are not profitable (such as lighthouse lighting, for which users cannot be charged). Some goods are unattainable to people with low incomes (such as food and housing). Governments spend on these products because they provide collective benefit, and so everyone in society must share the burden by paying taxes. It is the law.

Having laid down the law, governments then make exceptions and excuse some individuals from paying. In the United States, the federal government makes allowances for low-income individuals and families, effectively freeing them from the tax burden. They are considered too poor to participate in the tax system. Similarly, some one thousand years ago, the Franks who lived in the coastal villages of France were exempt from paying tribute to their German rulers for the simple reason that they faced England, thought to be the Isle of the Dead. Living in proximity to the dead was considered so onerous that, in compensation, area residents were freed from monetary payments to the authorities.193

Exceptions such as these are within the boundaries of the law. It is those individuals who are eligible to pay taxes but do not that operate outside legal limits. They are tax evaders, and societies penalize their behavior. Tax evasion and its concomitant punishment also appear in some visions of the afterlife. Two selected visions from different historical periods are examined in this vignette: ancient Egypt and contemporary Hollywood.

Ancient Egyptian society had a highly sophisticated tax system. People's taxes filled government coffers and thus enabled both the

143

lavish lifestyle of the rulers as well as the funding for projects such as construction, irrigation, and shipbuilding. In addition, a system of policing tax evaders was in place, together with consequent punishment for tax evasion. Since Egyptians viewed the afterlife as a mirror of earthly life, those who policed evaders in life were believed to continue doing so after death. Tomb drawings confirm that tax evasion was believed to be a part of the afterlife, as was the punishment doled out by authorities. In the Saqqara region of Egypt, a vizier who lived around 2400 BCE is depicted in his tomb drawings as living out his afterlife fully and happily. In some scenes he spears fish while his servants are trapping a hippopotamus; in other scenes he is presiding over judgment of tax delinquents, exactly as he did on earth.194

Fast forward several millennia, and meet Joe Black in the film *Meet Joe Black*. In this American romantic drama of the 1990s, Joe is the identity that Death takes on when he visits earth where, among other things, he punishes a man for engaging in tax fraud. Here is the story.

Bill Parrish is a charismatic and much-loved businessman who created and then transformed Parrish Communications into a successful global enterprise. Around his sixty-fifth birthday, Bill has a heart attack. Death comes to earth to escort Bill to the other world, but upon meeting him, Death is so impressed that he decides to postpone their voyage. He wants to stay on earth for a while, mostly to learn from Bill but also to experience life. He offers Bill a deal: a few more days of life in exchange for allowing Death to shadow him and learn from him. The offer is accepted. However, in order to mingle on earth, Death needs a physical body. As he reviews the options, a handsome young man (played by Brad Pitt) is killed in a car accident nearby, and Death immediately takes over his body. To it he adds a name, Joe Black, and with that identity proceeds to live life.

During several intense days on earth, Death (aka Joe) tastes peanut butter for the first time, learns to knot a tie, falls in love, and even experiences sex. He also learns that Bill's future son-in-law, Drew, is dishonest. Drew had been playing both sides in a buyout deal. He managed to convince Bill to agree to a merger with John Bonahue, a buyer who plans to dismantle and sell off bits of the company Bill spent his life building. Drew also manipulated the board of trustees of Parrish Communications to force Bill into retirement. But this is Hollywood, and Death steps in to save the day.

Joe Black's parting gift to Bill is to impersonate an IRS agent. Under that guise, he confronts Drew. In an accusatory tone, Joe says he has been investigating Drew and Bonahue for some time now and has come to learn of tax evasion and other improprieties. Drew has broken the law and now faces punishment. Defeated and slumped in a chair, Drew mummers, "Who would have guessed—you, an IRS agent!" To which Joe responds, "Well, you know…death and taxes!"

By impersonating an IRS agent, Death rights a wrong. Even though the fraud took place on earth, it took someone from the afterlife to come along and impose justice. Clearly, Death knew all about tax evasion and justice.

All Embezzlers Go To Hell

Bernie Madoff is an embezzler. He swindled investors, deceived those he advised, and committed fraud of enormous proportions. His Ponzi scheme was the biggest in history, costing thousands of innocent people some $60 billion. Yes, he is incarcerated for life, but still, those he swindled want to know: will Bernie Madoff go to hell?

If that question were posed to Dante, the fourteenth century Florentine poet, his response would unequivocally be affirmative. In his *Inferno*, Dante describes nine circles of hell. He set up special chambers where financial wrong-doers go after death. This is where they get their due, reaping in the afterlife what they sowed in their lifetimes. In Cantos 21-22 and 26-27 of the *Inferno*, Dante describes the specific parts of the eighth circle (the Bolgia 5 and the Bolgia 8) where fraudulent advisers and those with so-called sticky hands reside—hands to which money stuck as it was pocketed during illegal transactions. Dante's vision of these chambers does not stop with a sticky environment. Since fraudulent financial activities took place in secret, away from others who might witness them, so, too, embezzlers' souls are condemned to live away from others, where their presence is virtually secret and unknown to other souls. And since they took advantage of others in the course of their illegal earthly activities, in hell they, in turn, are victims of exploitation, repeatedly, by demons. All the while, the grafters' souls are engulfed by flames.

Dante's attention to embezzlers and grafters reflects the society in which he lived and wrote. His hometown Florence was a medieval headquarters of the financial industry—dynamic, competitive, and thriving. Creative investors flocked there to join wealthy investors. Together, they transformed the city into a concentration of venture capital where abundant monetary transactions made *loans, interest,* and *investment* household words. But where there is an opportunity for quick creation of wealth, there is also opportunity for illegal activities. In fact, Florence of that era was also known for its financial corruption, graft, misappropriation of funds, and other illegal activities. Unlike contemporary financial industries, which are regulated and operate under the watchful eye of the law, Florence's lax rules provided fertile ground for corruption and theft.

Sidebar 9.1: Bribery in the Chinese Afterlife

Some visions of the afterlife reflect the rule of law and the legal system believers experienced on earth. In China, where bribing government officials was part of daily reality, folk religion suggests that, after dying, the dead spent some fifty days (and sometimes even up to three years) going from official to official in the afterlife bureaucracy, standing on trial and giving bribes in order to change the outcome of their sentence.195

10

Employment, Occupations, Overtime Work, and Earnings

A popular American television show, *Six Feet Under*, glorifies the death industry by putting a human face to life behind the scenes at a funeral home. The show resonates with viewers in part because the subject is familiar. Not only are many people associated with the death industry as direct consumers for loved ones, or as passive attendees of funerals, but many also participate in the industry as producers. Numerous jobs deal with dying, either directly or indirectly. Some people work as morticians and others build caskets. Nurses tend to the dying, lawyers prepare their wills, priests administer their last rites, and journalists write their obituaries. Others mow cemetery lawns, grow flowers for wreaths, and print Hallmark's sympathy cards.

That there should be employment associated with the afterlife is not surprising since death is a rite of passage that, like marriage and birth, is associated with production of goods and services. The relevant question for this book is: what about employment *in* the afterlife? In other words, do people work after they die?

If they do, then do they retain their earthly occupations? How big is the labor force in the afterlife, and what is the unemployment rate? Is there competition for jobs and is there equilibrium in the labor market? Are there wages in the afterlife, and, if not, how are workers compensated? And then, do dead workers have bargaining power? Do they belong to unions?

Many of these questions cannot be answered given our current knowledge of the beyond. However, some answers are gleaned through selected visions of the afterlife that might induce readers to update their resumes before dying.

Dead Tinker, Dead Tailor, Dead Soldier, Dead Sailor describes postmortem occupations as depicted in myths and religions.

Even in the world of the dead, some workers have multiple jobs. *Holding Down Two Jobs* explores the differing work responsibilities of Etruria and Charon.

Worker productivity depends on the division of labor in the workplace as well as the extent of teamwork. In *The Dead Benefit From Teamwork,* a story illustrates how teamwork makes souls more productive in heaven than in hell. Similarly, *Asleep at the Wheel (at the Gates of Hades)* explores the effect on productivity of a lapse in Cerberus's attention at work.

There are many ways to remunerate people for the work they perform. *Angels Earn Their Wings* describes how angels in heaven get paid.

Sometimes workers receive no payment. *Zombie Slaves Are Free Dead Labor* shows how slave labor in Haitian Voodoo belief crosses the boundaries between the living and the dead, and in *Seventy Heavenly Wives Equal Seventy Heavenly Workers,* the Hausa views of women's work in the afterlife are described.

A word of explanation: economists define employment as work for pay. The last two vignettes in this chapter refer to work but contain no mention of pay. Even without a monetary or non-monetary compensation, the work performed is considered a marketable activity since someone somewhere trades it in a market. (For example, a Native American hunter is said to work at skinning buffalo. Even if he does not get a paycheck, skinning is nevertheless treated as a job because it is a marketable activity that can be exchanged in the market.)

Dead Tinker, Dead Tailor, Dead Soldier, Dead Sailor

Tinkers repair pots, tailors sew clothes, soldiers protect their country, and sailors serve on ships. They are all employed in the provision of services. As such, they work in the services sector, one of the three sectors into which all economic activity falls (the other two are agriculture and industry/manufacturing). All workers can be grouped by the sector in which they are employed. Such a grouping is known as the *industrial classification* of the labor force.

Afterlife visions from across the globe and from different historical periods reveal a variety of jobs that the dead are believed to perform. It is not surprising that those postmortem jobs reflect the industrial classification of the labor force of their earthly societies.

The Industrial Classification of the Afterlife Labor Force

The most elaborate descriptions of afterlife workers and occupations are from the agricultural sector. Farming activities described in writings and drawings by ancient Egyptian and Babylonian societies, as well as in oral myths of contemporary rural societies in Africa and Asia, include hoeing, irrigating, sowing, reaping, and harvesting. Fishing activities show up on hieroglyphics depicting skinny boats paddling on the Nile, and Inuit folklore depicts spear fishing of seals along the Canadian coast. Postmortem hunting appears in most Native North American myths.

Manufacturing jobs appear in afterlife visions of the above societies as activities related to the agricultural sector. All the above methods of food procurement have linkages to other economic activities. Animal skinning is linked to the production of clothing and teepees, which both use skins as inputs. Similarly, fishing among dead Egyptians stimulates the boat-building industry. Although these linkages spin off from agricultural activities, the souls who manufacture clothing, tepees, and boats belong to the afterlife manufacturing sector.

151

Food procurement also stimulates spinoff activities in the services sector. Once food is grown or caught, there are workers who prepare it and serve it. Cooks and waiters show up in afterlife visions, especially at banquets hosting gods and other dignitaries. Vivid scenes of the Mesopotamian afterlife are described in the *Epic of Gilgamesh*, in which the dead serve meat roasts and baked goods to guests, and pour cool water from water skins for them to drink.196

The services sector includes much more than food industries. It is an umbrella sector, encompassing the broadest range of jobs. This includes the transportation workers who populate afterlife visions throughout the millennia. Early examples include Charon, who ferries souls across the river into the land of the dead in the poetry of Homer and Virgil. Medical workers appear in Australian aboriginal mythology, in which some deceased people become shamans in the next life, acquiring the ability to cure the sick. They perform that function among the dead and can also return to earth to tend to the living. Finally, a variety of bureaucratic workers show up in visions of the afterlife that span centuries and continents. They include the ancient Egyptian scribes who keep track of souls by writing in a ledger and the magistrates who dole out justice in Plato's and Socrates's plays about the afterlife (*Gorgias* and *Phaedo*, respectively). Comprehensive and full-fledged bureaucracies existed in the Mesopotamian City of the Dead, where political and administrative jobs on earth are replicated to the minutest detail.197 Across the globe in Asia, the Taoist view of the afterlife is regimented, filled with judges who pronounce sentences. If the deceased wants to appeal a severe sentence, a petition gets submitted to officials and generals, each of which specialize in a particular complaint.198 Similarly, believers in Confucianism envision Tian, the Confucian paradise, as a place where some souls are selected to serve as clerks and attendants, as well as overseers of harvest and regulators of the change of seasons.199

The Structural Transformation of the Economy

The industrial classification of the labor force is useful for understanding the structure of an economy. By observing how the distribution of workers changes over time, economists can track the evolution of key economic variables. Typically, as economies expand and develop, they become more industrialized and less agricultural. That means the proportion of workers in agriculture decreases as the proportion in industry increases in response to growth in that sector. As agricultural workers shift into industrial jobs, they satisfy the manpower demands of the growing economy. After even more economic growth, the labor force becomes increasingly service-oriented, since new job creation tends to be in the services sector (banking, transportation, insurance, tourism, and so on). This process of long-term change, first identified by Nobel laureate Simon Kuznets, has come to be known as the *structural transformation* of the economy. It is used to explain why the United States presently has over three quarters of its workers employed in services, when at the turn of the twentieth century it had a highly industrial labor force, and one hundred years before that the agricultural sector predominated.

Like other earthly economic phenomena, the structural transformation of world economies is reflected in their populations' visions of the afterlife. Thousands of years ago, afterlives were believed to be agricultural. This makes sense, since those visions reflected earthly life of the era. For that same reason, contemporary rural African peoples (including the Ashanti and the Dinka), for whom agriculture is still a huge part of daily life, also envision an agricultural afterlife.

By contrast, Western views of the afterlife as expressed by contemporary popular culture are overwhelmingly non-agricultural. Indeed, in *The Simpsons*, Homer Simpson goes to an industrial hell where production assembly line technology is in effect. In the movie *Ghost Town*, a dead dentist keeps checking his blackberry, and in *Defending Your Life* soul chauffeurs drive the newly dead around Judgment City in huge buses, showing a vibrant afterlife transportation industry.

Do Earthly Occupations Carry Over to the Afterlife?

A lawyer's joke: a lawyer dies and goes to heaven. Souls flock to see the new arrival, lining the streets and elbowing each other to get a better view. One soul, straining his neck to catch a glimpse, asks another: "Who is this man? Why's he so important? Popes have come to heaven and they never drew such crowds." The other soul responds: "It's a lawyer. No one has ever seen one of them here before."

This joke implies that the lawyer's soul continues to be identified with the practice of law, even in the hereafter. The same is implied by art and literature depicting afterlife visions. The Egyptians, for example, believed that a farmer on earth will be a farmer in the afterlife, he will not become a fisherman. Similarly, the Greeks believed that King Minos of Crete, who was a cruel judge on earth, would continue his profession in hell, judging which sinners would inhabit the different parts of hell.

Burial customs also support the idea that earthly occupations carry over. Burying the dead with the tools of their trade enables them to continue with their earthly work. If a man was a priest, the Maya of Mesoamerica buried books in his grave; if he was a sorcerer, he was buried with his divine stones.200 Similarly, the rural Bagondo peoples of the Philippines bury their men facing east, so that when the sun rises they know it is time to go to work in the fields. (Women are buried facing west, so that when the sun sets they know it is time to go cook).201

Such occupational symmetry between life on earth and in the hereafter makes for an uncomplicated vision of eternity. But what if dead workers want to change occupations? What if they feel trapped and unfulfilled, and want to try something new after being fishermen or judges for a few hundred years? The postmortem envisioned by Elizabeth Stuart Phelps in the 1800s offers the possibility of such career changes. In her book, *Beyond the Gates*, Phelps describes the occupational flexibility of the dead as she observed it during her visit to heaven.202 Rather than being locked into their earthly roles, souls can start new jobs and choose new occupations. An application of this view might be: a shoemaker does not have to make shoes in the hereafter but can become a poet instead, if he is so inclined. If the dead in Phelps' heaven were to partake in such easy occupational transformations, the industrial classification of the afterlife labor force would not reflect the one they left behind on earth.

Sidebar 10.1: A Bedouin Camel for Afterlife Work

Hundreds of years ago, Bedouins of North Africa made their living with camels transporting their goods for trade. After the death of a relative, a well-to-do family would tie up a camel by the grave of the deceased and leave it there to starve and die, thus ensuring their loved one would have the means to pursue his occupation in the afterlife.203

Holding Down Two Jobs

In both Roman and Greek mythologies, there is a transporter who ferries the dead across a river and into the underworld. In the former his name is Etruria and he crosses the Acheron; in the latter, it is Charon and the river is the Styx. In addition to their names, the two men also differ with respect to their jobs.

The Roman Etruria is depicted in art and literature as old and twisted, often with a mallet in one hand. The mallet is the tool he uses in his other job, that of torturing souls once they get to the nether-world. He is in charge of hitting souls on the head the moment they leave their physical bodies.

While Etruria has two jobs in the netherworld, working both in the transportation industry as well as the torture business, the Greek Charon has only his transportation job. Principles of rational behavior, together with labor market analysis, can be used to explain their different employment situations.

Supply of Etruria's Labor

In both ancient Roman and ancient Greek practice, the dead are buried with a coin in their mouth to pay for the river crossing. If Etruria and Charon want to earn more than that coin for their services, they have two options. They can either increase the price of the boat ride or they can ferry more souls across (as per the equation: Total Revenue = Price of each crossing x Quantity of crossings). In reality, neither of these options is under their control. Increasing price is not feasible since they have no way of *a priori* informing the living about the price change, and at the point of transaction, the dead have no money other than the coin their relatives placed in their mouths. Similarly, increasing the number of souls that are ferried across the river is also beyond their control. The two ferrymen are limited by the demand for their services. In the aftermath of a war on earth, or a plague, or widespread starvation, demand rises. Otherwise, the death rate is largely constant in the short run (barring improvements in health and sanitation that prolong life spans).

Although Etruria and Charon cannot increase their income from their ferrying work, they can supplement it with part-time jobs. The fact that Etruria has a second job while Charon doesn't might be due to the fact that he supplies his labor to the labor market for additional work.

Why doesn't Charon offer his labor to the part-time market to supplement his earnings? Perhaps he doesn't need to. The price of the crossing might be higher among the Greeks than the Romans. Or dead Greeks are more generous and give tips. Perhaps expenses in the Roman underworld are higher than in the Greek Hades. And perhaps Etruria has a family to support while Charon does not. The possibilities are many.

Demand for Etruria's Labor

Even though both ferrymen are paid by souls, they both have employers who put them in charge of the crossing. Etruria's boss is Pluto, the lord of the underworld, the one who oversees all activities in the realm of the dead. Why did he hire Etruria for transporting as well as torturing, instead of hiring two different workers for the two jobs? Since Roman mythology provides no answers, economics offers the following possibilities. Perhaps Pluto reviewed the labor supply and found no worker as efficient, reliable, and capable as Etruria. Or perhaps no other worker agreed to Pluto's working conditions.

By contrast, in the Greek underworld, the ruler Hades relies on the Furies to perform torturing services. These three serpent-maned and winged sisters mercilessly torment those who sinned. Hades did not offer that job to Charon for several possible reasons. Charon might not be skilled at torture, so his labor productivity would be lower than that of the Furies. Alternatively, the workload for torturers might be so high that one ferryman, working part-time, cannot satisfy the demand (read: Greeks sinned more than Romans and so required not one but three torturers). Again, the possibilities are many.

The Dead Benefit From Teamwork

Organizations benefit from teamwork among their workers. Both individual and group productivity increases when workers cooperate and collaborate. A story from the afterlife illustrates this point.

The text below is of unknown origin. It appeared in my email inbox as a group mailing in 2010 that I was asked to pass on. I have no idea to whom to attribute this and have no citation for it. But given its content, it seems too good not to be included in this book.

A holy man was having a conversation with God one day and said, "God, I would like to know what Heaven and Hell are like." God led the holy man to two doors. He opened one of the doors and the holy man looked in. In the middle of the room was a large round table. In the middle of the table was a large pot of stew, which smelled delicious and made the holy man's mouth water. The people sitting around the table were thin and sickly. They appeared to be famished. They were holding spoons with very long handles that were strapped to their arms, and each found it possible to reach into the pot of stew and take a spoonful. But because the handle was longer than their arms, they could not get the spoons back into their mouths. The holy man shuddered at the sight of their misery and suffering. God said, "You have seen Hell." They went to the next room and opened the door. It was exactly the same as the first one. There was the large round table with the large pot of stew which made the holy man's mouth water. The people were equipped with the same long-handled spoons, but here the people were well nourished and plump, laughing and talking. The holy man said, "I don't understand." "It is simple," said God. "It requires but one skill. You see, they have learned to feed each other, while the greedy think only of themselves."

Asleep at the Wheel
(at the Gates of Hades)

According to Greek mythology, Cerberus guards the entrance to the abode of the dead. His job is to ensure that no one, dead or alive, goes in or out without permission. As the only guard of Hades, Cerberus has a huge responsibility, and it is only as a result of his unique physical features that he can perform his duties.

Cerberus is a dog with not one head but three. Encircling his limbs and torso are hissing vipers, and he has the tail of a dragon. Those who approach him are immediately scared off when they see his ferocious teeth, smell his bad breath, and hear his shrill howls. With those features, Cerberus successfully performed his job duties with just a few exceptions—the times when he fell asleep at the wheel, so to speak.

It first happened when the famous singer Orpheus managed to sneak past him by playing his magical lyre. The music put the dog to sleep long enough for Orpheus to enter Hades in search of his newly deceased lover. It happened a second time when Psyche, Cupid's lover, was on a mission to retrieve a magic box (the Box of Beauty) from Persephone, the queen of the underworld. Psyche offered Cerberus a delicious cake, and while he was distracted she slid past him.

These two lapses did not provide sufficient reason for Lord Hades, the ruler of Hades, to fire his guard. Not even when Cerberus was kidnapped by Hercules, and the gates of hell were left agape, did Lord Hades hire a replacement. Assuming there were other creatures that were willing and able to perform guarding functions (in other words, who supplied their labor to the labor market), the fact that Lord Hades did not demand their services implies that he was sufficiently satisfied with Cerberus's overall job performance. And why shouldn't he be? He had no productivity concerns with his guard. We know from Greek mythology that Cerberus worked around the clock without tiring, slacking off, or demanding vacation time. Lord Hades also had no cost concerns with Cerberus, who did not demand an unreasonable remuneration package. He was paid with the bones of the dead, which the dog ate at his workplace, never taking time off for meals. And with plenty of people dying, there was no concern about covering the costs of guard service. Lord Hades must have performed a cost/benefit analysis and decided that, despite Cerberus's minor lapses and absences, the benefit he got from his guard outweighed the cost.204

Angels Earn Their Wings

While alive, workers are typically paid for their labor by cash, check, or bank transfer. In the afterlife, wages tend to be in some form other than money. An example of such payment is the wings that angels receive in exchange for a job well done.

According to polls, three quarters of Americans believe that angels exist.205 Some think of angels as spirits in the service of a supreme being, engaged in one of their many jobs: protecting people on earth, escorting the dead to the postmortem, and serving in God's army. Others just feel cozy by thinking of their huggable rounded bodies. With so many believers, it is not surprising that a movie about an angel sweeping down to earth continues to be immensely popular, many decades after it was made.

It's a Wonderful Life was directed by Frank Capra in 1946. It starred Hollywood icon James Stuart as George Bailey, a well-meaning family man in a small Massachusetts town during the 1930s. When Bailey gets depressed by the world around him and considers suicide, angels get to work. The Chief Angel intervenes in worldly affairs by sending one of his angel workers down to earth to rescue George from himself. The name of that angel is Clarence Oddbody.

At the time of his mission, Oddbody was an Angel Second Class, but if he succeeds in saving Baily, his payment will be a promotion and a set of wings. Having waited long for such an opportunity, Oddbody is eager to get to work. After lengthy deliberation, Oddbody conjures up and executes the following scheme.

Having identified Bailey at a deserted spot on earth, contemplating suicide, Oddbody jumps into a nearby body of water and begins to pretend he is drowning. Bailey instinctively jumps in to rescue him. They begin to talk. Oddbody then gradually and ingeniously turns the tables and proceeds to convince George not to attempt suicide. He does so by taking George on a journey into a hypothetical world in which George did not exist, and showing him how many bad things would have happened to his family, friends, and neighbors had he not been present in their lives. The experience with Oddbody helps George put his own life in perspective and he soon regains his previous *joie de vivre*. Mission accomplished.

With his job successfully completed, Oddbody departs earth and goes to the heavens to report back and to collect his due. How do we know that the Chief Angel was satisfied with Oddbody's performance and that he believes the job merits the pay? We know because we hear a "dingdong, dingdong" sound at the end of the movie. We are told in the movie that whenever a church bell rings, it means an angel has received wings. Payment has been made in full.

Like Cerberus in Greek mythology, Oddbody received a non-monetary payment. Unlike Cerberus, his is a one-time payment, not a recurring one.

Zombie Slaves Are Free Dead Labor

Slavery is a system of labor relations in which workers have no rights. They are traded, like property. Their masters can do with them whatever they please, including force them to work without pay. Despite being universally illegal, slavery persists in its modern reincarnation—namely, human trafficking. A form of slavery also persists in the afterlife.

In the Caribbean nation of Haiti, a unique mixture of Voodoo religion, cult, and magical practice is deeply ingrained in the population. Haitians believe that when a person dies, one half of their soul becomes a spirit. It is the other half that runs the risk of being enslaved by knowledgeable sorcerers. Following a complex process that includes magical applications of poisons and some forced grave openings, that half of the soul gets packaged in a bottle.206 The bottle is then sold to people who have a malicious intent and expect to profit from the contents. Profit is possible because it is believed that the bottled soul can be instilled into the living, thereby transforming them into passive and submissive individuals who are partially dead. With the aid of a little magic, these zombies, as they have come to be known, are then easily controlled and exploited in the workplace.

Why would an employer want to hire a zombie worker? By definition, zombies are uncreative and lacking in initiative and enthusiasm—all characteristics that should make workers less desirable. The answer lies in the nature of the work zombies typically perform. They work as agricultural laborers in the Haitian countryside, doing tasks that require no skills, only raw physical strength. In fact, creativity and initiative are unwelcome distractions. Zombies follow orders unquestioningly, and that is considered a plus.

Zombie labor is similar to traditional slave labor. Both kinds of workers perform marketable activities that can be purchased in the labor market (such as ploughing and digging). There is no monetary payment for work performed. The basic housing, food, and medical care zombies and slaves both typically receive is not payment in kind but rather a maintenance cost incurred by the owners. With respect to supply of labor, neither slaves nor zombies voluntarily offer their labor to their masters. They are not free to choose their employers, to negotiate their remuneration packages, or to resign. With respect to demand for labor, masters do not sign contracts with slaves and zombies that describe job responsibilities and rewards. Instead, they purchase a slave by making a one-time payment, just as they purchase a zombie spirit in a bottle from a sorcerer. All additional expenditures having to do with the zombie (or slave) are made on the basis of a cost/benefit analysis that considers the person's work output relative to his total cost.

Voodoo believers in Haiti live in fear of becoming zombies after they die, because they associate zombies with slave labor.207 Given the country's history of colonization and slavery, and its highly agricultural economy, this aspect of voodoo beliefs is easy to understand. It is the magical process by which one becomes a zombie that is harder to understand and accept, leading skeptics to question what role drugs and mental retardation play in some workers' exploitation by their bosses. Still, the issue is of sufficient concern in Haiti that the penal code specifically prohibits the creation of zombies.208

Sidebar 10.2: Slave in Life, Slave After Death

Throughout history, the wealthy and/or powerful tried to ensure they would have access to free labor in the afterlife. Sardanapalus, the last king of Babylon, had his concubines and slaves burnt before he died so they could be buried with him,209 Celtic slave-owners buried their slaves for the same purpose,210 and one Mongol leader, Mangou Khan, had twenty thousand people killed to accompany him in his journey into the afterlife.211

Seventy Heavenly Wives Equal Seventy Heavenly Workers

Zombies and slaves are not the only people who work without pay. Across the world, urban women typically cook meals, drive carpools, clean houses, and balance checkbooks, in addition to their paid employment. Rural women worldwide perform backbreaking work in the fields and then scramble to prepare meals with limited ingredients, raise children, and perform remaining household chores. While such female labor is usually voluntary, and is the result of a division of labor that is both culturally determined and/or specifically devised in their households, nevertheless it takes place in the absence of a paycheck.

In the United States, the net beneficiaries of such household arrangements and divisions of labor are typically husbands, who rarely participate equally in household and child-related chores.[212] However, while American men may get a good deal in life, Hausa men get an even better deal in the afterlife. They don't get just one wife to perform household chores, without pay, but they get seventy.

The Hausa peoples inhabit several modern countries of West and Central Africa. Before they became Muslim in the fourteenth century, the Hausa adhered to an animist religion whose magical elements continue to permeate their beliefs, especially among the uneducated rural populations. An anthropological study conducted in the 1970s reports that Hausa villagers believe if men lead good lives, they will go to Allah's Kingdom in the postmortem, where they will each be granted seventy wives.[213] These are not the houris—the almond-eyed pure ladies described in Chapter 3. They are not the seventy-two virgins waiting for Muslim men in heaven (that the Western press has popularized in reference to terrorists). No, according to Hausa beliefs, these women are simply wives, like the wives men have on earth.

Hausa wives provide pleasure and emotional support for their husbands. However, their main contribution to their husband and their household is economic. As in numerous African communities, village women are producers. They produce and raise children, the family's most important asset. They engage in subsistence farming, growing food for the family. They also produce household goods and services, such as cooking meals, collecting water, tending to livestock, cleaning, and other household chores. Women are also sellers. They sell their labor for pay when they can, and, especially in West Africa, they sell the agricultural output their household produces. According to development economists, in addition to household and child-related chores, women do 60%-80% of agricultural work in Africa (for which they receive no direct payment).214

Since the Hausa believe the afterlife is a continuation of life on earth, the men expect to engage in the same work after death as they did in their earthly lives, and they expect their wives will do their same daily chores. But there is one difference: now there are seventy wives for each man. The afterlife for husbands promises to be superior to earthly life, because they will have more wives to do their bidding— both when the sun comes up and after it sets.

To Western men, having multiple free female workers at their beck and call may seem like a heaven worth dying for. However, upon closer inspection, they may change their minds. The fact is that, according to contemporary Islamic teachings, men are allowed to have multiple wives only if they can treat them all equally well financially, emotionally, and in every other way. Assuming that stipulation extends into the afterlife, then doing the math yields overwhelming results. If a man smiles at one wife, he must smile at them all; if he praises one, he must praise sixty-nine more. The implications of this Islamic stipulation make for an exhausting afterlife in which the opportunity cost of time is high for each man with multiple wives.

11

Economic Expansion and Recession

Less than a decade into the new millennium, Americans were overwhelmed by negative economic news that took most people by surprise. These included lingering recession, double-digit unemployment, bursting bubbles, and bank failures. A year or two later, economic expansion, fiscal policy, stimulus package, and deficit spending became household terms. It was a period in which macroeconomic concepts, usually confined to textbooks, filled airspace on talk shows and dotted newspaper pages. Macroeconomics was and still is all around us.

It's also associated with the afterlife.

Saving For a Rainy Day or Spending Like There's No Tomorrow describes economic activities that resulted in eternal punishment in medieval Europe, whereas today they are viewed as crucial for economic expansion.

In *Recession, Hades, and Persephone's Despondent Mother*, a Greek myth explains how events in the underworld affect earthly recessions.

To counter a recession, governments introduce expansionary fiscal policies. *Ghosts and the Stimulus Package (Fiscal Policy I)* refers to a story by Charles Dickens in which the dead offer prescriptions to stimulate the earthly economy.

Hey Dead Man, You Want Some Land by the Nile? (Fiscal Policy II)) shows how the ancient Egyptians' views of the afterlife include a form of fiscal policy that is still used by governments across the globe.

Saving For A Rainy Day or Spending Like There's No Tomorrow

Ask an average person strolling down New York's Fifth Avenue what they consider to be a deadly sin, and their response is likely to be "murder." The same question posed to a random Florentine crossing the Ponte Vecchio in the 1300s would probably elicit a response that referred to one of the Seven Deadly Sins described by Christian teachings. While the definition of these sins, also called "capital vices," has fluctuated and evolved over the centuries, by the Middle Ages it included avarice, sloth, and gluttony among others. Each of these sins has economic components.

Take avarice, for instance. Avarice refers to greed. It also refers to the pursuit of wealth—rather, the unbounded desire for the unbounded accumulation of wealth. In pre-capitalist times, this was viewed as a sin of excess. The Bible says that avarice is at the root of all evil, and the medieval church upheld that view.215 So did the literature of the period. Poet Dante used the tools of his trade, namely verse on paper, to describe avarice as a grave sin punishable harshly in the afterlife. In the *Inferno*, Dante presents his version of hell as divided into nine circles, four of which correspond to four of the deadly sins. The circle corresponding to avarice is described in Canto 7 as populated with hoarders—greedy people who accumulate money and store it. They are sinners because they fail to share their wealth with those they supposedly love: their families. By hoarding, they show disrespect for the blood ties that bind them to others, as well as the responsibilities that come with those ties. Even if they have the financial capacity to help their family members, hoarders refuse.

As punishment, Dante places hoarders in the fourth circle of hell, just above those accused of gluttony and just below those full of wrath and sullenness. Not by coincidence, another group of people share the fourth circle: those who spend too much and too extravagantly (in Dante's words, they "spend without measure"216). Such prodigality is on par with avarice because those who spend too freely and excessively will have no money left for those to whom they are responsible. They will have wasted their wealth without preserving it for their families in a future time of need.

Thus, spending too much (prodigality) and spending too little (hoarding, or, in Dante's words, having "closed fists") both relegate individuals to the fourth circle of hell. Since these earthly sins both involve money and its uses—they are two sides of the same coin—Dante condemns spenders and hoarders to spend eternity together. As punishment, spenders are required to roll big weights towards the hoarders while shouting, "Why do you hoard?" and the hoarders must roll weights of similar size towards the spenders, yelling, "Why do you waste?" Their souls then physically clash, move away from each other, and repeat the process again and again. Forever.

Fast forward to the twenty-first century and to mainstream macroeconomic theory. Hoarding and spending are part of contemporary economies no less than they were in fourteenth-century Florence. However, in the latter they were viewed with disdain, whereas today they are perceived as essential for economic growth. Hoarding is now called saving, and spending is called consumption. By definition, all of one's disposable income is devoted to these two activities. Both activities stimulate the economy and cause it to grow, albeit in different ways.

Consumption causes growth because each dollar (or florin, the coin used in the fourteenth-century Republic of Florence) spent on goods and services translates into income for some factor of production (labor or capital or land). That income is in turn spent on other goods and services that then also translate into income for yet other factors of production. Every time consumers spend on goods and services, their demand sends a signal to producers to produce more. In order to respond to this market signal, firms hire additional workers and pay them wages, which the workers then use for new purchases. Thus, expenditure by consumers spreads through the economy, inducing cyclical waves of production and consumption. This circular flow of economic activity describes the mechanism by which consumption stimulates the economy.

Dante failed to recognize this expansionary effect of consumption. By punishing prodigality in the *Inferno*, he missed an opportunity to underscore just how stimulating consumer spending can be. Sinners who, in Dante's words, "spend without measure" by continuously purchasing a broad range of goods and services actually enabled the Florentine economy to grow by way of the circular flow of economic activity. Had Dante's description of the tortures awaiting prodigal spenders succeeded in modifying their earthly behavior, the expansionary benefit of their expenditure would have been lost to Florence, and its economic and political power would have been greatly diminished.

Dante also overlooked the stimulative effect of savings on the economy. It, too, takes place by way of the circular flow mechanism. Savings refer to that part of people's disposable income that is not consumed. Typically people don't consume all their income but rather put some aside for future use. When those savings are placed in a bank (or in other financial institutions) for safekeeping, they not only earn interest for the saver but they also become available to potential borrowers in the form of loans. Firms borrow from banks in order to fund their investments. Borrowing enables firms to expand their productive capacity and to adopt innovative technologies, resulting in more, different, and better products and production methods. However, the increase in output typically cannot be achieved without employing additional workers. The wages these newly hired laborers receive enable them to consume and save, thus stimulating the economy in the circular fashion described above.

In his description of hell, Dante seems to have supported the Church's view on two matters critical in determining the quantity of savings in the Florentine economy. The first one has to do with avarice. By relegating hoarders to hell, Dante perpetuated the view that avarice is sinful. He missed the opportunity to extol the transformational capacity of savings as they become absorbed in the circular flow of economic activity. Of course, this capacity is contingent upon lending out those savings (if the money is just stored under the proverbial mattress, it becomes a dead resource, impotent and unproductive). Those who lend out their accumulated savings will want to earn interest. They are, after all, rational individuals who are cognizant of the opportunity cost of their money. However, by charging interest, they again face the wrath of the Church. This is the second matter with economic consequences about which the Church had an opinion. Medieval Christianity condemned usury (charging interest) no less than other sins. Fortunately for the Florentine economy, the city was replete with moneylending activity despite the Church's teachings. Even if those credit transactions occurred under notoriously unregulated and exploitative conditions, they nevertheless enabled many business endeavors and, when invested productively, fueled economic growth. Rather than devising imaginative punishments for hoarders and usurers in hell, Dante might have served Florence better by encouraging them to put their savings to work while still alive.

The fact that Dante did not extol the macroeconomic virtues of consumption and savings indicates that he chose not to criticize the potent Church on that particular matter, or, perhaps more likely, that he did not grasp concepts such as the circular flow of economic activity.

Sidebar 11.1: Hanging Usurers in Medieval Italy: the Case of Enrico Scrovegni

Art of the period is replete with images of greedy dead men hanging in hell with moneybags around their necks, indicating that they lent, made, and hoarded money during their lifetimes. Among the most famous of these depictions are Pieter Brueghel's *The Sin of Avarice*, Taddeo di Bartolo's *Last Judgment*, and Giotto's *Last Judgment*.

Both Enrico Scrovegni and his father Reginaldo were known to be usurers who lent out money to religious authorities and anyone else who could pay their interest rates of 30%-40%.217 Scrovegni lived in Padova in the early fourteenth century, at the same time as Giotto, and even became one of his patrons. He used the earnings from his business to build the Arena Chapel in Padova and support Giotto in his decoration of the interior. It is said that he did this in order to atone for his sin of usury. Despite Scrovegni's philanthropy, Giotto painted moneylenders as hanging with moneybags, and Dante, in the *Inferno*, placed Enrico's father in the ninth circle of hell for his moneylending activities.

Recession, Hades, and Persephone's Despondent Mother

The opposite of economic expansion is contraction. It refers to a situation in which the Gross Domestic Product shrinks as firms decrease production, lay off workers, and possibly even go out of business. When workers have less income, their consumption and savings decrease. Government tax revenue also decreases, since there is less taxable income as a result of the layoffs. Firms see little incentive to expand production at a time when people aren't buying, so total investment goes down. Firms also have less capacity to invest, given the decrease in personal savings that translates into less available credit for business borrowing. Given how interrelated all sectors of the economy are, a contraction in one corner quickly proliferates into another in a self-perpetuating downward spiral. When a contraction persists, it is called a recession.

Such a contraction occurs in a Greek myth in which macroeconomics meets a despondent mother.

According to the myth, Persephone is a beautiful young goddess, the daughter of Demeter and Zeus. One day, while playing outdoors, she is spotted by Hades, the god of the underworld, who happens to be visiting earth. Lord Hades immediately falls in love with her and decides to take her back to his kingdom. Zeus gives permission for the marriage, but no one remembers to ask or even inform Demeter. Instead, Hades merely grabs Persephone from the garden where she is picking flowers and carries her, screaming, into the underworld. Over time, Persephone becomes a good and loving wife, as well as a good queen of the dead. She still misses her mother but has learned to live without her.

Demeter, on the other hand, does not adjust to the new reality. She searches for her daughter everywhere (except the underworld) but finds no trace of her. After she learns that Zeus had condoned the marriage without consulting her, Demeter vows to punish everyone until Persephone is returned to her. Since she is the goddess of fertility, Demeter is responsible for growth and prosperity on earth. Every year she blesses the world to ensure bounty. Now, as punishment, she refuses to give that blessing, and the effect is immediate and disastrous. The sunshine does not reach the earth, the soil does not produce crops, and no rain falls to irrigate the land. Drought and famine spread far and wide. Demeter refuses to back down, forcing Zeus to undo the damage he caused. He sends a messenger to Hades to negotiate a deal. It is agreed that Persephone will spend four months per year in the underworld and the rest of the time on earth. While she is absent, Demeter inevitably becomes sad and depressed. Those are the winter months, when nothing grows from the soil. When Persephone returns in spring, she brings life with her. Crops grow, flowers blossom, the grass turns vibrant green, there is plenty.

While this Greek myth explains how seasons came to exist, it also explains, albeit without economic terminology, how recession plays out. Barren land and famine easily send an economy in a downward tailspin. When land does not produce, the principal source of suste-nance and income for the ancient Greeks dries up. There is no food with which to feed themselves and no surplus food to barter or sell. Without income from such sales, the farming population cannot purchase goods such as carts and cloth. As the demand for goods decreases, suppliers respond by cutting back on production and laying off workers. In this way, the village carpenter becomes unemployed, as do the innkeeper and the metal worker. The subsequent decrease in their incomes ripples through the economy. They can no longer afford to make purchases, reinforcing the contraction of the economy that began with the farmers and continues by way of the circular flow of economic activity. Soon the general population becomes destitute, consumption halts, previous savings are used up and no new saving takes place, investment stops, producers go out of business, and mere survival becomes the daily goal.

Such a recession on earth has secondary effects on the underworld. The unabated recessionary spiral of the earthly economy eventually shortens life spans. People die of hunger, cold, and lack of medical attention. The more people die, the more people enter the underworld, and the more crowded it becomes. Such an increase in the population density of the dead puts pressure on the existing infrastructure, raising a new set of economic problems that Lord Hades must solve. Perhaps it is as a result of these possible problems that Hades so readily agreed to share his wife with Demeter.

Ghosts and the Stimulus Package
(Fiscal Policy I)

Ebenezer Scrooge. Even young children recognize the name, and cringe. It has become associated with greed, stingy business practices, and the lack of human benevolence. Ebenezer Scrooge is the main character of Charles Dickens's *A Christmas Carol*. His personal characteristics were later adopted by Walt Disney for the creation of Donald Duck's Uncle Scrooge. The cartoon figure is often depicted sitting atop a mound of gold coins, fingering them with gusto, playfully throwing them up in the air, and counting them over and over again. Dickens's original character also keeps his money stashed away in his home, where only he can enjoy it. He is an old man, selfish, mean, alone, and very rich. He maximizes his utility both by accruing wealth and by hoarding it.

What does Scrooge have to do with the afterlife? Most readers do not recall him dying in *A Christmas Carol*, much less going to a heaven or hell. Rather, Ebenezer Scrooge is well and alive in the story, living out his life on earth in a typical London row house of the mid-nineteenth century. It is his creator Dickens who dips his imagination into the afterlife and creates ghost characters that travel to earth, replete with economics lessons.

The story begins when the ghost of Bob Marley, Scrooge's equally greedy business partner, appears to him just before Christmas of the year in which he passed away. Marley's ghost is in chains. In a voice laden with regret, he tells Scrooge that death brought him no peace and that he is condemned to roaming about, tortured by the memory of his miserly ways. He warns Scrooge that three visitors will come to him and he should heed their advice and change his priorities while he still has time. If and only if he does that, perhaps he might avoid Marley's fate in the afterlife.

Soon after, the first ghost visitor crosses over to earth to pay Scrooge a visit. His name is the Ghost of Christmas Past, and as his name suggests, he takes Scrooge on a journey into his past. The ghost points out all those individuals who once brought joy to Scrooge. He also points out that not one of them is still a part of the old man's life, that Scrooge pushed them all away, replacing them with a relentless drive to amass wealth.

After the first ghost leaves, the Ghost of Christmas Present arrives. He takes Scrooge on a trip into town, where the streets bustle with activity and excitement as shoppers seek out baked goods and presents with which to celebrate Christmas.

Finally, the Ghost of Christmas Yet To Come arrives to take Scrooge into his future, to show him how lonely and dreary future holidays will be if he doesn't change his attitude and his behavior.

And change them he does. The next day, Scrooge becomes generous and starts spending his money on other people.

Readers of all ages experience a surge of emotion after reading *A Christmas Carol* because it confirms that good prevails over bad and that redemption is possible. Those reading with an economics lens might experience an additional feeling: relief. They might be relieved that the economy is being stimulated. When Scrooge visits his butcher the day after his ghostly encounters, and proceeds to buy the biggest turkey for his former partner's impoverished family, he is stimulating the economy. When later that day he turns over a large sum of money to charity, he is again stimulating the economy. In both cases, Scrooge's expenditure represents an infusion of money into the circular flow of economic activity. His expenditures translate into an increase in aggregate demand, which sends signals to producers to increase production and to hire more workers. In this way, Scrooge's expend-iture ripples through the London economy and beyond, setting off a cyclical expansion thought the British economy.

In *A Christmas Carol*, a man is induced to increase his consumption by a subtle nudge from three afterlife visitors. In contemporary Britain, the inducement to increase consumption comes from the central government in the form of fiscal policy. Through such policy, government becomes involved in the economy in order to achieve goals such as economic growth and full employment. One tool of fiscal policy—taxation—induces consumers to behave in a way that will help achieve those goals. This is because, as rational decision makers, people consume more goods and services when they have more money to spend. That requires an increase in their disposable (after tax) income. Paying less in taxes has the same effect on disposable income as earning more. It induces people to consume more, and in the process they inadvertently stimulate the economy by way of the circular flow of economic activity.

In *A Christmas Carol*, the three Ghosts of Christmas come to earth and convince a stingy man to engage in consumption. By whispering in Scrooge's ear and enticing him to spend his money, the three ghosts in effect play the role of a government that, through fiscal policy, induces taxpayers to increase consumption and thus contribute to the achievement of macroeconomic goals.

Hey Dead Man, You Want Some Land Down by the Nile? (Fiscal Policy II)

Expansionary fiscal policy is not limited to increasing consumption through taxation. A similar effect can be achieved by increasing government expenditure. By examining the *Egyptian Book of the Dead* with an economic lens, the presence of fiscal policy in the afterlife is evident.

From the pharaoh to the village pauper, everyone who could afford it was buried with his or her own personal copy of the *Egyptian Book of the Dead*. As mentioned in earlier chapters, these books were papyrus scrolls containing words written by scribes and illustrated by artists. At first, the books were commissioned by the wealthy and were highly personalized. In later centuries, they became prefabricated, and only the name of the buyer was added upon purchase. The book not only provided information on the passage to the new life but it also described the next life. The illustrations portrayed the afterlife activities that await the deceased while the accompanying hieroglyphics provided explanatory text.

The longest copy of the *Egyptian Book of the Dead* was prepared for a man called Ani who resided in Thebes around 1240 BCE. Known as the *Papyrus of Ani,* it contains over sixty spells and a multitude of colored illustrations on a seventy-eight-foot scroll.218 There are depictions of Ani reaping corn, Ani driving oxen that tread out the corn, Ani ploughing a field near a stream, and also a heap of white corn and wheat that is three cubits high.219 These postmortem agricultural scenes provided intricate details of both inputs (hoes, rakes, irrigation) and output (crops, fish, fertile land).220 Since Egyptians believed that each image in the *Egyptian Book of the Dead* has the power to become real, they hoped the image of fertile land will result in afterlife fertile land; the image of abundant crops will result in afterlife abundant crops.

Economists might wonder how Ani expects to obtain the land he plans to cultivate in the afterlife. By what distribution mechanism are afterlife plots allocated among the dead? Ani surely did not ponder that question, since the answer was obvious to him and to other Egyptians. As mentioned in previous chapters, it was a widespread belief that when people die, their hearts are weighed against a feather. If the heart is not full of sin and does not tip the scales, the person can proceed to the Field of Rushes, where his/her existence mirrors his/her life on earth.221 However, to replicate their earthly existence, the dead must have land on which to cultivate crops, so the ancient Egyptians came to believe that afterlife authorities granted plots of land to the dead.222 Although there are no details as to the mechanism by which land is distributed or who gets which plot, the fact that land is allocated ensures that the dead are enabled to provide for their afterlife sustenance. On that land they will tend the crops, plough, and harvest. The nearby river will provide irrigation and a mode of transport for trading agricultural products. In the absence of a land grant, the dead cannot replicate the earthly life they led in the Valley of the Nile.

Such beliefs about the afterlife are replete with macroeconomic concepts. When the afterlife authorities give out land to the dead upon their arrival to the Field of Rushes, they are *de facto* putting fiscal policy into action. They are using part of their government revenue to underwrite land transfers. The land grants constitute government expenditure aimed at enabling dead farmers to provide for their own sustenance (no different from the U.S. federal government use of food stamps and unemployment insurance programs to help people provide for themselves on earth).

Giving out land grants in the Egyptian afterlife dovetails with the dual fiscal policy goals of economic growth and full employment. These are achieved through the circular flow of economic activity, although the stimulus originates with the government rather than with households (by way of consumption and savings) or firms (by way of investment). By giving out land grants, authorities enable people to work, earn, and spend. The expansionary effects of those activities then proliferate throughout the economy.

Left unanswered in the *Egyptian Book of the Dead* is the question of where the afterlife authorities get the money to fund land grants. On earth, fiscal policies are funded by government revenue obtained largely through taxation. If that fails to cover planned expenditure, then governments supplement tax revenue by borrowing and then engaging in deficit spending. There is no information in the *Egyptian Book of the*

Dead on whether land grants in the afterlife were funded by tax revenue and whether deficit spending occurred. Given the absolute power that earthly pharaohs had, coupled with riches beyond the imagination of commoners, few people questioned where and how authorities got the money to spend on irrigation, pyramids, and ceremonies. Since the afterlife was believed to mirror life on earth, the seemingly endless wealth of earthly rulers was probably assumed to carry over beyond the grave.

12

Money and Banking

Workers are paid for their labor, and firms are paid for the goods they sell. Such transactions are facilitated by money.

Money refers to anything that is commonly accepted for payment. Salt, deerskin, and shells have all served as money at some point in history. Also, goods and services have served as payment in what are called *barter systems*. However, as economies grew more complex, currency (paper bills and coins) replaced other forms of payment.

Money shows up in afterlife visions that span cultures and centuries. Sometimes it shows up in non-currency forms, sometimes as real or imitation currency. There is no discernable pattern, so it cannot be said that afterlife visions associated with old traditions relied on non-monetary transactions but those of modern societies exclusively use currency.

The multiple uses of money in the hereafter are discussed in *Money Makes the (After)World Go Round*.

Checks are an acceptable form of payment for earthly transactions. According to a story about an Irish wake, it seems that they are also acceptable in the afterlife (*Cash or Check*).

In *Banks in Hell*, the Bilgamesh Bank and the Bank of Hell are offered as examples of banking institutions in afterlife visions.

Banks keep records of monetary transactions with a variety of accounting methods. Some of these also show up in the afterlife, as discussed in *Keeping Track of Souls with T Accounts*.

The vignette *Reneging on Loan Payments* asks what happens to debts of the dead. Do they cancel out or do they follow the dead into the netherworld?

Money Makes the (After)World Go Round

According to economic theory, anything can serve as money as long as it satisfies three requirements: it must be a unit of account that enables a consistent way of measuring the value of goods; it must be an acceptable medium of exchange that makes trade among individuals more efficient than barter; and it must serve as a store of value that can be used for future purchases. Since coins satisfy all these requirements, they have come to serve as money across societies.

The ancient Greeks believed coins also served as money in the afterlife. They buried their deceased with a coin in the mouth because the function of money was believed to carry over. The fact that one coin was the agreed upon price for crossing the Styx River indicates that it was a unit of account. The fact that Charon accepted payment with a coin implies that it served as a medium of exchange. Finally, the fact that additional coins were sometimes given to the departed, in case of unforeseen future need, indicates that they were also a store of value.

In addition to coins, some non-monetary goods serve as a medium of exchange in transactions having to do with the afterlife. Food shows up as acceptable payment in Dante's *Inferno,* when Cerberus the three-headed dog demands that souls pay him for permission to enter Hades (the price is a handful of mud, fed into each of his mouths). Food also shows up as payment in the television show *The Simpsons,* when a devil from the netherworld bought Homer Simpson's soul with a donut. Finally, food shows up in beliefs of contemporary societies, such as among the Bagobo of the Philippines, who bribe the dead with food offerings so they will stay away and not haunt the living.223

Clothing also shows up as payment for admission into the underworld, first in Sumerian mythology from c. 3000 BCE. Ereshkigal, the Queen of Darkness who rules the netherworld, demands that the dead pass through seven gates in order to reach her kingdom. At each one they must pay with an article of clothing or a piece of jewelry.224 Payment with articles of clothing persists in the modern era in West Africa. According to Ashanti legend, a woman called Amokye stands guard at the entrance of the land of the dead. At her side is a basket where all newcomers must deposit an article of clothing in order to enter.225

Literature, popular culture, and legends dealing with interpersonal exchanges show clearly how food, clothing, and jewelry serve as a medium of exchange in postmortem matters. What is less clear is whether those goods, like coins, also satisfy the other requirements to earn the designation of money. There is no evidence that they serve as a unit of account—that is, that an article of clothing or an edible portion is a widely acceptable way of measuring value. We also cannot infer that they serve as a store of value, because there is no reason to believe that the value individuals put on clothing, donuts, or food is shared by others (acceptable across their society) or that it can be used for future value (especially given the perishable nature of food). However, we can infer that for the societies under discussion, the non-monetary goods that the living give up in order to obtain access to the underworld has value for them. And where there is value, there is opportunity cost.

Opportunity Costs Lead to the Creation of Substitute Money

To ensure the deceased have the means to pay for crossing the river Styx and for entry into the netherworld, their loved ones must give up coins, clothes, and jewels. Also, to ensure the deceased retain goodwill towards their surviving relatives, the living must give up some of their food and time. Since clothes, coins, food, and time are all scarce resources, the living incur an opportunity cost when they allocate them to the dead. Clearly, when the Bagobo peoples of the Philippines congregate at the burial sites to appease the dead, they are giving up other activities that have value (that enable them to earn income or gain utility). When they feed the souls of the deceased, they take scarce food away from the living. Burying a loved one with sufficient clothing to be used for payment in the afterlife means that surviving Sumerians and Ashanti have less to wear.

Undoubtedly, the highest opportunity costs are incurred when coins are buried with the dead, since they have the most alternative uses on earth. The more coins survivors bury, the less they have left for themselves to use as a medium of exchange and as a store of value.

To avoid this opportunity cost, societies and religions have created an ingenious money substitute that is believed to serve all the functions of money in the afterlife but not on earth. According to scholar Hiroshi Obayashi, who studied the afterlife across religions, such fake money is "backed not by bullion but by the religious merit and ritual prowess of the living."226

Asian societies have buried substitute paper money with their departed for centuries. According to Chinese Confucian belief, in heaven people will need Heaven Notes (also known as Spirit Money) to bribe overlords, purchase favors, and maintain a comfortable standard of living.227 In addition to those traditional uses, modern Koreans bury or burn contemporary Notes with their dead as a sendoff,228 while modern Chinese believe the Notes will enable dead men to pay for prostitutes in the afterlife.229

Such substitute money is readily available for purchase. Indeed, an entire micro economy has emerged around printing fake money for the explicit purpose of burning at funerals. While loved ones might feel better about burying or burning fake money, they have not eliminated the opportunity cost altogether. They paid for the fake money with real money, money that could have been used for the purchase of other goods and services.

Sidebar 12.1: Non-Monetary Price of Entry Into Heaven: Murder

According to the beliefs of the indigenous hunter-gatherer Society Islanders of the South Pacific, rulers and leaders are the only mortals allowed to enter the Place of Light and Joy after they die. There is one exception. Entertainment workers, including singers, dancers, and actors, are allowed to enter but only if they pay a very steep admission price: they have to have their babies killed.[zzz]

Cash or Check

Cash and checks are used interchangeably as payment for goods and services. Economists include them both in the narrowest definition of money, M1, because of their *liquidity*. (Liquidity refers to the ease with which an asset can be transformed into a medium of exchange and used for payment.) In addition to currency (bills and coins), checking accounts in banks are also highly liquid.

Are cash and checks also interchangeable in the afterlife? This question is explored in a short story offered by University of Notre Dame professor William Evans, which is summarized below.231

> Three Irish brothers congregate at the wake of their deceased eldest sibling. One of them raises the question of money in the afterlife. "Who knows," he says, "maybe our brother could use some in Heaven."
>
> Since no one had proof one way or the other, the brothers decide to err on the side of caution. They agree that each one will place a hundred dollars in the dead man's casket.
>
> On the day of the burial, the first brother approaches the casket and places a one-hundred-dollar-bill in his brother's jacket pocket. Then the second approaches and does the same. The youngest brother is the most creative of the three. After pausing respectfully by the casket, he reaches in and picks up the two hundred-dollar bills, replacing them with a check for $300.

Banks in Hell

Contemporary commercial banks have two functions: they serve as depositories for people's savings, and they provide loans to borrowers. In this way, banks bring lenders and borrowers together in what is called a *fractional reserve banking system* (where a fraction of the bank's deposits are lent out).

These modern functions of the banking system appear in afterlife visions of the Mesopotamian peoples who lived, since about 5000 BCE, in roughly the area of present-day Iraq. They were highly sophisticated peoples excelling in astronomy, writing, technology, and social organization. The first book ever written was composed in tablet form in Mesopotamia. It is in that book, called *Epic of Gilgamesh,* that a bank is first mentioned: the Bank of Bilgames. Bilgames is the name of the Sumerian King (later known as Gilgamesh) in the early versions of the book, dating from between 2750 and 2500 BCE. According to the story, Bilgames is responsible for introducing the practice of giving offerings to dead ancestors.232 The Bank refers to the place where the offerings were made. It was believed that such offerings then accumulate and are available, as credit, to be withdrawn by the dead in the afterlife when needed. In this way, the Bank of Bilgames serves the dual modern role: it is both a depository for some (in this case, the living) and a source of credit for others (the dead). This is the closest approximation of credit card use in the afterlife.

Fast forward over five thousand years. In contemporary China, Taoists and Buddhists alike celebrate the Festival of Ghosts, when, according to their beliefs, all their ancestors come out to pay a visit. As part of the festivities, paper money is burned in temples for the benefit of the dead. In addition to the Heaven Notes described in an earlier vignette, there are also bills drawn on the Bank of Hell.233 It is believed that if a relative is in hell, waiting for rebirth, this money can be used to build up merit. The greater the accumulated deposits at the bank, the more credit can be withdrawn and the better and sooner his/her rebirth will occur. If the dead are already in heaven, then the deposits of paper money will provide them with more happiness.

Like the Mesopotamian Bank of Bilgames, the Chinese Bank of Hell serves the two functions of modern banks. Some people make deposits and others make withdrawals. However, contrary to modern banks, some of their customers are alive while others are dead.

Sidebar 12.2: U.S. Government Sends Checks to Dead People

In October 2010, the United States government sent out checks for $250 to some fifty million Americans in an effort to stimulate the economy (as part of an economic recovery package). Of those checks, 72,000 were sent to dead people.234 Might this information be used by economists and historians, one day in the distant future, as evidence that the Obama administration believed there are banks in the afterlife?

Keeping Track of Souls with T Accounts

Banks keep track of their monetary transactions by using T accounts in which their accountants list the value of their assets and their liabilities. According to Zoroastrians, a similar system of precise recording is used in the afterlife.

The prophet Zoroaster lived in the Middle East, possibly one millennium before Christ, and founded a religion that was at the root of later religions such as Christianity, Islam, Hinduism, and Buddhism. Unlike other beliefs of his time, Zoroaster introduced a dualistic view based on the force of good (the Wise Lord or Ahura Mazda) and the force of bad (Evil Spirit or Angra Mainyu). These two forces battle each other for the souls of all people. And therein lie the accounting and the math.

After death, a soul stays by its corpse for three days. During that time, the life of the deceased is evaluated by two mythical genies, or angels, who stand in judgment. They use a ledger in which they enter good deeds as credits and bad deeds as debts. The two columns are then compared, and judgment is made on the Accountant's Bridge (also known as Chinvat Bridge), at the entrance to the underworld.235 If the balance sheet indicates more credit than debt, the soul travels to a good place (accompanied by a beautiful maiden with two dogs). However, even the slightest tilt in favor of debt sends the soul straight to hell. If a person's credits and debt cancel each other out, then the soul enters a state of limbo until the apocalypse occurs.236

In her study of hell, Alice Turner discusses the precision with which the credits and debts are entered according to Zoroastrian beliefs. She says, "Neither prayer, sacrifice, nor the grace of Ahriman can influence the legal outcome of the mathematical trial."237 Such strict accounting systems have carried over to the present and are at the core of good banking practices.

Reneging on Loan Payments

The last words Socrates uttered before dying in 399 BCE were to his friend Crito, urging him to clear a debt he owed to Asclepius.238 Even though Socrates owed a mere rooster, he wanted all debts repaid before going to the afterlife. Perhaps he believed indebtedness would impact the quality of his afterlife. If so, he would not have been alone in his belief.

During the Roman era, Celts believed that all business accounts and debt claims were transferred to the postmortem.239 They expected a very active afterlife, one where all earthly activities continue as before. In such a worldview, debt repayment cannot be avoided by mere death, and the same forces hounding debtors in life will hound them in death. In modern times, the LoDagaa peoples of Ghana also believe their debts follow them to their final resting place. To get there, they must cross a river and, as in many other cultures, they must pay for the crossing. However, if they are debtors, their payment is not accepted until someone on earth pays off their debts.240

Some views on afterlife debt are location dependent. In Dante's vision of hell, for example, debts are remembered for eternity, whereas in heaven people forget the debts they have to others and others have to them. This duality is echoed many centuries later by author Margaret Atwood, in her non-fiction book *Payback*. Writing about debt, she states that, "In Heaven, there are no debts—all have been paid, one way or another—but in hell there's nothing but debts, and a great deal of payment is exacted, though you can't ever get all paid up...So Hell is like an infernal maxed-out credit card that multiplies the charges endlessly."241

It seems that debtors fare the best in contemporary societies with inter-generational transfers of debt obligations. Rather than death erasing one's debts, or debts preventing entry into the afterlife, earthly obligations are simply transferred to one's estate. Those who inherit the assets also inherit the debt, ensuring that debt remains in the world of the living and does not encumber the dead.

189

13

Equality, Inequality, and Income Distribution

Some people are rich and some people are poor. While there is undoubtedly less overall income inequality in Western countries in the twenty-first century than there was in ancient Egypt or medieval Europe, it nevertheless persists.

What about inequality in the afterlife? Does death obliterate all differences between people, or do earthly inequalities carry over? The vignette entitled *Is Death the Great Equalizer?* shows there are beliefs in support of both views.

When income discrepancies between rich and poor in society are large, governments intervene to alleviate poverty with a variety of macroeconomic policies. *Redistribution of Income (Fiscal Policy III)* shows how religious figures invoke the afterlife in their efforts to address issues of poverty and income distribution.

Sometimes market forces bring about a reduction in inequality, with no intervention by government or religious leaders. *Designer Mummification: From Saks to K-Mart* explores the process by which the price of mummification went down over time, reducing the inequality between rich and poor in terms of access to the afterlife.

"Just so you know, I'm taking all this with me into the afterlife."

Cartoon 13.1: Inheritance and Inequality in Ancient Egypt

Is Death the Great Equalizer?

Many factors are responsible for fostering socio-economic inequalities in society. Some are inherent in individuals (such as education, inheritance, and innate abilities) while others are a product of social circumstances (including unemployment and discrimination). Are these factors irrelevant in the postmortem, leading to the elimination of inter-personal inequalities? In other words, is death the great equalizer? As with most questions pertaining to the afterlife, there is no single answer.

According to *Topper,* an American television show popular during the 1950s, inequalities carry over into the afterlife. The show is about an upper-class bank executive named Cosmo Topper and his adventures with the former owners of his home, Mr. and Mrs. Kerby. In the first episode of the series, the three characters end up in a haunted country inn. There are some muffled sounds coming from a location below the stairs. Topper is surprised, he thought they were alone in the building. Turning to Mr. Kerby, he asks him to go downstairs and investigate. To Topper's surprise, Kerby refuses, saying that the sounds are probably made by ghosts. And they must be low-class ghosts since, in old houses, servant quarters are typically located below the stairs. Mr. Kerby refuses to associate with low-class ghosts.

Did I mention that Mr. and Mrs. Kerby are dead? In the television show, they are ghosts. Cosmo Topper is the only living person who can see them and talk with them.

And even though Mr. Kerby is dead, he still clings to the earthly class cleavages with which he is familiar, indicating that earthly inequalities persist in the postmortem.

This view is not unique to *Topper.* All visions of the afterworld in which earthly life continues after death, and in which personal characteristics (as well as social circumstances) are retained, inequality persists. Egyptians, Etruscans, and other ancient peoples typically adhered to this view, as do many contemporary societies whose beliefs are ingenious localized mixtures of traditional ancestor worship and modern religious teachings.

Afterlife visions in which inequalities carry over lack the concept of punishment and reward that is central to the most widespread contemporary religions. In Christianity and Islam, for example, the ultimate destination of the soul has nothing to do with socio-economic status on earth but rather depends on earthly behavior with respect to goodness and sin. And then, once within their appropriate destination (heaven or hell), souls are equal with respect to each other. Coupling life in the next world with goodness and faith on earth precludes carrying over earthly socio-economic hierarchies.

Sidebar 13.1: The *Danse Macabre* Portends Afterlife Equality

The Danse Macabre appeared in fourteenth-century Europe, at the time of the bubonic plague. It consisted of several individuals, dressed as skeletons, dancing and playing instruments as they passed in procession through towns. By personifying death, the Danse served to familiarize people with what awaits them and, in the process, underscore that death is inevitable for everyone, no matter how rich and powerful or poor and downtrodden. However, the upper classes of medieval Europe did not like the Christian idea that in hell the rich and the poor are equal, that they coexist side-by-side and intermingle for eternity. This was so distasteful to them that it acted as a deterrent against sinful behavior. Alice Turner, in her study of hell, states that Jesuit priests described hell in such a way that scared the upper classes into good behavior, just to avoid spending eternity with the poor who were assumed would go to hell.242

Redistribution of Income (Fiscal Policy III)

Efforts to reduce poverty on earth sometimes invoke the afterlife. Two very different religions, Buddhism and Christianity, both teach that charitable behavior towards the less fortunate is rewarded by a good afterlife. At the same time, failure to be charitable by those who have the means results in an unpleasant afterlife. Buddhist teachings about reincarnation, as well as Biblical lessons about charitable giving, share a common goal (to help the poor by alleviating poverty) and an incentive for achieving it (reward or punishment in the afterlife). There is a positive externality associated with reducing poverty: inequality between income groups is also reduced.

According to Buddhist beliefs, if a man accumulates wealth over his lifetime, he will be reborn into a higher position of wealth and social status in the next life. This bump up in the hierarchical ladder happens if, and only if, two conditions are met: first, the wealth cannot be accumulated by immoral or illegal ways; second, the individual cannot be greedy throughout his life and must generously distribute his wealth to those who are less fortunate. If one or both of those conditions are not met, then rebirth will be at a lower socio-economic status. The fear of such an outcome makes compliance high. Economist Fredrick Pryor, in his comparative study of the relationship between economics and religion, states that Buddhists perceive wealth as a means of gaining merit in society, since there is an understanding that much of it will be given away to the poor.243 In other words, by adhering to Buddhist teachings that dictate the rich must redistribute some portion of their wealth among the poor, the rich alleviate poverty, decrease inequality, and, in the process, become meritorious.

Similarly, the Christian fear of future retribution for bad earthly behavior goes a long way towards ensuring compliance with the Church's goal of wealth redistribution. Believers learn the lesson on proper behavior with respect to inequality from the Gospel of Luke.244

The story goes as follows. Lazarus was a beggar who lived outside the gates of a rich man's home. Lazarus had nothing, and the rich man lived lavishly and extravagantly. He could have shared some of his wealth with Lazarus but didn't. After they both died, it was Lazarus who was embraced by heavenly bliss and the rich man who was tormented with fire and who craved even just a drop of water from Lazarus's fingertip. The message of the story is clear: Lazarus was rewarded because he accepted his poverty without resorting to illegal activities to reverse his fate. The rich man was punished because he did not share his wealth with those in need.

By controlling the behavior of believers, early Buddhist and Christian religious leaders met their goals of poverty eradication and income redistribution. Today, attempts at such control are less successful; societies cannot rely on individuals to voluntarily give up their assets for the sake of others. Governments have stepped in to alleviate poverty and adjust the unfairness associated with inequality.

Economists typically shy away from talking about fairness. It is considered a normative concept, one that refers to how things should be, while economics deals with positive concepts, which describe the way things are. Still, to the extent that governments intervene in the economy to redress inequality, it is to increase fairness in society. Such government intervention entails redistributing income across society. It consists of taxing those with higher incomes and using the revenue to fund transfer payments to those with lower incomes (via social security, welfare, and unemployment benefits). Transfer payments are part of total government expenditure, and thus an integral component of fiscal policy. Across western capitalist countries, redistributive macroeconomic policies that take from those with high incomes and give to those with low incomes have been successful in decreasing the gap between rich and poor.

In the past, religions used fear of afterlife retribution to alter earthly behavior in the interest of equality. Today, Washington uses the Internal Revenue Service and its recourse to legal sanctions to ensure that the rich contribute to making society more equitable. In the former, the penalty takes place in hell; in the latter, it takes place in a federal prison.

Designer Mummification: From Saks to K-Mart

Because they have more income, the rich can buy goods that the poor cannot afford. However, if prices of those goods decrease, then more poor people can afford to buy them, even if their income has not changed. When it comes to consumption, the *de facto* effect of a price drop is the same as an increase in income. Through a decrease in prices, the poor have access to goods they previously could not afford, and, as a result, inequality decreases, with no government intervention or religious prescriptions guiding redistributive actions. That is what happened in ancient Egypt with respect to mummification of the dead.

Ancient Egyptians prepared bodies of the deceased using a complex process of preservation. They believed that the soul returns, after a short journey, to inhabit the body. In order to ensure that it can house the soul for eternity, the body needed to be prepared by priests and their helpers in a meticulous process that took some seventy days. First, internal organs were removed and set aside in four jars (to be buried later). After the empty body dried out for forty days, it was bandaged with linen. During these preparations, a head priest, known as the Reader, recited prayers, cast magic spells, and provided information to both body and soul about their future voyage. In the end, the body became a mummy and was ready for burial with all the paraphernalia it might require in the next world. Without mummification, a dead body was unable to receive its soul, and so the deceased could not enjoy an afterlife.

During the early Egyptian dynasties of the Old Kingdom (c. 2686-2181 BCE), it was only the pharaoh and his innermost circle that were believed to have an afterlife, because they were the only ones who could afford to undergo the mummification process. The funerary literature, then called the *Pyramid Texts*, focused on chants and spells to ensure that the pharaoh got resurrected and protected in his new life. Later, during the Middle Kingdom (c. 2055-1650 BCE), members of the nobility also wanted a piece of the afterlife action. They were wealthy enough to buy slaves and land and precious metals. Now they wanted to buy something that was far more valuable than the sum of those posses-sions—namely, an eternal life. To satisfy their demand, entrepreneurs surfaced who could offer a less elaborate type of mummification. These entrepreneurs acquired the skills of embalming and learned the ritual steps. At the same time, the funerary texts that priests formerly read now became tailored for the privileged outside the pharaoh's inner circle. They became known as the *Coffin Texts*. Finally, by the time ancient Egypt moved into the period of the New Kingdom (c. 1550-1069 BCE), the spells and chants were adjusted even further for a larger spectrum of deceased. By now these had been complied as the *Book of the Dead*, so information on what to expect and how to behave became readily available. Now everyone could learn the correct password needed to pass through the seven gates of the afterlife. No longer were the elite and powerful priests required for the embalming process. In the words of Alan Segal, author of the comprehensive tome *Life After Death*, mummification had become an industry, and, in the process, there was a democratization of immortalization.245 Over time, the possibility of embalmment and its concomitant afterlife had reached the common man.

In this way, equality in access to eternity came to ancient Egypt. What was once designer mummification, limited to wealthy demanders, became accessible to the masses. What was once associated with wealth, power, and class became a possibility for the less privileged. The ultimate in death attire went from elitist to plebian, from Saks Fifth Avenue to K-Mart. And this was not because the incomes of the poor increased. Rather, it was because the prices of embalmment came down.

14

International Economics

Imagine if Alexander the Great, Oliver Cromwell, Abraham Lincoln, and Nikita Khrushchev took an economics class together at Afterlife University. Their assignment is to prepare a report on the earthly global economy of the twenty-first century. From the vantage point of Cloud #33146, they look down to earth and what do they see?

They see a world in which economic ties between countries are stronger and more numerous than during any of their lifetimes. Goods, money, and people cross borders, leading to unprecedented international integration and economic interdependence. This new globalization is enabled in part by innovative technology that has decreased the price of global transportation and communication. Production possibilities include the entire world, as firms seek to lower costs by outsourcing production processes. Consumption possibilities also include the entire world, as consumers are no longer limited by local availability. As a result, people in remote corners of the world now wear the same clothes, get informed from the same Internet sites, and use mobile phones to connect with each other. Similar tastes and choices bind people of different national, racial, and linguistic backgrounds. The Cold War has ended, but wars over scarce resources continue across the globe. The market system has prevailed, although government involvement in economies has persisted. Previously less developed countries such as India and China have become economic powerhouses; previously more developed countries such as Greece and Italy have succumbed to economic malaise. Old countries have disintegrated, new countries have been created.

The four dead leaders are not impressed by what they see on earth. Each has an air of ennui, having seen it all—in the afterlife. Alexander the Great says, "Going to war for scarce resources? The afterlife is full of warriors preparing for such battles." Cromwell adds, "Outsourcing?

I know all about outsourcing. My compatriot souls told me how they engaged in outsourcing centuries ago!" Abraham Lincoln joins in, "So now different races get along on earth? In heaven they've been getting along forever." And Nikita Khrushchev, who until his death refused to believe there is a heaven, adds to the dialogue, "Alas, I knew the Soviet system would collapse. The jokes they tell about communism in the afterlife have all become reality."246 The vignettes in this chapter describe what it is that the four leaders saw in the afterlife that led to their conclusions.

Wars and the Competition for Afterlife Resources shows how some societies believe their dead countrymen continue to fight wars, just as they did on earth.

Globalization and the Outsourcing of Sin describes the seventeenth-century practice of hiring sin eaters to liberate people from their earthly peccadilloes.

Black and White: How Diversified is the Afterlife contains a discussion of racial, linguistic, and other forms of diversity in the afterlife.

Three Cold War Leaders Walk into a Bar [in Heaven] offers afterlife jokes that mock Soviet economic weaknesses and hint at the sources of the system's eventual demise.

Wars and the Competition for Resources

Throughout history, countries have gone to war in competition over scarce resources. This economic rationale for war is compelling because the winners are awarded with an immediate augmentation of their productive capacity through the absorption of new lands (with their precious raw materials), people (with their physical and intellectual power), and capital (such as industrial sites and machinery), as well as all pre-existing infrastructure, trade routes, urban centers, and more. In this way, victorious countries acquire the means for economic growth and development.

To the extent that war is a way of obtaining new resources on earth, then those who believe the afterlife mirrors earthly life also believe wars are a feature of eternity. According to myths and legends, as well as the evidence from burial sites, it seems that those believers who are accustomed to using guns and swords and arrows in their earthly competition for scarce resources also expect to do so after they die. Being rational individuals, they also believe they should be prepared for such wars.

Although afterlife visions differ in how best to prepare, they shared the focus on the warrior. This is especially clear in pre-modern societies that relied on labor-intensive warfare in which the quality and quantity of the troops were crucial to the outcome on the battlefield. Some afterlife visions focused on improving the quality of eternal warriors and others focused on expanding their numbers.

Nordic myths are especially colorful when it comes to the quality of dead troops. These myths focus on the Vikings who lived in Scandinavia from the eighth to the eleventh century. According to the Edda (the collection of old Norse legends in poems and prose), when soldiers die, they go to a heaven called Valhalla.247 Valhalla translates to "Hall of the Slain," and only those who die in battle are allowed entrance. In this heaven, dead warriors spend their days battling each other and heal their wounds during the nights so they can continue fighting again the next day.248 The purpose is to keep honing their skills in preparation for real battles that are expected to occur in the afterlife. They will be similar to earthly battles—fighting other Europeans for scarce resources by attempting to control trade routes and sources of plunder. Vikings were warriors, explorers, and traders known for their seafaring abilities and their ferocity. Battle filled the days of Viking warriors on earth, and it would fill them after death, too.

Another way of qualitatively ensuring military advantage in afterlife wars was devised by the Celts, who creatively combined logic and mythology to develop burial customs appropriate for their needs and conditions. The Celts were a militarily successful people who repeatedly poked at the boundaries of the Roman Empire and at one point spread east as far as Greece, plundering and collecting tribute everywhere they went. Although the Celts cremated most of their dead, the evidence from numerous burial sites indicates that their soldiers met with a different end. They were buried in full warrior attire, ensuring their preparedness for future wars.249 In addition, they were laid to rest facing in the direction from which their biggest danger (usually the Romans) was likely to come. While that direction changed, depending on where in Europe the burial took place, the relevant fact is that the soldiers were ready to pounce and fight, even if dead.

Although keeping soldiers prepared is important, not all ancient societies viewed it as the primary way to prepare for afterlife warfare. Some focused on the number of warriors, believing that the sheer size of an army could overwhelm afterlife enemies.

This view was popular among Chinese emperors. The most famous example of such military excess is associated with Emperor Ch'in Shih Huang Ti (aka Qin Shi Guangdi), who lived in 259-210 BCE. His imperial mausoleum, located just outside of Xian, is guarded by thousands of life-size terracotta warriors, horses, chariots, and war implements, all lined up in oversized pits. This impressive preparation for afterlife battle must be seen in the context of the times. Emperor Ch'in lived during what is referred to as the Warring States Period. He was the first emperor who, through war after war, managed to unite the multitude of little states that permeated what is now Chinese territory. Emperor Ch'in also conquered the land and the peoples of Mongolia and Vietnam, and to protect his empire from outside invaders he built a barrier that has come to be called the Great Wall of China. All his military accomplishments required a strong army. Given his earthly experience, coupled with indigenous Chinese religious beliefs that promised and promoted the afterlife, Emperor Ch'in ensured he was equipped for battle and ready to continue his warring activities in the afterlife.

Back to the Afterlife University. Having spent so many centuries in the postmortem, Alexander the Great has had occasion to witness all the above war preparations by soldiers and their commanders. As a result, the huge expenditures contemporary earthly governments incur to ensure military preparedness do not surprise him at all.

Globalization and the Outsourcing of Sin

American businesses outsource their legal services to India, and French companies maintain call centers in Francophone Africa. Outsourcing occurs when firms contract out a business process to an external firm rather than perform it in-house. They make that decision on the basis of a cost/benefit analysis that considers numerous factors.

If it is possible to hire someone to write legal briefs and answer telephones, then why not hire someone to assume one's sins by…eating them! The employer avoids hell in the future while the sin eater enjoys payment in the present. A mutually beneficial transaction occurs that makes everyone better off.

As incredible as it sounds, such sin eaters actually existed. In early seventeenth-century England, where the population lived in terror of the final judgment described in frightening detail by church represent- atives, entrepreneurial individuals began offering a valuable service. These were the so-called sin eaters, who ate the sins of the dying or the newly deceased, liberating the soul to go into the afterlife cleared of all their bad behavior.250 For a fee, they eliminated the fear of an eternity in hell.

Not surprisingly, there was a demand for sin eating services. The dying were rational, after all. They pursued their self-interest and sought to maximize their well-being, especially on their deathbed. If a product existed that could make their afterlife more pleasant, they demanded it. Anyone who could afford to hire a sin eater did so.

And the supply was abundant. Individuals with no other source of income were grateful for the opportunity to earn some money. All they had to do was eat some bread and drink some wine. Those foods had been placed on and near the chest of the deceased in order to absorb the corpse's sins. The sin eater then swallowed the food, along with the sins. The transaction was so simple that every British village had a ready supply of sin eaters.

And thus, through the market mechanism, the dying hired a third party to carry their sins into the afterlife rather than keep them in house. Performing a cost/benefit analysis indicated that the benefit of hiring a sin eater far surpassed the cost. It also indicated that the cost of an eternity in hell was by far greater than the cost of hiring a sin eater.

Back at the Afterlife University, Oliver Cromwell recounted how he met numerous souls from seventeenth- century Britain who were benefici- aries of transactions with sin eaters. As a result, he was not impressed with the earthly firms that decreased their costs by outsourcing legal services to Indian lawyers. While globalization in the twenty-first cen- tury may have enabled outsourcing across the globe, Cromwell didn't think the fundamental economic rationale behind the practice had changed over four centuries.

Black and White: How Diversified is the Afterlife?

The seven billion people on earth encompass a multitude of races, ethnicities, and nationalities. To varying degrees, this diversity of the global population is replicated within many individual countries, as international migrations have brought new peoples to locations where they previously did not live and inter-marriages have produced offspring that blur traditional racial and ethnic boundaries.

Is this diversity mirrored in the afterlife? Specifically with respect to race: is there an afterlife exclusively for Caucasians and another for Negroids, and yet another for Mongoloids? Or do the dead of all races spend eternity together?

According to the Bible, after the last judgment people of all races (as well as nations, tribes, and languages) will gather in heaven around God's throne.251 There they will spend eternity, together, in harmony. This biblical view of harmonious racial diversity has appeared, albeit in modified form, throughout literature and popular culture. In her bestselling series, *Vampire Chronicles*, Anne Rice describes such inter-racial harmony. Her main character, a vampire called Lestat, is taken to hell by Memnoch the Devil.252 To his amazement, Lestat finds souls of all races and all times coexisting. Black and white and Asian all move together, feeling equally lost and confused. Those from ancient times are dressed in togas and those from the Borneo hills wear a loincloth, but still, all get along.

Getting along implies contact and interaction. Even a minimal amount of interaction involves simple economic transactions such as basic trade and barter. Such interaction requires the capacity to communicate. Thus, if the afterlife is indeed characterized by the harmonious coexistence of racial groups, it follows that these people, coming from diverse countries across the globe, communicate with each other through a common language. Such a language lubricates interactions between a deceased black Nigerian and a white Ukrainian.

There have been claims that the dead do indeed share a common language. Cicero, the Roman orator from the first century BCE, as well as Giles of Rome, a fourteenth-century scholar, both believed that all souls speak the same language.253 No matter where people come from, once they die there is a lingua franca that enables them to communicate. While both men fall short of naming that language, others step in to fill the gap. The Islamic religion specifies that Arabic is the only language in heaven, the only one in which the choirs of angels sing.254

By contrast, novelists Daniel Quinn and Tom Whalen offer a vision with multiple languages. In *A Newcomer's Guide to the Afterlife*, a how-to book intended for the recently dead is published in English and all other Indo-European languages (and modified versions of the book exist in most Afro-Asiatic languages).255

Abraham Lincoln looks down to earth and sees that, over two centuries after the American Civil War, the liberated black slaves and their former white masters live in relative harmony. They engage in economic transactions enabled by their shared English language, the same language that lubricates trade throughout the global economy. For centuries, Lincoln has experienced the harmonious way racial groups interact in the afterlife, so he is unimpressed with twenty-first-century racial harmony on earth.

Sidebar 14.1: Nationalities in the Afterlife

A joke that circulates across Europe leaves no doubt as to the belief that the dead retain their nationalities and national characteristics: *In heaven, the cooks are French, the policemen are English, the lovers are Italian, and it is all run by the Germans. In hell it's reversed. The English are cooks, the French are the police, Germans are the lovers, and the Italians manage everybody.*

Sidebar 14.2: Religious Diversity in Heaven

Religious beliefs dictate that heaven is only open to believers. Islamic heaven is populated by Muslims, not Jews or Parsees. So, too, Christian heaven contains no agnostics or Shintos. While these heavens may contain racially and linguistically diverse populations, they are not characterized by religious diversity. Author Stanley Elkin takes a contrarian position. In his comic view of life after death, *The Living End*, Elkin describes the architecture of paradise as consisting of a mixture of minaret-spiked mosques, rounded domes of classical synagogues, tall pagodas, and big cathedrals.[256] In other words, religions exist side by side in the same afterlife, rather than each religion having monopoly power in its own afterlife.

Three Cold War Leaders Walk Into a Bar (in Heaven)

It's the early 1980s and the Cold War is in full swing. Menachem Begin, Ronald Reagan, and Leonid Brezhnev are the leaders of Israel, the United States, and the Soviet Union, respectively. They are all still alive. Each gets an unexpected opportunity to visit Heaven for a meeting with God. Each is granted the right to ask only one question. Begin gets to go first.

Begin: "God, you who know everything, can you tell me: when will Israel be at peace with the Palestinians?"

God: "In one hundred years."

Begin is overcome with emotion and begins to cry.

God: "Why are you crying, Menachem?"

Begin: "Because I won't be around to witness it."

Begin leaves the meeting place, hunched over. It is the turn of Ronald Reagan.

Reagan: "Please God, tell me, when will all nine Supreme Count justices be Republican appointees?"

God: "In two hundred years."

Like Begin, Reagan is overcome with emotion and begins to cry.

God: "Why are you crying, Ronald?"

Reagan: "Because I won't be around to witness it."

Hunched over and demoralized, Reagan leaves the meeting place, and Leonid Brezhnev brushes past him for his turn with God.

Brezhnev: "Comrade God, I want to know, when will the Soviet command economy overtake the American market system?"

God does not respond. Instead, overcome with emotion, he begins to cry.257

We can infer from this joke that God knew of the deplorable state of the Soviet economy and that it could not be fixed, not even until the end of eternity and the end of his reign. He knew the system would self-destruct. He knew about the limitations of command economies. He knew what Western economists, specializing in the Soviet economic system, failed to predict. While the fall of the Berlin Wall, the symbolic beginning of the Soviet collapse, took most people by surprise, God knew it was coming.

The Soviet Union had a command economy in which directives for micro and macro level economic activity came from the government. Central planning determined what is produced and how. Government ownership was the norm, enabling firms and enterprises to operate with a so-called soft budget constraint, relying on the state to cover their deficits. In addition to holding property rights, governments also controlled and managed virtually all economic activity. Contrast that with market economies, in which households and firms, through supply and demand, determine prices and therefore determine the allocation of economic resources.

Several jokes toy with elements of the Soviet system that caused its economy to collapse.258

Q: What would happen in heaven if communism were introduced?
A: At first nothing. But later there would be a shortage of halos, clouds, and angels.

Here the focus is on the notorious shortages that plagued the Soviet economy. There was insufficient production of goods to satisfy demand (halos). There was insufficient housing to accommodate everyone comfortably (clouds). And there were not enough appropriately skilled workers for the jobs that needed doing (angels). The reason for these shortages is that allocation of resources took place by government planners rather than in the market. In the absence of a product market, a housing market, and a labor market, prices and quantities are not determined by supply and demand but rather by government bureaucrats. They cannot be as efficient as the market in determining how to allocate scarce resources.

Inefficiencies are further illustrated by the joke below:

Q: Would you rather go to a communist hell or a capitalist hell?
A: Definitely a communist hell. There would be less torture, since shortages of oil, malfunctioning furnaces, and lazy demons keep it all from functioning.

A lack of spare parts and bottlenecks in production diminished capital inputs and contributed to a crumbling infrastructure. Lazy workers were the result of Soviet labor policy that promoted full employment at all costs. Not that laziness did not exist among workers elsewhere, but the fact that no one could be fired (other than for political reasons) eliminated the incentive to work hard and served to institutionalize low productivity.

This low labor productivity is illustrated in a joke that links the Soviet economy and the afterlife:

> It is 1975. Every decade or so, souls from heaven get to visit earth, just to get a look at how things have changed since they died. A group of dead Japanese factory workers want to learn about the Soviet economy. They arrange to spend a day visiting a shoe factory on the outskirts of Moscow. They make the transition to earth seamlessly and show up at the factory. After the necessary introductions, the Japanese begin their escorted tour. Everywhere they go, the Japanese souls see Soviet workers sitting around, reading the newspapers, listening to radios, and discussing soccer teams. A few hours into their visit, the factory host announces a lunch break and asks the souls if they want to continue observing the workers some more in the afternoon. After conferring with each other, the Japanese souls respond, "We appreciate being allowed to visit your factory, but we really don't feel right participating in your strike."

What seems like a strike to the hard-working Japanese souls is a normal working day in Soviet factories.

Low productivity of labor and other resources, together with shortages and inefficiencies, are the characteristics of the Soviet economy that ultimately resulted in an implosion from within. Coupled with political and economic pressures from outside the country, this implosion led to the demise of the Soviet system.

After reaching the afterlife in 1971, Khrushchev hears enough jokes mocking the Soviet reality to suspect that the Soviet economic system was untenable. At some point, he begins to wonder if his beloved motherland needs an infusion of some market economic principles. To learn more about the market economy, he goes to the heavenly library to read the *Wealth of Nations* by Adam Smith, the eighteenth-century Scottish philosopher. There he learns that economies thrive when their people pursue their own self-interest. In so doing, it is as if an invisible hand comes into the economy to set everything right, resulting in optimal prices, employment, and output. Smith, Khrushchev learns, promotes a free market economy with no government interference in domestic economic affairs.

He scans other books on Adam Smith and capitalism that line the heavenly library shelves. He learns that even free market systems are not without problems. Market failures such as negative externalities, poverty, unequal distribution of income, and long-term unemployment repeatedly occur and require government attention. He comes across a poem by Stephen Leacock, a Canadian political scientist and writer, that brings a smile to his face. In "A Resurrection of Adam Smith," Leacock calls on Smith to come out of his grave and justify some of his ideas about the invisible hand.259 The poem ends with the verse below.

> Smith, come up from under the sod,
> Tell me what did you do with God?
> You never named him, I understand,
> You called him (Book IV) an invisible hand;
> You gave him the system all geared and speeded,
> With none of his Interferences needed.
> It wasn't worthy of a man of your size,
> Smith—come up and apologize.

Khrushchev leans back in his chair and sighs. Wisely, he notes that no economic system is without flaws, but alas, the Soviet system is more flawed than the market system.

Sidebar 14.3: Chinese Workers Want a Communist Afterlife

This is not a joke.

When the Chinese government reformed the economy and introduced widespread market liberalization, growth rates skyrocketed. The Chinese economic transformation of the past few decades has been deep and broad. It was a time of profound change, and while most people benefited, some workers suffered, having lost their jobs and secure incomes. Tim Harford, the author of *The Undercover Economist*, writes that the upheaval was so unsettling that a nostalgic group of workers from Sichuan came to hope and believe that in the afterlife there is a factory run by deceased communist leader Mao Zedong along socialist principles. Harford reports on claims that some of the workers killed themselves so as to join their beloved leader as soon as possible.260

15

Even Dead People Just Want to Be Happy

Throughout history and across societies, earthly economic conditions repeatedly show up in visions of the afterlife. The most common condition is scarcity—the lack of sufficient resources to satisfy human wants. Scarcity occurs both at the individual and aggregate levels and, as such, dictates both personal and social choices.

For those who believe in life after death, that which is perceived to be scarce on earth is also perceived to be scarce in the afterlife, indicating that its value is maintained across the life/death divide. A snapshot view of selected societies yields the following examples of how earthly scarcity repeatedly shows up in visions of the afterlife.

In ancient Mesopotamia, there was concern about low population numbers relative to invading neighbors whose demographic advantages translated to economic advantages. Hence, Mesopotamian visions of the afterlife included large families and rewards for those with many children. Celts and Vikings, as well as more recent rural populations in Africa and South America, were concerned with food production and famine. Since they never had enough to eat on earth, their afterlives were characterized by an overabundance of food. Those Native North Americans who could not hunt enough seals or buffalo to satisfy their needs envisioned an afterlife overpopulated with animals. The peoples of the Middle East, who battled barren soil and overwhelmingly dry weather, looked forward to an afterlife filled with water resources for drinking and irrigation (in fact, both the Bible and the Qur'an describe heaven as filled with lush green gardens and rivers, exactly the opposite of the land where their holy books originated). Societies with warring neighbors envisioned an afterlife as a walled location, protected from intruders (such as the Islamic heaven that is depicted as a garden surrounded by a wall). Medieval Europe was ravaged by battles as well as disease, both of which got left behind by those who went to Christian heaven. Gold and jewels were scarce in the Renaissance, hence their dominance in artistic depictions of heaven.261

These and other examples point to a correlation between economic conditions on earth and qualitative afterlife experiences as envisioned by believers. The evidence of correlation is even stronger if we observe societies over time and trace the changes in economic conditions and the corresponding changes in afterlife visions.

Take, for example, Etruscan society. Early tomb paintings from the sixth and fifth centuries BCE depict an afterlife filled with drinking, sports, games, music, and other happy activities. Later, in the fourth century BCE and onwards, the scenes become somber, showing battles, snakes, and anxiety on people's faces. The Etruscans' vision of their collective afterlife underwent a fundamental change that coincided with the loss of their dominant economic and political position.262 Battles with neighboring peoples became common, output decreased, and hunger spread.

Across the world, Chinese folk beliefs prescribed the burial of loved ones with animals and coins. These specific items were believed to be useful in the afterlife. Today, burials are more likely to include a laptop, a bottle of Viagra, and chicken nuggets in a box with golden arches.263 What happened to change the Chinese vision of their after-lives? Technological advances, urbanization, and globalization altered what people believe they will be doing in the afterlife.

For both the Etruscans and the Chinese, times changed, economic conditions changed, and overall earthly realities changed. Later, with a lag, their conceptualization of the afterlife changed, highlighting again the correlation between economic conditions and the way believers envision their afterlife.

This correlation, however strong, does not imply causation. Indeed, there is no way to prove that an economic downturn or expansion have in fact given rise to any particular afterlife vision.

Also, this correlation does not hold universally. Many old religions such as Islam, Zoroastrianism, Hinduism, and Christianity, cling to visions of the afterlife that are rarely updated and modernized. Instead, these old religions coexist side by side with contemporary popular culture, literature, and music that offer a parallel vision of the nether-world, one that is more in line with contemporary earthly existence. A few examples illustrate this point.

When the American Civil War decimated the standard of living and killed off a large portion of the labor force, survivors found solace in visions of the afterlife provided by author Elizabeth Stuart Phelps, who depicted heaven as filled with surplus goods and services, jobs, and leisure activities as they existed in the abundant pre-war economy. Many people embraced this view, despite their overwhelming adherence to the Christian churches whose afterlife visions were in clear contradiction. Similarly, during the late nineteenth century, the construction of the North American railway system linked previously inaccessible parts of the country and brought them into the national economy. As a result, jobs were created and trade flourished, and the overall economic expansion explains the popularity of a song entitled *Life's Railway to Heaven*, which compared heaven to a railroad station.264 It is likely that no Christian preacher spoke of heavenly trains and stations from the pulpit, but still the song resonated with the population and was seamlessly integrated into their worldview.

This coexistence of afterlife worldviews continues in the twenty-first century, as some old, organized religions compete with popular culture for the hearts and minds of the population when it comes to their afterlife beliefs. While emissaries of old religions describe heaven in words used by their forefathers, contemporary movies, television, media, and literature depict afterlives in which cell phones are used by souls to communicate with each other. Suits and ties that male souls wear in heaven point to consumer goods in the afterlife. Skyscrapers where souls reside reflect an afterlife housing industry. It is the new religions that more closely resemble popular culture when it comes to describing the afterlife as a reflection of the earthly economy. Evangelist Billy Graham, for example, implicitly referred to the transportation industry when he described heaven as the place where, "we will drive down the golden streets in a yellow Cadillac convertible."265

If You Want To Be Happy For the Rest of Your (After) Life...

Driving cars and chatting on cell phones indicate participation in the afterlife product markets. However, these activities are more than manifestations of economics in the afterlife. They indicate that modern humans expect to spend their afterlives doing something fun. They expect they will have occasion to drive convertibles. They expect they will have sex and use Viagra. They expect to go on vacation and eat good food. In other words, they expect to do that which brought them happiness in the course of their lives. They expect that they will be happy in the afterlife.

And why shouldn't people have such expectations? Western societies in the twenty-first century have experienced sustained economic growth for over several centuries, despite regular dips of the business cycle. The basic needs of food and shelter were satisfied long ago, and standards of living are at an all time high. People participate in the circular flow of economic activity insofar as they produce and they consume, they earn and they spend. They have consumer sovereignty and decide how to spend their money. Life expectancy has grown as many killer diseases have been conquered. Basic education and literacy have been achieved and, together with democratic political systems, have empowered the population. To the extent that the market system fails to provide sufficiently for all, governments step in with social policies and social networks that cushion the falls associated with economic downswings. Societies have moved so far beyond the satisfaction of basic needs that activities such as art and literature and music can flourish in sophisticated markets of their own. Of course there are exceptions to this rosy picture, and of course there is poverty, but on the whole, Western populations have never had it so good. And many profess to be happy.

Polls from across the world show that, indeed, people in Western societies largely identify themselves as happy. According to a Gallup World Poll of 2008, respondents in 140 countries were asked questions about their subjective well-being.266 North European countries came out on top, joined by Australia and New Zealand in the top ten and the U.S. is not far behind. Why are people in these countries happy?

Personal wealth, according to the poll, is not the most important determinant of individual happiness. That is not surprising, given the evidence provided by previous economic studies. As early as 1974, Richard Easterlin's cross-country comparative analysis showed that personal wealth is linked to happiness among people whose basic needs (such as food, shelter, and basic medical care) have not been met. At higher levels of income, when basic needs have been satisfied, personal wealth is no longer the primary source of happiness.267 This has come to be called the Easterlin Paradox. It has been confirmed with recent data by Carol Graham in her study of happiness across the world (which carries the following informative subtitle: *The Paradox of Happy Peasants and Miserable Millionaires*268).

So what makes people happy in Western societies, where GDP per capita is typically over $30,000 and basic human needs have generally been met for several generations already? Some value family. Others focus on love and affection. Satisfaction in the workplace is important to many, as is job security. Spirituality is cited as giving peace and strength. Intellectual stimulation and political freedoms are also included. And, of course, there are those who derive extreme happiness from consumption and other activities that money can buy. (As Geoffrey Miller notes in *Spent: Sex, Evolution and Consumer Behavior*, even though scientific evidence says that buying stuff does not lead to happiness, people who can consume continue to do so relentlessly.)

Irrespective of the source of happiness or the form it takes, people seem to share a common goal, and that is to be happy. In the United States, that is not a new goal. After all, the Declaration of Independence calls the pursuit of happiness an inalienable right, together with life and liberty. What has changed in the recent past is that the pursuit of happiness has become operationalized and concretized. Those who seek happiness now tend to have a demand for it—in other words, they are willing to pay to attain it. Suppliers emerge to supply a variety of goods and services to satisfy that demand. There are now happiness entrepreneurs that offer happiness makeovers.269 There is a plethora of self-help books and seminars that help people become happier. Cable television offers viewers the *Happiness Show* for entertainment and enlightenment. Providing happiness has become big business. Happiness-related economic activities pique the interest of responsive governments. Many have jumped on to the bandwagon by paying attention to the happiness quotient of their electorate. Indeed, French President Nicholas Sarkozy called for happiness to be used as an economic indicator, and the town of Somerville (in Massachusetts) included a question about happiness in the city census in 2011.270

In the aggregate, Western societies have a new orientation that has produced a new term: happyism.271

The 80% of Americans who believe in the afterlife might ask, "Why stop at death? Why not take the quest for happiness into eternity? Why not be happy both here and there?" It is a logical next step for people who want it all. If earthly happiness comes from close family ties, they hope to have those in the afterlife. If earthly happiness comes from shopping at the mall, then they'd like to use their credit cards in heaven.

How can people ensure afterlife happiness?

According to the Hopi Indians of North America, what a young bride wears in life will determine her happiness in the next life.272 At the time of her marriage, a Hopi woman is given special attire that she is expected to wear on her wedding day and also on any other important occasion throughout her lifetime. She must follow this dress code in order to ensure happiness in the afterlife.

Most people do not rely on their wardrobes for this purpose. To the extent that they seek to be happy for eternity, it is likely that they will adopt an economic way of thinking. Specifically, they will adopt behavioral rules of maximization that are at the heart of microeconomic theory. While firms maximize profits subject to cost constraints, and consumers maximize utility subject to income constraints, people who seek a good afterlife will maximize afterlife happiness subject to earthly behavioral constraints.

Maximize Happiness...

It has been said that there is no choice about death, but there is a choice about one's view of the afterlife.273 To the extent that people want to be happy in the afterlife, they will adopt a belief system that offers them the greatest possibility of achieving happiness. Assuming consumers behave rationally, they will choose the religion or belief system or mythology that offers them the best chance of the happiest afterlife.

Is it unlikely that people change religions or belief systems? Not at all. Throughout history, individuals have changed religious affiliation in order to assimilate, to marry, or to obey the will of some authority or master. Converting in order to maximize the possibility of eternal happiness seems no more or less valid a reason, especially given twenty-first-century Western propensities and sensibilities.

There is evidence that, with increasing frequency, people have been changing religions. According to a study by the Pew Forum on Religion and Public Life, America is in a period of unprecedented religious fluidity, in which 44% of adults have left the denomination they were born into.274 The most popular new American churches are large, contemporary, and evangelical.275 Most converts are attracted to what might be called "happy religions." They want to focus on the positive sides of religion, on how it can make them happy, not how it controls their earthly behavior. They want to be unencumbered. They do not want to live in fear or face punishment in the afterlife. They reject religions that profess a scary afterlife filled with pain and torture.

Scholars have reported on this new trend. As noted in an earlier chapter, John Micklethwait and Adrian Wooldridge wrote *God is Back*, in which they claim that "religion is becoming a matter of choice" as people now decide what they want to believe rather than being born into it or forced into it. Lisa Miller called this phenomenon our "promiscuous approach to religious identity."276 In reference to all the possible choices of afterlife beliefs, Nicholas Lezard said, "it's an eschatological free-for-all out there."277 Alan Segal notes that the First Amendment to the United States Constitution forbids the establishment of a state religion, thereby encouraging "competition among religions within the marketplace of ideas."278

Where there is demand, supply will respond. Given that people are searching for religions, facilitators come along to help in their search. KnockKnock has published a guide for potential converts called *Choosing a Religion*, which has simplified researching religious choices. It contains information on what they call "religious tourism," urging readers to try several out before committing.279 For convenience and efficiency, the book contains a chart of ninety-nine religions classified by characteristics such as dietary restrictions, time commitment, holidays, and cost—as well as the quality of the afterlife.

... *Subject to Constraints*

Economists know there are constraints on all desired activities. Because of scarcity, people cannot maximize *ad infinitum*, without incurring opportunity costs and facing tradeoffs. So, too, in pursuing happiness in the afterlife, people face constraints. The first constraint they face has to do with faith. People cannot hope to achieve afterlife happiness if they do not adhere to a system of beliefs that includes an afterlife as a definite outcome that follows death. So: people must become believers.

The second constraint happiness maximizers face has to do with behavioral prescriptions imposed by this faith. Belonging to a religion and believing in its views of the afterlife often entails modifying earthly behavior to conform to its rules. If a potential convert is made happy by wealth, he might be drawn to Buddhism, so he could be reincarnated as a rich man. However, after conversion he must conform to rules prescribed by Buddhist doctrine, including supporting those less fortunate and feeding the monks. Similarly, if a potential convert is a nature lover, she might consider converting to Islam to spend eternity in the horticulturally induced serenity of the heavenly garden's bucolic landscapes. However, her behavioral prescriptions will include Arabic language lessons and restrictions on alcohol. Finally, if a man wants to ensure his wife stays his wife for eternity, he might consider converting to Mormonism. One price he would have to pay is mandatory (temporary) missionary service.

Some constraints may be too big to overcome. They may entail prices potential converts do not want to pay. Every individual needs to conduct his or her own cost/benefit analysis to determine if the behavioral squeeze imposed on their earthly life is worth the promise of future happiness. People will need to consider the inter-temporal dimension, weighing present cost against future benefit, just as if they were considering placing their current savings into a mutual fund in expectation of future returns.

At the end of all this economic analysis, the potential convert will have identified the afterlife vision and requisite earthly behavior that they can live with. One day, an economics Ph.D. student will operationalize this process in order to identify the HAPI—the Human Afterlife Preference Index.

In the event that all existing belief systems fail to assure individuals that they have maximized their expected afterlife happiness, then American capitalism offers one final solution. It offers the possibility of starting a new belief system, one in which all the elements of the afterlife that one wants can be incorporated. It is easy to do. One doesn't even have to leave the comfort of one's kitchen table. The Internet offers a variety of sites offering to guide people through the process of creating their own religion. A particularly user-friendly one is www.startchurch.com. With little start-up funding, one can have a personalized afterlife that will provide the greatest chance of eternal happiness.

After all, human beings have the capacity to believe in anything. The seventeenth-century English poet John Milton made this point succinctly when he said, "The mind is its own place and in itself, can make a Heaven of Hell, a Hell of Heaven."280

"You picked the wrong religion, period. I'm not going to argue about it."

Cartoon 15.1: Pick Your Religion Wisely

Acknowledgments

When I tell people about this book, inevitably the first question they ask is if I believe in the afterlife. *Really* believe. After I explain that it doesn't matter if I do or don't, that I am simply an economist trying to understand how people think and behave, then the interesting conversations begin. Those conversations have provided a subtle but crucial dimension to my research. I am very grateful to all those friends, colleagues, and even strangers who candidly offered up their personal beliefs and disbeliefs, both about the afterlife as well as the ubiquity of economic principles.

There are some people whose contributions to this book are especially appreciated. Stephen Urice helped out with Egyptian hieroglyphics and, with the aid of his colleagues, answered all my esoteric queries about the Etruscan afterlife. Karen Mathews went beyond the call of friendship by researching Islamic and Catholic religious art and compiling photos and texts that were crucial to this study. Tom Burke's pointed comments on just how far to push the boundaries of economics were invaluable. Ben Liebman's enthusiasm about the application of my research to the classroom opened a world of possibilities for me. Brainstorming with Jim Stormes pointed out some leads in Catholic thought and practice. Thanks are also due to Bruce Harvey for alerting me to research on Polynesian and Maori beliefs. Pascal Goldschmidt introduced me to Japanese mourning practices, and Julian Kreeger's extensive knowledge of classical music proved invaluable in identifying afterlife themes. Larry Foglia introduced me to the Human Relations Area Files, and then Christianne Cunnar at the HRAF headquarters worked with me to find the sources I needed pertaining to afterlife views across the globe. Nenad Amodaj's suggestions, ranging from art to philosophy, broadened the scope of this book. Elissa Vanaver and Andy Hine provided an ongoing sounding board for both macro-level ideas as well as micro-level sentence structure. Lynthia Romney crafted book descriptions and Alexandria Szeman played a pivotal role in the title choice. Elisa Rodriguez-Vila showed extreme patience while designing yet one more version of the cover. Dori Pappas's attention to administrative details meant that I didn't have to think about them. Two work-study students helped out with this book: Mike Serra produced digital drawings and Anna Hidano checked sources. My heartfelt thanks to all!

As always, my family played a huge role in my research and writing. Richard has been invaluable as an inexhaustible source of articles and websites. No major idea in this book escaped our extensive dissection in the course of the past three years. Karla and Jelena read the first draft and offered conceptual and organizational suggestions. Aleksandra was my sounding board and never failed to say "this works" and "that doesn't." As most of my other accomplishments in life, this book would not exist without the support, wisdom, love and hand-holding of all these individuals.

Notes

1   According to the *New York Times* Book Review (April 10, 2011), the non-fiction bestseller list includes the following titles: *Heaven is For Real, 90 Minutes in Heaven, The Immortal Life of Henrietta Sacks,* and *I Hope They Serve Beer in Hell.* Two of those were also on the list on January 4, 2009.

2   Mark Johnston, *Surviving Death* (Princeton, N.J.: Princeton University Press, 2010), 3.

3   Robert Frank and Ben Bernanke, *Principles of Economics,* 4th ed. New York: McGraw Hill), 1.

4   Paul Krugman and Robin Wells, *Macroeconomics* (New York: Worth, 2006), 6.

5   The references in this paragraph refer to the following. Gary Becker and Guity Nashat Becker, *The Economics of Life* (New York: McGraw Hill, 1997); Daniel Hamermesh, *Economics is Everywhere,* 2nd ed. (New York: McGraw Hill, 2006); Bruce Madariaga, *Economics For Life* (Boston: Houghton Mifflin, 2006); Richard McKenzie and Gordon Tullock, *The New World of Economics: Explorations Into the Human Experience* (Homewood Il.: Richard Irwin, 1978); Steven Landsburg, *More Sex is Safer Sex: The Unconventional Wisdom of Economics* (New York: Free Press, 2007); Steven Levitt and Stephen Dubner, *Freakonomics* (New York: William Morrow, 2005); *Seussisms for Success: Insider Tips on Economic Health from the Good Doctor* (New York: Random House, 2009).

6   Dr. Sanjay Gupta, the medical correspondent for CNN, wrote a book entitled *Cheating Death* in which he writes of visits to a "gray zone" where people are neither truly dead nor truly alive.

7   Lynne De Spelder and Albert Strickland, *The Last Dance* (Palo Alto: Mayfield Publishing Co., 1983), 19.

8   The undead include apparitions, banshees, ghosts, ghouls, poltergeists, shades, and vampires. The dead who are in danger of becoming undead are those who have unfinished business on earth, who died early, who were murdered, and who are witches. Richard Taylor, *Death and the Afterlife: A Cultural Encyclopedia* (Santa Barbara, Ca.: ABC-CLIO, 2000), 383-384.

9   Richard Schweid, *Hereafter: Searching for Immortality* (New York: Thunder's Mouth Press, 2006), 237-239.

10   Mary Roach, *Spook: Science Tackles the Afterlife* (New York: W. W. Norton, 2005), 97-100.

11   Richard Dawkins, *The God Delusion* (Boston: Houghton Mifflin, 2006); Sam Harris, *The End of Faith* (New York: W. W. Norton, 2005); Victor Stengar, *The Failed Hypothesis* (New York: Touchstone Books, 1994).

12   Alan Segal, *Life After Death* (New York: Doubleday, 1989), 15.

13   Kenneth Kramer, *The Sacred Art of Dying* (New York: Paulist Press, 1988), 94.

14   Daily Mail Reporter, "Prehistoric Child is Discovered Buried with 'Toy Hedgehog' at Stonehenge," *Mail Online* (October 10, 2008), www.dailymail.co.uk/news/article-1073210, accessed January 30, 2010.

15   *New York Times*, July 21, 2009.

16   *Miami Herald*, March 18, 2010.

17   Created by Knock Knock, *The Savvy Convert's Guide to Choosing a Religion* (Venice, Ca.: Knock Knock, 2008), 36.

18   Kramer, *Sacred Art of Dying*, 178.

19   *Encyclopedia of Death and Dying*, www.deathreference.com, Ars Morendi, accessed May 28, 2010.

20   Nerina Rustomji, *The Garden and the Fire: Heaven and Hell in Islamic Culture* (New York: Columbia University Press, 2009), 158.

21   Randy Alcorn, *Heaven* (Carol Stream, Il.: Tyndale House), 51.

22   Jane Idelman Smith and Yvonne Yazbeck Haddad, *The Islamic Understanding of Death and Resurrection* (Albany: State University of New York Press, 1981), vii.

23   *The Big Religion Chart*, www.religionfacts.com/big_religion_chart.htm, accessed on November 4, 2009.

24   In his study of the Jewish afterlife, Raphael discusses the premodern Jewish book of the dead, the Maavor Yabok, as well as the Italian rabbi Immanuel Ha-Romi, a contemporary of Dante, who wrote a text on his visionary journey into the postmortem world. Raphael also says, "it is not that Judaism lacks a belief in the afterlife. Rather, the contents of many of these earlier teachings have been lost due, in part, to the changing nature of modern Jewish society." Assimilation led to the decrease of commitment to the study of Judaism. When the center of Judaism shifted from Europe to America, English-speaking Jews assimilated to American society and the commitment to study old Judaism was lost. Simcha Paull Raphael, *Jewish Views of the Afterlife*, 2nd ed. (Lanham: Rowman and Littlefield, 2009), 13, 15, 218.

25   Segal, *Life After Death*, 17.

26   Rebecca Price Janney, *Who Goes There? A Cultural History of Heaven and Hell* (Chicago: Moody Publishers, 2009), 22.

27   Raymond Moody, *Reflections on Life after Life* (Bantam, 1985). His book was followed by Melvin Morse's, *Closer to the Light* (Ivy Books, 1991), and more recently by Don Piper's *90 Minutes in Heaven* (Revell, 2004).

28   Roach, *Spook*, 80.

29   Culture as per definition on http://oxforddictionaries.com, accessed January 20, 2011.

30   Robert Hughes, *Heaven and Hell in Western Art* (New York: Stein and Day, 1968), 13.

31   Lisa Miller, *Heaven: Our Enduring Fascination With the Afterlife* (New York: HarperCollins, 2010), 224.

32   Miriam Van Scott, *Encyclopedia of Heaven* (New York: St. Martin's Press, 1998), 168.

33   *The Big Religion Chart*, www.religionfacts.com/big_religion_chart.htm, accessed on November 4, 2009.

34   www.religionstatistics.bravehost.com/statofrell.htm, accessed May 22, 2009. [This site is no longer in existence.]

35   "What People Do and Do Not Believe In" Harris Interactive Poll, December 2009, www.harrisinteractive.com/vault/Harris_Poll_2009_12_15.pdf, accessed May 21, 2011. Also, James L. Garlow with Keith Wall, *Heaven and the Afterlife* (Minneapolis: Bethany House Publishers, 2009), 234.

36   Cited in Mark Johnston, *Surviving Death* (Princeton, N.J.: Princeton University Press, 2010), 3.

37   "What People Do and Do Not Believe In" Harris Interactive Poll.

38   Cited in Janney, *Who Goes There?*, 206.

39   "Poll: One Out of Three Believers in Ghosts," Associated Press, AP online, accessed on October 26, 2007.

40   "The Decline in Believers" Harris Interactive Poll, January 2003, November 2008, cited in Garlow, *Heaven and the Afterlife*, 108.

41   Segal, *Life After Death*, 8-9. Segal cites the paper by Andrew Greely and Michael Hout in *American Sociological Review*, 66 ("Americans Increasing Belief in Life After Death: Religious Competition and Acculturation," 1999).

42   For example, see Judith Chevalier and Fiona Scott Morton, "State Casket Sales Restrictions: A Pointless Undertaking?" *Journal of Law and Economics* 51, no. 1 (2008): 1-23.

43   Wen Chung Chang, "Religious Giving, Non-religious Giving and After-Life Consumption," *Topics in Economic Analysis and Policy*, 5, no. 1, Article 13 (2005), www.bepress.com/bejeap/topics/vol5/iss1/art13, accessed November 20, 2008.

44   Fredrick Pryor, "The Roman Catholic Church and the Economic System," *Journal of Comparative Economics* (1993); Fredrick Pryor, "A Buddhist Economic System: In Practice," *American Journal of Economics and Sociology* (1991); and Jomo K. S., ed., *Islamic Economic Alternatives* (New York: Palgrave Macmillan, 1991).

45   McKenzie and Tullock, *New World of Economics*, 150-151.

46   Corry Azzi and Ronald Ehrenberg, "Household Allocation of Time and Church Attendance," *Journal of Political Economy* 83, no. 1 (February 1975): 27-56.

47   Scott Gordon, "Economics in the Afterlife," *Journal of Political Economy* 88, no. 1 (February 1980): 213-214.

48   This phrase is attributed to Stephen Landsberg, *More Sex*, ix.

49   This paragraph draws on Brennan and Waterman's criteria for determining if economics can be adopted as a framework for analysis. Geoffrey Brennan and A. M. C. Waterman, eds., "Introduction: Economics and Religion," *Economics and Religion: Are They Distinct?* (Boston: Kluwer Academic Publishers), 7-8.

50   John Taylor, "Life and Afterlife in the Ancient Egyptian Cosmos," in John Taylor, ed., *Journey Through the Afterlife* (Cambridge: Harvard University Press, 2010), 17.

51   E. A. Wallis Budge, *The Egyptian Book of the Dead* (London: Penguin Books, 2008), 321 (sheet 35).

52   Robert Garland, *The Greek Way of Death*, 2nd ed. (Ithaca: Cornell University Press, 2001), 71.

53   See http://www.griffith.ox.ac.uk/gri/carter/ for a complete list of tomb contents.

54   http://www.griffith.ox.ac.uk/gri/carter/.

55   Budge, *Egyptian Book of the Dead*, 53-54.

56   Budge, *Egyptian Book of the Dead*, cxxix-cxxx.

57   Richard Taylor, *Death and the Afterlife* (Santa Barbara, Ca.: ABC-CLIO, 2000), 197.

58   Unless stated otherwise, the information on hell and heaven in the next few paragraphs comes from Miriam Van Scott, *Encyclopedia of Hell* or *Encyclopedia of Heaven*, both published in New York by Saint Martin's Press, 1998.

59   Alice K. Turner, *The History of Hell* (Orlando, Fl: Harcourt, 1993), 3.

60   Turner, *History of Hell*, 180.

61   Mark Twain, "Captain Stormfield's Visit to Heaven," in Howard Baetzhold and Joseph McCullough, eds., *The Bible According to Mark Twain* (New York: Simon Schuster, 1995), 146.

62   Van Scott, *Hell*, 4.

63   Bruce Henderson, *Window to Eternity* (West Chester, Pa.: Crysalis Books, 1987), 49.

64   Van Scott, *Hell*, 246.

65   Van Scott, *Hell*, 95.

66   Turner, *History of Hell*, 178.

67   *Koran* 6/160, http://quran.com/6/160, accessed May 14, 2011.

68   Becker and Becker, *Economics of Life*, part seven; Herbert Simon, "Bounded Rationality," in John Eatwell, Murray Milgate, and Peter Newman, eds., *Utility and Probability* (New York: W. W. Norton, 1990).

69   David Letterman, *An Altogether New Book of Top Ten Lists* (New York: Pocket Books, 1991), 32.

70   *New York Times*, July 24, 1999, cited in Miller, *Heaven*, 186.

71   Peter Potter, ed., *All About Death* (New Canaan, Ct.: Bull's Eye Book, 1988), 177.

72   Van Scott, *Heaven*, 25.

73   Turner, *History of Hell*, 28.

74   Randy Alcorn, *Heaven* (Carol Stream, Ill.: Tyndale House), 426.

75   Alcorn, *Heaven*, 446.

76   Anthony DeStefano, *A Travel Guide to Heaven* (New York: Doubleday, 2003), 6-7.

77   John Romer, "Introduction," in Budge, *Egyptian Book of the Dead*, xxvii.

78   Elizabeth Stuart Phelps, *Beyond the Gates*, (1883, Boston: Houghton Mifflin and Co, 1883, repr., Kessinger Publisher, United States), 153-155.

79   Sylvia Browne, *Afterlives of the Rich and Famous* (New York: HarperOne, 2011), 111, 250, 272, 276.

80   Gordon, "Economics in the Afterlife," *Journal of Political Economy* 88, no. 1 (1980): 213-214.

81   www.metrolyrics.com/heaven-lyrics-talking-heads.html, accessed on May 14, 2011.

82   William Shakespeare, *Hamlet*, Act 3 Scene 1, lines 78-80.

83   Potter, *All About Death*, 80.

84   Thomas Cathcart and Daniel Klein, *Heidegger and a Hippo Walk Through Those Pearly Gates* (London: Penguin Books, 2009), 95.

85   Some two years later, in 2006, Piper's book was followed by Bill Wiese's *23 Minutes in Hell*. In this case, Jesus came to Wiese one night and took him on a visit to hell.

86   Schweid, *Hereafter*, 159.

87   Cited in Dinesh D'Souza, *Life After Death: The Evidence* (Washington D. C.: Regnery Publishing, 2009), 64.

88   Miller, *Heaven*, 176.

89   Schweid, *Hereafter*, 172.

90   Based on Gallup poll of 2005, cited in Miller, *Heaven*, 203.

91   *New York Times*, August 21, 2009.

92   Van Scott, *Hell*, 168.

93   Paul Arden, *God Explained in a Taxi Ride* (London: Penguin Books, 2007), 54.

94   Geoffrey Chaucer, *The Canterbury Tales* (New York: Oxford University Press, 1985), 394-397.

95   Schweid, *Hereafter*, 74.

96   Taylor, *Journey Through the Afterlife*, 105.

97   Gary Becker, "A Theory of Marriage: Part I," *Journal of Political Economy* 81 (1973): 813-846 and "A Theory of Marriage: Part II," *Journal of Political Economy* 82 supplement (1974): s11-s26.

98   McKenzie and Tullock, *New World of Economics*, 120.

99   McKenzie and Tullock argue that when love is present, both husband and wife will be more likely to care about how the other feels, and so will be more motivated to behave in a way that is conducive to the success of the marriage contract. McKenzie and Tullock, *New World of Economics*, 129.

100 Cited in Janney, *Who Goes There?*, 204.

101 Henderson, *Window To Eternity*, 21.

102 Emanuel Swedenborg, *Heaven and Hell* (West Chester, Pa.: Swedenborg Foundation, 2000), 329, 348.

103 Henderson, *Window to Eternity*, 32.

104 Richard Eyre, "The Church of Jesus Christ of Latter-Day Saints," in Christopher Jay Johnson and Marsha McGee, *Encounters With Eternity* (New York: Philosophical Society, 1986), 139-140.

105 Eyre, "The Church of Jesus Christ of Latter-Day Saints," in Johnson and McGee, *Encounters With Eternity*, 142.

106 John Casey, *After Lives* (Oxford: Oxford University Press, 2009), 385.

107 Van Scott, *Heaven*, 188.

108 George Smith, *Nauvoo Polygamy: But We Call It Celestial Marriage* (Salt Lake City: Signature Books, 2008), 412.

109 This point is disputed. According to Smith, if a widower remarries, he can have two wives in the afterlife, while women can only be sealed to one man for eternity. Smith, *Nauvoo Polygamy*, 412.

110   The analysis in this vignette is limited to heterosexual couples not only to conform to Mormon teachings but also for simplicity.

111 Van Scott, *Heaven*, 188.

112 This is true for normal goods—that is, goods for which demand increases when income goes up. For inferior goods, income increases result in a decrease in demand.

113 Ellen Basso, *The Kalapalo Indians of Central Brazil* (New York: Hold, Rinehart and Winston, 1973), 58.

114 Spell 110 from the *Book of the Dead* belonging to Horemakhbit, Papyrus of the New Kingdom, 20th Dynasty (about 1186 BCE - 1069 BCE), located at the National Museum of Antiquities in Leiden, Netherlands.

115 Garland, *Greek Way of Death*, 72.

116 *New York Times*, March 16, 2010.

117 This practice, so widespread that it evoked a government crackdown in 2006, indicates both wishful thinking as well as contingency planning. *Guardian online*, www.guardian.co.uk/artanddesign/2009/nov/14/chinese-paper-offerings-afterlife, accessed April 12, 2010.

118 Schweid, *Hereafter*, 72.

119 Incidentally, contrarian ideas such as this led to his excommunication and execution by the Catholic Church. Van Scott, *Heaven*, 78.

120 Henderson, *Window To Eternity*, 84, 89.

121 Garlow, *Heaven and the Afterlife*, 167.

122 Alcorn, *Heaven*, 352.

123 Richard Eyre, "The Church of Jesus Christ of Latter-day Saints," in Christopher Jay Johnson and Marsha McGee, *How Different Religions View Death and Afterlife*, 2nd ed. (Philadelphia: Charles Press, 1998), 99.

124 Van Scott, *Heaven*, 188.

125 Smith and Haddad, *Islamic Understanding of Death*, 164-165.

126 Van Scott, *Heaven*, 157.

127 Smith and Haddad, *Islamic Understanding of Death*, 164-165.

128 Swedenborg's views on marriage are encapsulated in Emanuel Swedenborg, *Heaven and Hell*, 294-306.

129 Hemmingway wrote this in a letter to F. Scott Fitzgerald in 1925; cited in Lisa Miller, *Heaven*, 215.

130 See, for example, the Etruscan Matrimonial Sarcophagus from Vulci, dating to the fourth century BCE and currently housed in the Boston Museum of Fine Arts.

131 Potter, *All About Death*, 165.

132 Mark Twain, "Captain Stormfield's Visit to Heaven," 165.

133 Van Scott, *Hell*, 148.

134 Thomas Paine, http://www.brainyquote.com/quotes/authors/t/thomas_paine_4.html, accessed August 9, 2011.

135 Mark Twain, "Captain Stormfield's Visit to Heaven," 155-156.

136 Mircea Eliade, *Death, Afterlife, and Eschatology*, Part 3 of From Primitives to Zen (New York: Harper Row, 1974), 26-27.

137 A. R. Williams, "Animals Everlasting," *National Geographic* (November 2009).

138 Miller, *Heaven*, 202.

139 *Tufts University website*, http://enews.tufts.edu/stories/1297/2001/07/09/BestPet/, accessed July 25, 2010.

140 Cited in Garland, *Greek Way of Death*, xx.

141 Ptolemy Tompkins, *The Divine Life of Animals* (Crown Publishers, 2010).

142 Cynthia Rylant, *Dog Heaven* (Blue Sky Press, 1995).

143 Ian Stevenson, *Twenty Cases Suggestive of Reincarnation* (Charlottesville: University Press of Virginia, 1974).

144 This evidence is discussed in Fred Frohock, *Beyond, On Life and Death* (Lawrence: University Press of Kansas, 2010), 57-58.

145 Roach, *Spook*, 27-28.

146 Mary Roach writes that this custom can easily lead to fraud as poor people sometimes try to convince wealthy families that one of their members has been reincarnated into the poor family. Roach, *Spook*, 27-28.

147 Schweid, *Hereafter*, 89.

148 Taylor, *Death and the Afterlife*, 31.

149 Taylor, *Death and the Afterlife*, 242.

150 Smith and Haddad, *Islamic Understanding of Death*, 89.

151 Basso, *Kalapalo Indians*, 56-59.

152 Richard Irving Dodge, *The Plains of the Great West and Their Inhabitants* (New York: G. P. Putnam's Sons, 1877), Chapter 13.

153 James Fennimore Cooper, *The Last of the Mohicans: A Narrative of 1757* (Albany: State University of New York Press, 1983), 349. The phrase "happy hunting grounds" has been introduced in this fictional account of the Mohicans, and it is unclear if it is a translation of one of the languages or if it is made up. Either way, it has been part of the English language reference to Native people's views of the afterlife. The name has persisted over time, albeit with some controversy.

154 Sheila Blair and Jonathan Bloom, eds., *Rivers of Paradise: Water in Islamic Art and Culture* (New Haven: Yale University Press, 2009), 3.

155 "The Devil and Homer Simpson" was first aired in 1993. It was part of the Treehouse of Horror IV episode of *The Simpsons* (Halloween special).

156 Bruce Woodcock, *The Selected Poems of William Blake* (Hertfordshire: Wordsworth Editions, 1994), 202.

157 Incidentally, a similar fate befell Prometheus, whom Zeus had chained to a rock. Every day an eagle devoured his liver and every night it regrew. However, Prometheus was not sent to hell but rather lived on earth, allowing Hercules to save him after a few years.

158 Dina Tiniakos, Apostolos Kandilis, and Stephen Geller, "Tityus: A Forgotten Myth of Liver Regeneration," *Journal of Hepatology* 53, no. 2 (August 2010): 357-361. See also, Carl Power and John Rasko, "Wither Prometheus's Liver? Greek Myth and the Science of Regeneration," *Annals of Internal Medicine* 149, no. 6 (2008): 421-426.

159 Smith and Haddad, *Islamic Understanding of Death and Resurrection*, 85-86.

160 Marjana Tomic Canic, "Wizardry of Tissue Repair and Regeneration: A Tale of Skin Cells When Their Magic is All But Gone," research presentation to the National Institutes of Health, March 7, 2012, *NIH website,* http://videocast.nih.gov/summary.asp?Live=10497.

161 Van Scott, *Hell,* 177.

162 Isaac Asimov, "The Last Answer", www.thrivenotes.com/the-last-answer, accessed July 8, 2010.

163 Miller, *Heaven,* 232.

164 www.religionfacts.com/islam/beliefs/afterlife.htm, accessed June 21, 2011.

165 Phelps, *Beyond the Gates,* 120.

166 Segal, *Life After Death,* 12.

167 Turner, *History of Hell,* 32.

168 Mark Twain, "Captain Stormfield's Visit to Heaven," 156.

169 Mark Twain, "Captain Stormfield's Visit to Heaven," 156.

170 Dodge, *Plains of the Great West,* 285-286.

171 Dodge, *Plains of the Great West,* 286.

172 Clare Gibson, *Ancient Maya* (New York: Metro Books, 2010), 42.

173 Letterman, *Top Ten Lists,* 32.

174 Ian Frazier, "The Temperature of Hell: A Colloquium," *New Yorker* (July 20, 2009): 35-36.

175 Frazier, "The Temperature of Hell," 35-36.

176 Kramer, *Sacred Art of Dying,* 54, 73, 90-91.

177 If not the child, then it is the closest relative of the deceased. Harold Courlander, *A Treasury of African Folklore* (New York: Marlow and Co, 1996), 288.

178 Taylor, *Death and the Afterlife,* 125.

179 Taylor, *Death and the Afterlife,* 39.

180 Taylor, *Death and the Afterlife,* 102.

181 Eliade, *Death, Afterlife, and Eschatology,* 33.

182 Diana Eck, *Banaras: City of Lights* (New York: Knopf, 1982), 341-342.

183 Van Scott, *Hell,* 197.

184 Budge, *Egyptian Book of the Dead,* clix.

185 Judith Berling, "Death and Afterlife in Chinese Religions," in Hiroshi Obayashi, ed., *Death and Afterlife: Perspectives of World Religions* (New York: Greenwood Press), 186.

186 Berling, "Death and Afterlife in Chinese Religions," in Obayashi, 186.

187 David Eagleman, *Sum, Forty Tales From the Afterlife* (New York: Pantheon Books), 52.

188 Van Scott, *Hell,* 244.

189 Taylor, *Death and the Afterlife,* 13.

190   Patricia Lysaght, *The Banshee: the Irish Death Messenger* (Boulder, Colorado: Roberts Reinehart Publisher, 1986).

191   Jason Boyett, *Pocket Guide to the Afterlife* (San Francisco: Jossey Bass, 2009), 194-195.

192   Garland, *Greek Way of Death*, 8, 134.

193   Pierre Grimal, ed., *Larousse World Mythology* (London: Paul Hamlyn, 1965), 389-390.

194   Segal, *Life After Death*, 43.

195   Taylor, *Death and the Afterlife*, 248.

196   Jerrold Cooper, "The Fate of Mankind: Death and Afterlife in Ancient Mesopotamia," in Obayashi, ed., *Death and Afterlife: Perspectives of World Religions*, 25.

197   Segal, *Life After Death*, 96.

198   Taylor, *Death and the Afterlife*, 248.

199   Van Scott, *Heaven*, 98-99, 250.

200   Gibson, *Ancient Maya*, 131.

201   Lydia Mary De Leon, Manobo, http://literalno4.tripod.com/manobo_frame.html, accessed November 30, 2010.

202   Phelps, *Beyond The Gates*, 135-136.

203   Miller, *Heaven*, 87.

204   Non-Greek myths involving Cerberus, such as those originating in the Roman *Aeneid*, state that more than two mortals managed to slip by the guard.

205   In Britain, Canada, and Australia, the percent of people who believe in angels are in the 30s. *Economist* (December 20, 2008): 36.

206   A pharmacological theory for the creation of zombie-like characteristics was presented by Wade Davis and Richard Evans Schultes in *Passage of Darkness: The Ethnobiology of the Haitian Zombie* (Chapel Hill, Nc.: University of North Carolina Press, 1988).

207   Hans Ackerman and Jeanine Gauthier, "The Ways and Nature of the Zombi," *Journal of American Folklore* 104 (1991): 466–494.

208   Fred Frohock, *Beyond, On Life and Death* (Lawrence: University Press of Kansas, 2010), 84.

209   This was described in Lord Byron's play entitled *Sardanapalus* (1821).

210   Taylor, *Death and the Afterlife*, 122.

211   Taylor, *Death and the Afterlife*, 125.

212   Among other literature on the male/female contributions to the household, see Arlie Russell Hochschild, *The Time Bomb: When Work Becomes Home and Home Becomes Work* (New York: Metropolitan Books, 1997); Arlie Russell Hochschild, *The Second Shift* (New York: Avon Books, 1989).

213   Ralph Harold Faulkingham, *Political Support in a Hausa Village* (Ann Arbor, Mi.: University Microfilms, 1971), 115.

214 Michael Todaro and Stephen Smith, *Economic Development*, 10th ed. (Boston: Pearson Addison Wesley), 450.

215 *The Holy Bible*, 1 Timothy 6:10 (New York: Meridian, 1974).

216 Dante Alighieri, *The Divine Comedy, Volume One: Inferno* (Penguin Classics, 2002), Canto 7.42.

217 Anne Derbes and Mark Sandona, *The Usurer's Heart: Giotto, Enrico Scrovegni, and the Arena Chapel in Padua* (College Park, Pa.: Penn State Press, 2008).

218 John Taylor, *Journey Through the Afterlife* (Cambridge: Harvard University Press, 2010), 13.

219 Budge, *Egyptian Book of the Dead*, 321 (sheet 35).

220 Taylor, *Death and the Afterlife*, 1.

221 William Murnane, "Taking It With You; The Problem of Death and Afterlife in Ancient Egypt," in Obayashi, ed., *Death and Afterlife: Perspectives of World Religions*, 43.

222 Murnane, "Taking It With You," in Obayashi, 43.

223 Van Scott, *Hell*, 136.

224 Boyett, *Pocket Guide to the Afterlife*, 108.

225 Van Scott, *Heaven*, 26.

226 Judith Berling, "Death and Afterlife in Chinese Religions," in Obayashi, 189.

227 Van Scott, *Heaven*, 250.

228 *New York Times*, November 23, 2009.

229 Tania Branigan, "Essentials for the Afterlife," *Guardian*, November 14, 2009.

230 Robert Wright, *The Evolution of God* (New York: Little Brown and Co, 2009), 68.

231 William Evans, "M1 in the Afterlife," *Journal of Political Economy* 1124, 1, (2006), back cover.

232 Andrew George, trans., *The Epic of Gilgamesh* (London: Penguin 1999), 178.

233 Taylor, *Death and the Afterlife*, 105.

234 Stephen Ohlemacher, "72,000 Stimulus Checks Went to Dead People," *Huffington Post*, October 7, 2010.

235 Turner, *History of Hell*, 16-18.

236 Instead of an apocalypse, Janney says souls in limbo await subsequent judgment. Janney, *Who Goes There?*, 18.

237 Turner, *History of Hell*, 18.

238 Kramer, *Sacred Art of Dying*, 115.

239 Taylor, *Death and the Afterlife*, 123.

240 Boyett, *Pocket Guide to the Afterlife*, 180.

241 Margaret Atwood, *Payback: Debt and the Shadow Side of Wealth* (Toronto: Anansi, 2008), 168.

242 Turner, *History of Hell*, 173-174.

243 Frederick Pryor, "A Buddhist Economic System- In Principle," *American Journal of Economics and Sociology*, 49, no. 3 (1990): 345.

244 *The Holy Bible*, Gospel of Luke (16:19-31) (New York: Meridian, 1974).

245 Segal, *Life After Death*, 55.

246 Khrushchev said that there is no heaven because cosmonaut Yuri Gagarin circled around the world and went into space and found nothing there. There was no garden, only darkness. Raphael, *Jewish Views of the Afterlife*, 23.

247 Turner, *The History of Hell*, 106.

248 Boyett, *Pocket Guide to the Afterlife*, 126.

249 Taylor, *Death and the Afterlife*, 123.

250 Van Scott, *Hell*, 262.

251 Van Scott, *Heaven*, 65.

252 Ann Rice, *Memnoch The Devil* (New York: Ballantine Books, 1995), 378.

253 Van Scott, *Heaven*, 121.

254 Smith and Haddad, *Islamic Understanding of Death*, 89.

255 Daniel Quinn and Tom Whalen, *A Newcomer's Guide to the Afterlife* (New York: Bantam Books, 1998), 106.

256 Stanley Elkin, *The Living End* (Champaign, Il.: Dalkey Archive Press, 2004), 24.

257 There are many variations to this joke. See Ben Lewis, *Hammer and Tickle: A History of Communism Told Through Communist Jokes* (London: Weidenfeld and Nicholson, 2008), 223.

258 Lewis, *Hammer and Tickle*, 133.

259 Stephen Leacock, "A Resurrection of Adam Smith," in Caroline Postelle Clotfelter, ed., *On the Third Hand, Humor in the Dismal Science* (Ann Arbor: University of Michigan Press, 1996), 126.

260 Tim Harford, *The Undercover Economist* (New York: Random House, 2007), 236.

261 Hughes, *Heaven and Hell in Western Art*, 117.

262 Taylor, *Death and the Afterlife*, 132.

263 *Guardian online*, www.guardian.co.uk/artanddesign/2009/nov/14/chinese-paper-offerings-afterlife, accessed April 12, 2010.

264 Miller, *Heaven*, 5.

265 W. C. Martin, *A Prophet With Honor: The Billy Graham Story* (New York: W. Morrow, 1991), 126; cited in Miller, *Heaven*, xviii.

266 Lauren Sherman, "World's Happiest Places," www.Forbes.com, May 5, 2009, accessed May 9, 2009.

267 Richard Easterlin, "Does Economic Growth Improve the Human Lot?", in Paul David and Melvin Reder, eds., *Nations and Households in Economic Growth: Essays in Honor of Moses Abramovitz* (New York: Academic Press, 1974).

268 Carol Graham, *Happiness Around the World* (New York: Oxford University Press, 2009).

269 *New York Times*, November 27, 2008.

270 *New York Times*, May 1, 2011.

271 Steve Salerno, "Ignorance of Bliss," *Skeptic Magazine*, 16, 1 (2010): 53.

272 Mischa Titiev, *Old Oraibi: a Study of the Hopi Indians of the Third Mesa* (1944; repr., New York: Kraus Reprint Co., 1971),196.

273 Joel Slemrod, "Thanatology and Economics: The Behavioral Economics of Death," *American Economic Review*, 39, no. 2 (May 2003): 371-375.

274 Study by Pew Foundation cited in Michael Paulson, "More Americans Changing Religious Denominations, Study Finds," in www.boston.com, February 25, 2008, accessed December 9, 2010.

275 Cathy Lynn Grossman, "Biggest U.S. Churches Contemporary, Evangelical," www.usatoday.com, September 17, 2009, accessed December 9, 2010.

276 Miller, *Heaven*, xiv.

277 Nicholas Lezard, "Life After Life Explained," *Guardian*, June 13, 2009.

278 Segal, *Life After Death*, 6.

279 KnockKnock, *Convert's Guide*, 27.

280 John Milton, *Paradise Lost*, http://www.notable-quotes.com/m/milton_john.html, accessed May 14, 2011.

References

Abdel Haleem, M. A. S., trans. *The Qur'an*. Oxford: Oxford University Press, 2010.

Alcorn, Randy. *Heaven*. Carol Stream, Il.: Tyndale House, 2004.

Alighieri, Dante. *The Divine Comedy, Volume One: Inferno*. London: Penguin Classics, 2002.

Baetzhold, Howard and Joseph McCullough, eds. *The Bible According to Mark Twain*. New York: Simon Schuster, 1995.

Becker, Carl. *Breaking the Circle: Death and the Afterlife in Buddhism*. Carbondale: Southern Illinois University Press, 1993.

Beed, Clive and Cara Beed. "A Christian Perspective on Economics." *Journal of Economic Methodology* 3, no. 1 (1996).

Bell, Rob. *Love Wins*. New York: Harper One, 2011.

Bering, Jesse. "Intuitive Conceptions of Dead Agents' Minds: The Natural Foundations of Afterlife Beliefs and Phenomenological Boundary." *Journal of Cognition and Culture* 2, no. 4 (2002).

Blair, Sheila and Jonathan Bloom, eds. *Imagies of Paradise in Islamic Art*. Austin: University of Texas Press, 1991.

Blair, Sheila and Jonathan Bloom, eds. *Rivers of Paradise: Water in Islamic Art and Culture*. New Haven: Yale University Press, 2009.

Blake, William. *The Marriage of Heaven and Hell*. Oxford: Benediction Classics, 2010.

Bonfante, Larissa. "Etruscan Couples and Their Aristocratic Society." In *Reflections of Women in Antiquity*, edited by Helene Foley. New York: Gordon and Breach, 1981.

Bonafante, Larissa, ed. *Etruscan Life and Afterlife*. Detroit: Wayne State University Press, 1986.

Boyett, Jason. *Pocket Guide to the Afterlife*. San Francisco: Jossey Bass, 2009.

Bremmer, Jan. *The Rise and Fall of the Afterlife*. London: Routeledge, 2002.

Brennan, Geoffrey and A. M. C. Waterman. *Economics and Religion: Are They Distinct?* Boston: Kluwer Academic Publishers, 1994.

Budge, E. A. Wallis, ed. *The Egyptian Book of the Dead*. London: Penguin Classics, 2008.

Bulfinch, Thomas. *Mythology.* New York: Dell, 1967.

Casey, John. *After Lives: A Guide to Heaven, Hell and Purgatory.* Oxford: Oxford University Press, 2009.

Cathcart, Thomas and Daniel Klein. *Heidegger and a Hippo Walk Through Those Pearly Gates.* London: Penguin Books, 2009.

Chang, Wen-Chung. "Religious Giving, Non-Religious Giving, and Afterlife Consumption." *Topics in Economic Analysis and Policy* 15, no. 1, Article 13 (2005).

Chopra, Deepak. *Life After Death: The Burden of Proof.* New York: Three Rivers Press, 2006.

Coleman, Graham with Thupten Jinpa, ed. *The Tibetan Book of the Dead.* New York: Penguin, 2005.

Courlander, Harold. *A Treasury of African Folklore.* New York: Marlowe and Co., 1996.

Dawkins, Richard. *The God Delusion.* Boston: Houghton Mifflin, 2006.

D'Souza, Dinesh. *Life After Death: The Evidence.* Washington D.C.: Regnery, 2009.

Derbes, Anne and Mark Sandona. *The Usurer's Heart: Giotto, Enrico Scrovegni, and the Arena Chapel in Padua.* University Park, Pa.: Penn State Press, 2008.

DeStefano, Anthony. *A Travel Guide to Heaven.* New York: Doubleday 2003.

Eagleman, David. *Sum, Forty Tales from the Afterlife.* New York: Pantheon Books, 2009.

Eire, Carlos. *A Very Brief History of Eternity.* Princeton: Princeton University Press, 2010.

Eliade, Mircea. *Death, Afterlife, and Eschatology.* New York: Harper and Row, 1974.

Evans-Wentz, W. Y., ed. *Tibetan Book of the Dead.* New York: Metro Books, 2008.

Fraiser, James. *The Golden Bough.* New York: Macmillan, 1924.

Frazier, Ian. "The Temperature of Hell: a Colloquium." *New Yorker* (July 20, 2009).

Frohock, Fred. *Beyond: On Life After Death.* Lawrence, Ks.: University Press of Kansas, 2010.

Gaiman, Neil. *The Graveyard Book.* New York: Harper Collins, 2008.

Garland, Robert. *The Greek Way of Death.* 2nd ed. Ithaca: Cornell University Press, 2001.

Garlow, James L. with Keith Wall. *Heaven and the Afterlife.* Minneapolis: Bethany House Publishers, 2009.

George, Andrew, trans. *The Epic of Gilgamesh.* London: Penguin 1999.

Gibson, Clare. *The Hidden Life of the Ancient Maya.* New York: Metro Books, 2010.

Gordon, Scott. "Economics in the Afterlife." *Journal of Political Economy* 88, no. 1 (1980).

Gray, John. *The Immortalization Commission: Science and the Strange Quest to Cheat Death.* New York: Farrar, Strauss and Giroux, 2011.

Grimal, Pierre, ed. *Larousse World Mythology.* London: Paul Hamlyn, 1965.

Hamilton, Edith. *Mythology*. New York: Warner Books, 1999.

Hitchcock, Mark. *55 Answers to Questions About Life After Death*. Colorado Springs, Co.: Multnomach Books, 2005.

Hrung, W.B. "After-life Consumption and Charitable Giving." *American Journal of Economics and Sociology* 63, no. 3 (2004).

Hull, Brooks B. and Frederick Bold. "Hell, Religion, and Cultural Change." *Journal of Institutional and Theoretical Economics* 150, no. 3 (1994).

Hughes, Robert. *Heaven and Hell in Western Art*. New York: Stein and Day, 1968.

Iannaccone, Laurence. "Voodoo Economics? Reviewing the Rational Choice Approach to Religion." *Journal for the Scientific Study of Religion* 34, no. 1 (1995).

Janney, Rebecca Price. *Who Goes There? A Cultural History of Heaven and Hell*. Chicago: Moody Publishers, 2009.

Johnson, Christopher Jay and Marsha McGee, eds. *How Different Religions View Death and Afterlife*. 2nd ed. Philadelphia: The Charles Press, 1998.

Johnson, Christopher Jay and Marsha McGee, eds. *Encounters With Eternity*. New York: Philosophical Library, 1986.

Johnson, Mark. *Surviving Death*. Princeton: Princeton University Press, 2010.

Kelsey, Morton. *Afterlife: The Other Side of Dying*. New York: Crossroad Publishing, 1979.

Kselman, Thomas. *Death and the Afterlife in Modern France*. Princeton: Princeton University Press, 1993.

Knock Knock. *The Savvy Convert's Guide to Choosing a Religion*. Venice, Ca.: Knock Knock, 2008.

Kramer, Kenneth. *The Sacred Art of Dying*. New York: Paulist Press, 1988.

Kyu, Lee Kwang. "The Concept of Ancestor Worship in Korea." *Asian Folklore Studies* 43, no. 2 (1984).

Leonard, John, ed. *John Milton Paradise Lost*. London: Penguin Classics, 2000.

Lewis, C. S. *The Great Divorce*. New York: HarperOne, 2001.

Long, Jeffrey with Paul Perry. *Evidence of the Afterlife*. New York: HarperOne, 2011.

Lucie-Smith, Edward. *The Glory of Angels*. New York: Collins Design, 2009.

Lysaght, Patricia. *The Banshee, The Irish Death Messenger*. Boulder: Roberts Reinhart Publishers, 1986.

Ma'sumian, Farnaz. *Life After Death: A Study of the Afterlife in World Religions*. Los Angeles: Kalimat Press, 1995.

Miller, Lisa. *Heaven: Our Enduring Fascination With the Afterlife*. New York: HarperCollins, 2010.

Mills, Antonia and Richard Slobodin, eds. *Amerindian Rebirth: Reincarnation Belief Among North American Indians and Inuit*. Toronto: University of Toronto Press, 1994.

Moody, Raymond. *Life After Life*. New York: HarperOne, 2001.

Murray, Sarah. *Making an Exit.* New York: St. Martin's Press, 2011.

O'Flaherty, Wendy Doniger, ed.. *Hindu Myths.* London: Penguin, 1975.

Obayashi, Hiroshi ed. *Death and Afterlife: Perspectives of World Religions.* New York: Greenwood Press.

Ortolja-Baird, Ljiljana, ed. *Heaven in Art.* New York: Watson Guptill Publications, 1998.

Phelps, Elizabeth Stuart. *Beyond The Gates.* Boston: Houghton Mifflin and Co, reprint of original [1883], 2009.

Phelps, Elizabeth Stuart. *The Gates Ajar.* New York: Ward, Locke and Co., reprint of original, 2010.

Potter, Peter, ed. *All About Death.* New Canaan, Ct.: Bull's Eye Book, 1988.

Pryor, Fred. "A Buddhist Economic System - In Principle." *American Journal of Economics and Sociology* 49, no. 3 (1990).

Pryor, Fred. "A Buddhist Economic System - In Practice." *American Journal of Economics and Sociology* 50, no. 1 (1991).

Pryor, Fred. "The Roman Catholic Church and the Economic System: A Review Essay." *Journal of Comparative Economics* 17, no. 1 (1993).

Quinn, Daniel and Tom Whalen. *A Newcomer's Guide to the Afterlife.* New York: Bantam Books, 1998.

Raphael, Simcha Paull. *Jewish Views of the Afterlife.* 2nd ed. Lanham: Rowman and Littlefield, 2009.

Roach, Mary. *Spook, Science Tackles the Afterlife.* New York: W. W. Norton, 2005.

Rustomji, Nerina. *The Garden and the Fire: Heaven and Hell in Islamic Culture.* New York: Columbia University Press, 2009.

Schweid, Richard. *Hereafter: Searching for Immortality.* New York: Thunder's Mouth Press, 2006.

Segal, Alan. *Life After Death.* New York: Doubleday, 1989.

Sheiman, Bruce. *An Atheist Defends Religion.* New York: Alpha, 2009.

Slemrod, Joel. "Thanatology and Economics: The Behavioral Economics of Death." *American Economic Review* 39, no. 2 (2003).

Stenger, Victor. *The Failed Hypothesis.* New York: Touchstone Books, 1994.

Stephenson, David. *Visions of Heaven: The Dome in European Architecture.* New York: Princeton Architectural Press, 2005.

Stevenson, Ian. *Twenty Cases Suggestive of Reincarnation.* Charlottesville, Va.: University of Virginia Press, 1974.

Smith, Jane Idelman and Yvonne Yazbeck Haddad. *The Islamic Understanding of Death and Resurrection.* Albany: State University of New York Press, 1981.

Smith, Joseph. *The Book of Mormon.* Berkeley: Apocryphile Press, 2005.

Swedenborg, Emanuel. *Heaven and Hell.* Westchester, Pa.: Swedenborg Foundation, 2000.

Taylor, John, ed. *Journey Through the Afterlife.* Cambridge: Harvard University Press, 2010.

Taylor, Richard. *Death and the Afterlife, A Cultural Encyclopedia.* Santa Barbara Ca.: ABC-CLIO, 2000.

Turner, Alice K. *The History of Hell.* Orlando, Fl.: Harcourt, 1993.

Van Scott, Miriam. *Encyclopedia of Heaven.* New York: St. Martin's Press, 1998.

Van Scott, Miriam. *Encyclopedia of Hell.* New York: St. Martin's Press, 1998.

Weiss, Brian. *Many Lives, Many Masters.* New York: Fireside Books, 1988.

Woodcock Bruce, ed. *The Selected Poems of William Blake.* London: Wordsworth Editions, 1994.